CULTURE WARLORDS

CULTURE
WARLORDS

MY JOURNEY INTO THE DARK WEB
OF WHITE SUPREMACY

TALIA LAVIN

hachette
BOOKS

New York

Hachette Books
Hachette Book Group
1290 Avenue of the Americas
New York, NY 10104

HachetteBooks.com
Twitter.com/HachetteBooks
Instagram.com/HachetteBooks

First Edition: October 2020

Published by Hachette Books, an imprint of Perseus Books, LLC, a subsidiary of Hachette Book Group, Inc. The Hachette Books name and logo is a trademark of the Hachette Book Group.

The Hachette Speakers Bureau provides a wide range of authors for speaking events.

To find out more, go to www.hachettespeakersbureau.com or call (866) 376-6591.

The publisher is not responsible for websites (or their content) that are not owned by the publisher.

Print book interior design by Thomas Louie.

Library of Congress Cataloging-in-Publication Data has been applied for.

ISBNs: 978-0-306-84643-4 (hardcover); 978-0-306-84644-1 (ebook)

Library of Congress Control Number: 2020940816

Printed in the United States of America

LSC-C

Printing 2, 2020

To my family, the Femme Collective, and all the black and brown and Jewish and Muslim and queer and trans kids, who deserve to grow up in a world without hate. And to Diane, the warrior.

¡No pasarán!
—Dolores Ibárruri

They were as one in their grief and in their
determination to continue the battle against fascism . . .
—Emma Goldman

CONTENTS

INTRODUCTION

There's a classic *New Yorker* cartoon that I like: It's from the early days of the internet, 1993, and it features a pooch sitting in an office chair at a blocky, Mac-looking computer, talking to another dog who's looking up at him, bemused. The caption: "On the internet, nobody knows you're a dog." Well, that may be true. But on the internet nobody knows you're a Jew, either, unless you announce it. And while writing this book, for the first time in my life, I spent a whole lot of time, a full year, not telling people I was a Jew, and listening to what they said when I didn't.

In order to look as deeply as I could into the world of white nationalism, I had to leave my own identity behind as often as not. In real life, I'm a schlubby, bisexual Jew, living in Brooklyn, with long brown ratty curls, the matronly figure of a mother in a Philip Roth novel, and brassy personal politics that aren't particularly sectarian but fall considerably to the left of Medicare for All. Over the course of writing this book, I had to leave my own skin. And sometimes what I found made me want to never return to it.

INTRODUCTION

Here are a few things I did over the course of working on this book.

I fabricated. A lot. Spectacularly. I invented identities from whole cloth purely because I needed to enter communities where my real self—Jewish, a journalist, a well-known fascism-hating Twitter loudmouth—was extremely unwelcome. And so I had to become other people, and invent them as I went along.

I pretended to be a slender, petite blond huntress who'd grown up on a white-nationalist compound in Iowa, looking for suitors on a whites-only dating site.

I pretended to be a down-and-out warehouse worker in Morgantown, West Virginia, who had become suicidal after his wife left him, only to be restored to his full self by becoming part of the white-nationalist movement—and willing to do anything to support his brothers in the cause.

I pretended to be an incel—an "involuntarily celibate" virgin, radicalized into a deep hatred of women by his lack of sexual success.

I infiltrated a Europe-based, neo-Nazi terror propaganda cell, called the Vorherrschaft (Supremacy) Division, by pretending to be a sexy young woman with an interest in saving the white race through violence, with the screen name "Aryan Queen."

I silently observed as neo-Nazis mused about what raping me would be like.

And, as myself, I went to dark places; I spoke to bad people and good people on the front lines of the battle for America.

As myself, I attended a conference for alt-right YouTubers in Philadelphia and was chased out of a casino.

I spoke to everyday antifascists defending their community in Charlottesville, Virginia.

I was rejected from joining a white-supremacist pagan ritual in the Albany area by the elders of a weight-lifting pagan cult called Operation Werewolf.

I listened to a terrible white-nationalist freestyle-rap diss battle.

I watched neo-Nazis post photos of trans children and Jewish children and black children and talk about killing them.

Every day for nearly a year, I immersed myself in chat groups and websites and forums where photos of lynchings were passed around like funny memes. Where "KILL JEWS" was a slogan and murderers were called "saints." On the anniversary of the Pittsburgh synagogue shooting, I watched them celebrate Robert Bowers, the murderer of eleven Jews at prayer, like a hero and a friend. I listened to strangers talk about killing kikes every day. I listened to strangers incite violence and praise murder and talk about washing the world with blood to make it white and pure. I listened to their podcasts. I watched their videos. I listened to their terrible music and watched them plan to meet and celebrate the racism that was their raison d'être.

And something snapped in me.

I admit it: I started this book angry at the racist right. I set out with the idea of writing a profane but intellectual, impassioned but clear book to spell out just exactly who these people are and what they want to do. Before I started writing, I was already the top Google search result for "greasy fat kike," thanks to neo-Nazi website the Daily Stormer. A hate group called Patriot Front had already sent my parents a postcard with the Nazi-era slogan "Blood and Soil." I had already had my relatives' names published on Gab, a white-supremacist-friendly social media site used by alleged Pittsburgh synagogue shooter Robert Bowers. I thought I was ready for what researching this book would do to me.

I wasn't.

As I write this now, I feel myself incandescent with the kind of anger that doesn't just last an evening. It's an old cliché that lovers shouldn't go to bed angry; well, for the past year I have gone to bed with my anger and woken up with my anger and gone about my day with my anger hot and wet like blood in my mouth.

It's not that I discovered that members of the racist far right are inhuman, or monsters beyond comprehension. They're not some entirely new species of being that requires forensic analysis and the dispassionate gaze of the scientist. They're not uniquely stupid or uniquely mired in poverty or uniquely beset by social problems or even members of any specific socioeconomic class. They're not monsters. They're people. Just people, mostly men and some women, all over this country and this world, who have chosen to hate, to base the meaning of their lives on hate, to base their communities of solidarity on hate, to cultivate their hate with tender, daily attention. They are just people, people with an entire alternate curriculum of history, who operate within an insular world of propaganda, built to stoke rage and incite killings and for no other purpose at all. There are rich men and poor men, tradesmen and office workers, teenagers and men cresting middle age. They eat and sleep and sometimes drink too much and sometimes are sober. They're lonely, some of them; horny, some of them; sometimes depressed and sometimes confused and sometimes joyful. They're people, just like you and me. They could work in the next cubicle over and you might not know it; sit one seat over in class from you and you might not know it; live in your neighborhood, play on your sports team, and you would never know that deep in the night they trade photos of lynchings like baseball cards, and laugh.

But I know them now, these men and women. I've seen what they write and how they talk and what they read and even how they sing. (Poorly.) It is precisely their humanity that angers me so much: The hate they promulgate and the violence they desire are the culmination of dozens or hundreds of small human choices.

They choose, every day and every day more of them, to create alternate identities that embrace the swastika and the skull mask and the Totenkopf, the worst of history and the worst of the present melding seamlessly. They choose to dream not of peace or of equality or of anything better than the sorry ragged world as it is, but of a worse world, riven by terror, awash in the blood of those they consider subhuman. Which means anyone not white; which means anybody Jewish; which means anyone who fights back against their putrid cancer of an ideology. Their dialogue is unremittingly puerile and violent. Everything about them goes back again and again to violence, as a hummingbird to nectar; it is what they crave, it fills them with a fleeting sense of virility and meaning. The fear they can instill makes them feel powerful; the murderers they celebrate are their brothers in arms. And I admit that as I researched this book and wrote it, the anger I felt calcified into a parallel hatred—one based not on skin color but on the sheer accumulation of vitriol I consumed and the way people I'd never met spoke about killing people who look just like my nieces and nephews, my cousins and aunts, my lovers, my friends, me. In a sense, I began to enjoy deceiving them, taking an acrid pleasure in my own duplicity.

But anger at these bigots was only part of what I felt. Some of my rage became directed at the people who oppose strong action against neo-Nazi organizing. I raged against white moderates—the people who don't believe in de-platforming Nazis from every perch they get, or facing down their marches, depriving them of audience and influence and a safe pedestal from which to spread their bile. The people who say: Ignore them! Let them march! Let them tweet, let them speak on campus, let them have their say and they will be defeated in the marketplace of ideas. The people who bill themselves as reasonable, who say: Let them air out their arguments. But the effect of these ideas when they are aired out is much like Zyklon B. Studying them as deeply as I have has made me realize no amount of such rhetoric is acceptable in the country's discourse, just as there is no acceptable amount of poisonous gas to let seep into a room.

To assert otherwise is an argument born of self-congratulation, the argument that being tolerant of violent racism is just another form of tolerance, and not a capitulation to the far right's own view of their legitimacy.

There are different strains of racist far-right ideas that I will discuss in the book—the milquetoast-seeming intellectual pablum of "identitarianism," which hides hate in tweedy language and makes a po-faced argument for the need for separate ethnostates for all, as if that constituted equality.

There's the straightforward violence of far-right accelerationism, which dictates the need for more and more terror attacks until American society devolves into a racial civil war. There is racism bound up in religious ideas, racism bound up in pseudoscience. And all of it is poison; and to allow any of it to be aired, particularly under the mealy-mouthed argument for "tolerance," is to give way to a movement that seeks absolute power and the total destruction of its enemies, who are its enemies by virtue of the immutable characteristics of their birth.

The more I grew to know this movement, the less patience I had for it; and still less for those who tolerate it. Studying the far right taught me what it means to have an enemy to whom one must give no quarter, because any ground given allows them to accrue power; and any increment of power they receive they will use toward violent ends. Over the course of the research that I did for this book and the gonzo journalism-cum-activism it entailed, I became radicalized. The violent far right has the sole goal of destruction, and allowing them to amass any power at all is to accede to that goal. To make peace with white supremacy, to give it room, to tender it mercy, is to assert that protecting black and brown and Muslim and gay and trans and Jewish people from violence isn't all that important or necessary. The marketplace of ideas breaks down when poison is sold in pretty packages, when hate is pressed into eager hands. Studying the far right taught me what hatred looks like, and taught me how to hate.

Hatred makes me itch inside; it's like wearing a too-small wool sweater over my soul. It doesn't come naturally to me, although anger does. It is painful to have your face pressed up for so long against the intellectual equivalent of aqua regia. I can feel my soul deformed, distended. It will hurt for a long time. But I know why I've done this, and it's hardly for money or fame; there are easier routes to both. It's for those children they want to kill, for my baby relatives, my cousins and aunts, my lovers, my friends, and me.

The poet Ilya Kaminsky describes the responsibility of being an author in his poem *Author's Prayer*:

I must walk on the edge
of myself, I must live as a blind man
who runs through rooms without
touching the furniture.

For a year, to write this book, I lived on the very edge of myself and beyond it. I became unrecognizable to myself. I lived in the world of hate and only from time to time emerged into a world that had love in it, and good cheese and olives, and my apartment in Brooklyn and the novels of Terry Pratchett and everything worth living for.

INTRODUCTION

My mind spun hellward for months, but I did these things to describe these people—white supremacists—and their culture and their motivations. To do so is to deprive them of the power to organize in total darkness, to operate as the terrifying bogeymen they would so like to be. It is to drag them by their hair into the light and let them scream. This is not a comprehensive accounting of the far-right and its history, nor even a full picture of the far-right's contemporary presence online. There are many areas I was not able to penetrate fully, from far-right women's groups, who are more elusive than their male counterparts, to the sprawling antigovernment militia movement that organizes primarily on Facebook, which overlaps significantly, though not perfectly, with white supremacist groups. This is an accounting of a sliver of a movement at a moment in time, a world I moved through as though it were a room whose walls were made of burning glass. I learned a lot, though there is always more to learn, and I learned what I cannot forgive. I will never forgive them for hating me and everyone I love as much as they do; I have friends neo-Nazis have publicly fantasized about raping and flaying and murdering and leaving for dead, and I will never forget that. I will never forgive them for making me hate them as much as I do, for folding a red loathing into my soul. So let *Culture Warlords*, such as it is, be part revenge, part explainer, and partly the story of what hate does to those who observe it and those who manufacture it. Let it be a manual that leads you to fight—for a better world for you, for me, for all the black kids and Muslim kids and Jewish kids and trans kids and brown kids, who deserve a world free of the verminous miasma of hatred. Let us hold it to the light—this wet, rotting, malodorous thing—and let it dry up and crumble into dust and be gone.

CHAPTER 1

ON HATING

In mid-June 2019, I opened a far-right chat room I had been monitoring for a few weeks on the messaging app Telegram. The chat room was called "The Bunkhouse"—I'd been informed by a source that it was filled with particularly violent rhetoric. And at four o'clock in the morning, hazy and sleepless, I found a discussion in the chat room about whether I was too ugly to rape.

For the previous hour or so, members of the Bunkhouse had been casually discussing sex with Jewish women. "I condone and endorse consensual relations with yentas," one wrote. (*Yenta* is a Yiddish word for "busybody" that has been coopted by some white supremacists as a slur for Jewish women writ large.) "But not BREEDING," wrote another. One minute later, a user asked: "Would anyone rape Talia Lavin?"

"I'd rape her with my double barrel," responded a user who went by the moniker "James Mason," an homage to an American neo-Nazi and child pornographer most famous for *Siege*, a book in which he advocates racist terrorism.

Most users found me too ugly to rape—"Talia Lavin's appearance makes me viscerally ill," "I can smell her through the monitor," "Talia Levin [*sic*] would make me wanna throw up my intestines." The conversation ended with an oblique expression of a desire to kill me. "No need to go into detail here," wrote one user about threats of violence. "Like anyone is ever going to think gee im glad we kept Talia lavin with us," responded another.

That night I nursed too much vodka and thought about how strange it was that a complete stranger had expressed the desire to rape me with a double-barreled shotgun. It's not like they knew I was lurking and reading that particular chat; I was a topic of discussion in absentia. I bemoaned the paucity of my own body of work, wishing that I was a worthier opponent—someone who truly merited this kind of vitriol. I'd written a feature for the *New Yorker* and another for the *New Republic* on far-right shenanigans, along with a few columns and op-eds for the *Washington Post* and *HuffPost*. While I'd done my best with the pieces, they hardly amounted to a substantive blow against a rising American fascist movement. I was mostly just a loudmouth on Twitter: Why was I taking up real estate in their heads? A member of the chat room started messaging me on Twitter, sharing sexually explicit fantasies about me having sex with dogs, and sharing the screenshots with the Bunkhouse, not knowing that I was watching.

The source who had initially recommended the group for my research had noted that it was full of "Siegeheads"—people who closely followed the work of neo-Nazi James Mason. Mason advocated terrorism to topple the American social order. The Bunkhouse was a group comfortable with discussing violence; actively militating for a race war; and prone to obsessive harassment and vendettas. Several members were part of the "Bowlcast," a podcast named for the bowl haircut sported by Dylann Roof, the young man who entered the

Emanuel African Methodist Episcopal Church in Charleston, South Carolina, in 2015 and murdered nine parishioners. Over and over again, members of the chat shared photos of Roof, often with a bandanna photoshopped onto his head that read KILL JEWS. On June 17, 2019, they celebrated the anniversary of "Saint Roof's" murders, and punctuated it with a kind of prayer litany of white-supremacist murder:

Heil Hitler.
Heil Bowers [Robert Bowers, who allegedly murdered eleven Jews in a Pittsburgh synagogue in 2018].
Sieg Heil.
Heil Roof.
Heil Breivik [Anders Breivik, a Norwegian neo-Nazi who murdered seventy-seven in a massive terror attack in 2011].
Heil McVeigh [Timothy McVeigh, the 1995 Oklahoma City bomber].

There was no one to de-escalate these men; it was a private group, one that existed for them to egg one another on, to venerate mass murderers and perhaps one day to emulate them. And over and over again, they posted my selfies, a photo of my feet, an old Google result about my dismal performance on the game show *Jeopardy!* They speculated about what my feet smelled like, how disgusting my body was. They didn't know I was lurking in their chat room; I was fair game regardless.

Feeling distressed, I texted Kelly Weill, a friend who works as a reporter on extremism for the *Daily Beast*, telling her my doubts about my own worthiness as an opponent to white supremacists. But Weill's response indicated just how small the cadre of journalists and activists who engage with the American far right is—and how such work or speech can attract obsessive attention from extremists. "These people see us as antagonists in the big character drama of their lives," she wrote to me.

To be publicly Jewish and female, and engaged in antifascist rhetoric—even in the form of caustic tweets—rendered me a vivid character in the imaginations of extremists. It placed me at the end of a hypothetical gun barrel, wielded by a stranger; thrust me deep into the thicket of racialized, anti-Semitic, and misogynist violence that made up the dark garden of their imaginations. Whatever extra humiliations I encountered were the price I paid for looking where others didn't care to, and it mirrored everything I'd resolved to fight against: the deep hatred of Jews and of women; the casual disregard for human life; the endless stream of incitement toward violence, gun lust, and the humiliation of their enemies.

The first time I experienced anti-Semitism, it was on the internet.

It's not that I don't look like a Jew. I absolutely do: My Ashkenazi heritage and anxious epigenetics are written all over me. I have long, brown, untamable curls I keep up in a bun most of the time so they don't blind me in an errant wind, and the matronly hips and bosom of a Jewess caricature, or a Venus of Willendorf. I have a nose that could be charitably called "aquiline" and more realistically just "big." I speak rapidly and gesticulate often, my voice expressing a hectoring, New York urgency, as if I have to get all the syllables out before I'm interrupted by someone else with an equally strong opinion. This is a fair bet in my family, in any case. During my travels as a young woman, through Iceland, Ukraine, and Russia, the attitudes of strangers toward my Jewishness were at worst a kind of "othering"—touching my hair, asking me if I was a Jew, playing "Hava Nagila" when I entered a room. I never felt any danger, just a perennial reminder that I was a Jew, and different.

I grew up like a Jew, too, in a fairly extreme way: in a Modern Orthodox enclave, in the town of Teaneck, New Jersey, where my neighborhood was dubbed "Hebrew Hills." I went to Orthodox Jewish schools, ate at kosher restaurants, went to Jewish summer camps. I watched Red Lobster ads on TV and thought it was an accurate reflection of the temptations of the vast world of non-kosher cuisine. Outside my kosher life, fat white shrimps tumbled endlessly into pools of glistening sauce, shot through a soft lens warmed to awaken desire. I knew about Christmas because to live in America in wintertime is to be immersed in an ambient, omnipresent Christmas, from which I was always excluded, pressing my nose against the windowpane, the glowing trees shimmering within. I knew that the president was Christian—that every president had been Christian. But within the sheltered confines of home and school and extra-curricular activities, I lived a quietly separatist life in suburban New Jersey, one in which every meaningful personal relationship I had was with a Jew.

Every element of my upbringing was steeped not just in biblical and Talmudic precepts but in the lessons of Jewish history. Such lessons were slanted through a school system whose project was to raise and sustain devout Orthodox Jews by evoking the tragedies of our history. Every Holocaust Remembrance Day, I sat through slideshows of emaciated bodies, set to maudlin ballads of Jewish loss. I learned about pogroms; I played Golde in a school production of *Fiddler on the Roof*; I learned in excruciating detail how the long and complex and illustrious history of the Jews in Europe had dissolved in blood

13

and gas and human ash. It wasn't just in school, either: The Holocaust had shaped not just Jewry more broadly, but my own family. My whole life was shaped by anti-Semitism, at a generation's remove.

My maternal grandparents, Esther and Israel Leiter, were born at the turn of the twentieth century in Galicia, a region that was then Poland but today is part of Ukraine. I was the child of a youngest child—my mother had been a surprise in my grandmother's forties—and I never heard the story of their Holocaust survival from their own lips. What I heard were suggestive snatches of what had already become family legend: that they had survived in the woods; that they had joined with the partisans; that members of their party had been apprehended and killed by Nazi searchers. My grandmother had given birth during the war and the baby died. A girl they traveled with was caught by Nazis between the trees and shot. They foraged for potatoes in frozen ground. My grandmother's shoes broke and she went barefoot in winter. My grandfather judged the calendar by the moon and shaped matzahs from mud when he thought it was Passover.

From what I knew—a story that took shape as my mother told me, piecemeal—the war had never left them entirely. My grandfather's brilliant brothers had been rabbis, as he was, and he never stopped mourning their loss. During my mother's childhood he was plagued by night terrors every night, and once or even twice a week, he would cry out, "*Polizei!*"—the German word for "police"—and herd his daughters out into the Brooklyn night. When they left the cramped apartment in Borough Park where my mother was raised, no longer capable of living on their own, my relatives discovered a cache of checks and bonds hidden under the floorboards of their bedroom. They had always been ready to run. The fear of slaughter because they were Jews never left them.

Still, all this had transpired on a continent I'd never visited, in a Poland of my imagination, a frozen waste of ruin and loss. In Teaneck I could choose between Chickie's and Schnitzel+ if I wanted to dine out on kosher schnitzel. At school I learned which blessings to recite before eating a cough drop, or a dinner roll, or a carrot. The reality of the branches cruelly bitten from my family tree made me realize that anti-Semitism was real, but it felt profoundly distant. Every summer, on Tisha B'Av, a solemn Jewish holiday of mourning and fasting, we sat on the floor to symbolize grief and heard the keening text memorializing the loss of the Temple, the Book of Lamentations, chanted aloud. All these lamentations, even those that afflicted my grandparents, and my mother through them, seemed rolled into one long and terrible past that I had emerged from, ready to triumph in a country that held no threat for me.

Until my adulthood, anti-Semitism was largely an abstract concept. It wasn't something I'd experienced personally, any more than a fish gasps for air in an aquarium, though all the world outside the glass is air. I lived a life secure in the assumed privilege of full whiteness, both in the way I passed physically through the world and in the way I found my identity as a Jew to be perceived by those I interacted with.

After I graduated from college, I spent a year in Ukraine, on a Fulbright grant. In part, I wanted to explore Eastern Europe at greater leisure than summer trips could afford me; in part, I was burrowing into my family's past, peering at the blood that watered my stunted, foreshortened family tree. I wanted to know about the love and creativity and tradition and passion that had sustained my family for generations—and the hatred that cut it short. I wanted to see what anti-Semitism had wrought for myself.

That fall, before the impossible cold set in and the sun still remembered the land, I took a grumbling Soviet-era overnight train from

Kyiv to Lviv and then a minibus out to Chemerintsi, the village where
my grandfather was born. The roads were impossibly bad—potholes
brocaded with broken asphalt—and the landscape velvet-lush. It was
time for the safflower harvest, and horse-drawn plows bit into the low
yellow hills. The only hint that nearly a century had passed since the
last of my family had lived here in the 1930s were the telephone poles
that stretched out over the steppe. Even here, in the green bed from
which a bloody family myth had sprung, no one sought to expel me.
The village was tiny—a clutch of houses spreading out like tendrils
around an onion-domed church alone on a hill. I stepped off the bus
and asked, rather boldly, to speak to the oldest person in the village.
Her name was Mama Svitlana, she was ninety, and her house smelled
like sour milk. She remembered little and spoke little, and when I
came back after winter finally ended, she was dead. Once again I
asked passersby for the oldest person in the village; this time they
showed me the street where the Jews had lived, and gave me a bag of
bruised, golden apples. What had happened during the war and after
hung between us; in the words of one old woman, "a time of calamity."
In a neighboring village, where family lore said my newlywed grandfather had worked briefly as a rabbi, a woman pointed at a street of
broken, empty buildings: "Before the war, there were Jews and there
were shops. Now, there are no Jews, and there are no shops."

When I returned home, I felt secure in my Americanness, in my
secular, cultural Judaism. I started work as an editorial intern at the
Jewish Telegraphic Agency (JTA), a venerable, century-old newswire,
supplying Jewish papers around the nation and the world with news
content. It had a tiny staff, and in my role as intern I blogged and
wrote newsletters and moderated web traffic and comments.

That was my first real encounter with anti-Semitism in its modern
incarnation, out of the jackboots and behind the keyboard.

ON HATING

I quickly discovered that one of the largest traffic drivers for JTA was Stormfront.org—a white supremacist website that was the largest hub for neo-Nazis on the internet at the time. When I asked coworkers about it, they responded simply: We were in the business of writing about Jews behaving badly (confirming their thesis about nefarious Jews); about Jews succeeding (confirming their thesis about the racial cunning that drives Jewish superiority); and about which celebrities and public figures were Jewish (allowing them to be added to the dossier). Articles about abuse, scandal, and intra-community disputes drew particular attention from Stormfront.

Then there were the threats against our writers.

One of my roles, as a jack-of-all-trades in a tiny office, was moderating the comments on JTA's articles. It's a ghastly job, no matter what publication you work for, but what I saw made my bones ache. Anonymous figures gave graphic descriptions of what they wanted to do to our writers: murder, dismemberment, torture. It was clear that the reasons they wished to do this had everything to do with the fact that we were Jews. There they were, the anti-Semites, in real time. They weren't in Poland; they weren't lost in the mists of decades past. They were telling me what they wanted to do to my coworkers—right now. There was fascism there—swastikas earnestly displayed, sinister intent, a deep hatred toward me, for being born where I was born, for growing up as I had. There was an embrace of Hitler and his Reich, and countless terms I had never heard before, tossed out under disposable usernames. The moment I saw it, I knew this was a battle I had to wage. I was going to learn what I needed, and I was going to fight.

Five years later, a Twitter follower of mine sent me a few screenshots from 8chan, a notorious anonymous message board that serves as a kind of sewer of the internet, a sprawling, chaotic channel for outright hate speech, dubious porn, and conspiracy theories, whose slogan is "Embrace infamy." The thread I'd been linked to featured users hypothesizing about whether Jews are a different species. And it featured pictures of me—lots of them.

The thread was titled "the mysterious jew/Neanderthal skull" (*sic*), and it was a feast of pseudoscience and bizarre anti-Semitism, liberally spackled, of course, with mentions of the Rothschilds. The idea that Jews are not *Homo sapiens*, but in fact more closely related to Neanderthals, would explain "the reason why these jews view us as entirely different and separate from them, as if we're literally different species," wrote one user. "All the folklore about 'people' that feast on humans depicts the same large hooknose of the jew," wrote another.

A third posted six pictures of me, juxtaposed against a crude diagram of *homo neanderthalus*. They were mostly old Twitter profile pictures: one from a photo session I'd done for a small Brooklyn blog and another from a 2015 appearance on *Jeopardy!*, my awkward smile inches from Alex Trebek's weathered, handsome face.

"Neanderthal phenotype certainly isn't defined by the skull shape alone," wrote the anonymous user, below the photos of me. "Their body tended to be wide and broad and robust in comparison to more modern types such as Cro-Magnon."

I looked down at myself and wondered if this was the reason I'd had so little success dieting. Once you start gazing into the abyss of the far right, pretty soon it turns its gaze right back on you. And its gaze is a fearsome thing, a twisted thing, one full of boredom and anger that have calcified into hatred. By that time, I had done a lot of gazing—and ranting, and writing, and reporting—in public. And I'd never hidden what I was and am: a Jew.

A Jew, yes. But not "the Jew"—the international Jew, the "eternal Jew," the "wandering Jew" of all the propaganda concocted against my people, over millennia. I am a small part of what so many see as a nefarious whole, bent on dissipation, destruction, and dissolution for our own inscrutable ends. In some ways, the internet, with its rapid dissemination of dubious words, seems made for a prejudice that works best in whispers and intimations. It's never been easier to spread such intimations, finding willing ears from San Diego to Pittsburgh and across the great length and breadth of this country. It's never been easier to, as a common neo-Nazi phrase puts it, "name the Jew."

I felt ready to fight it. My desire was to deracinate it, dry out the roots that grow so thick and strong in the murk of the internet's secret places, like poison mangroves. There is an anti-Semitic ecosystem of information in this country, a system that feeds on selectively plucked news stories and regurgitates them more and more biliously, until they are so caustic they burn. It utilizes the rhetoric of extermination and conspiracy, and its origins extend far back beyond the Trump era; anti-Semitism is an American prejudice, among the many that define this country.

There are occasions in America when anti-Semitism devolves into deadly violence. In 2018 and 2019 alone, two deadly shootings erupted in synagogues, with the slaughter of eleven congregants at the Tree of Life synagogue in Pittsburgh and the murder of a woman at a Chabad synagogue in Poway, California. But, for the most part, the role of anti-Semitism in far-right extremist thought is to serve as an ideological linchpin for white supremacy. Anti-Semitism is the keystone of a worldview that seeks to place white men above all others. The Jew—not any one Jew, necessarily, though any can be made to fit the mold of the "eternal Jew"—serves as a construct of a foe, cunning beyond human comprehension, and evil beyond imagining, a foe against whom no tactic is unjustifiable, and whom not fighting means the surrender of all one holds dear. As Jean-Paul Sartre put it in 1946, "If the Jew did not exist, the anti-Semite would invent him"; it is convenient to have an all-knowing foe, one who has schemed for millennia to oppress you, and thus serves as an explanation, and a foil, for all your ills.

In the white-supremacist movement, Jews have long served the function of scapegoat. Blame can be a motivating force: The specter of the perpetually scheming and diabolical Jew allows those invested in white supremacy to posit themselves as oppressed and righteous. Few people adhere to ideologies they believe to be unjust or untrue. This is equally true of those who believe that the white race alone belongs in the seat of power, who cheer the degradation of non-white people and uphold the justness of racist brutality. Many white supremacists begin as internet shock jocks—utilizing racist or anti-Semitic rhetoric primarily to provoke—but that is often only the beginning of an ideological journey that ends in deadly sincerity. In every era, there are individuals who are prone to question received narratives and ideals, and in every era, such thinkers bifurcate. There are those who use that questioning spirit to seek out truths with integrity and rigor, and others who allow themselves to be snowed by propaganda, to enter harmful, self-serving orbits of errant belief. And, in every era, the latter confuse themselves with the former.

In the age of the internet, the temptation exists as it always has. As noted by Anna Merlan in *Republic of Lies*, her recent book on American conspiracy theories, the tendency to seek hidden meanings and sinister patterns behind events in the news is part of the American psyche. Belief in conspiracy theories tends to spike in moments of particular social upheaval—but is otherwise consistent across decades, a steady, background throb in our social discourse.[1] Yet the internet has without question made it easier for conspiracy theorists to connect to one another, to build power through organizing and the steady rollout of ever-slicker propaganda. And anti-Semitic rhetoric has bloomed like a bog flower in the swampier parts of YouTube, Twitter, and Facebook. A further constellation of sites, like Minds and Gab, are marketed as "free-speech" havens for ideology excluded from mainstream social-media platforms, and have become beloved of white supremacists as venues to spread unchecked hate. There is, in addition, an explicitly white-supremacist network of news outlets, forums, and blogs.

What makes white-supremacist worldviews more comprehensive and textured than a simple animus toward nonwhites is their addition of the Jew, the nefarious foe who seeks to upend the natural racial order. Brutality, inequality, and a fiercely enforced racial caste system become weapons in the war against the Jew. Not all white-supremacist ideologies center on anti-Semitic conspiracy—but for many of the ideologues of organized racism, the Jew is as rhetorically indispensable as he is evil.

In the fall of 2019, I watched an anti-Semitic meme be born and rise in the far-right ecosystem. It was based on a musing in the manifesto of Dylann Roof, a white supremacist who at twenty-one murdered nine parishioners in an African-American church in Charleston, South Carolina. Roof's ire and the full force of his rage and contempt were concentrated on black people in his manifesto, but engaging with white-supremacist influences as closely as he did, he was unable to avoid the "Jewish Question" entirely. He wrote that Jews were "an enigma"—and that the chief problem with understanding the Jewish agenda was the success with which Jews had assimilated into whiteness. "If we could somehow turn every jew blue for 24 hours, I think there would be a mass awakening, because people would be able to see plainly what is going on."

In November 2019, a small channel on Telegram gave rise to a meme inspired by Roof's words. They wanted to truly "turn every Jew blue"—and set about photoshopping images and videos from the news and popular culture in order to do so. Opinion columnists, Supreme Court justices, tech executives, presidential advisers—all painted in various shades of blue. An image of the lawyers representing Christine Blasey Ford—the woman who testified that Supreme Court justice nominee Brett Kavanaugh had assaulted her in high school—painted blue was shared and viewed thousands of times. It showed the two lawyers flanking the snow-white Blasey Ford, rendered in her natural skin color; they were leaning in to her, painted in an almost violet shade of blue, as if asserting an unholy influence. It was a literalization of a persistent white-supremacist idea: that Jews are everywhere in the halls of power, subverting the popular will to their own nefarious ends. Over the course of researching this book, I learned about the thick, poisoned roots that gave rise to that meme, and countless memes like it. I learned about the system of texts, ideologies, and intellectual forebears that white supremacists draw on, the perennial remix of past and present hatreds they trade each day online. To understand the hatred of the present, I had to dive back into the past, and the pestilential blooms pressed into its dusty pages.

CHAPTER 2

THE JEWS

In many ways, contemporary white supremacy is not a new ideology. Its means of dissemination may be technologically novel, as it throws tendrils out across social-media sites, chat apps, and blogs. But its central ideas are a mélange of influences plucked from predigital decades—a bigot's pastiche that encompasses everything from nineteenth-century scientific racism to late-twentieth-century dystopian racist fiction. In 2019, many of the ideas put forth by the likes of Henry Ford, George Lincoln Rockwell, and William Luther Pierce have returned to a certain prominence. Copies of *The International Jew* are available online, both for free and for sale in dozens of separate iterations; at the time of this writing a handsomely bound paperback edition was for sale on Barnes & Noble's website. The florid segregationist tracts of the Confederacy and their Jim Crow heirs are a Google search away. *The Protocols of the Elders of Zion*, made wildly popular in the English-speaking world by Ford, is similarly easy to find.

Phrenology (or "craniometry") and race science have seen a resurgence online as well, described as "repressed" fields of study, driven out by political correctness. This was what prompted the anonymous 8chan posters to study my Neanderthal proportions and conclude that the Jew was neither *Homo sapiens* nor particularly sympathetic to members of that species. Everything old is new again online, and the worst of history, freed from its paper bonds and any context, floats in a void, to be plucked up and championed by hatemongers. Most online participants in white supremacy adopt a grab bag of principles from a variety of sources, recommended to them by YouTube talking heads, on forums, or in group chats, and pass the material along in turn.

These principles are fixated on antiblackness in particular; hatred of nonwhites is one of the founding ideologies of the United States, and is palpable in every element of the country's policies, politics, and economic conditions, from the mainstream to the radical fringe. The writer Adam Serwer calls this caste system the "racial contract" in America: the ways in which nonwhite subhumanity and white humanity are visible in every interaction between the state and its citizens, between nonwhite citizens and white citizens. But part of this racial contract in the modern era, as Serwer puts it, is that the subhumanity of nonwhites is a "codicil rendered in invisible ink": It works most effectively, he writes, "when it remains imperceptible to its beneficiaries."[1]

The chief distinction between members of the white-supremacist movement and the explicit and implicit antiblack racists of mainstream American politics is a gleeful reveling in the terms of the racial contract, and a desire to render injustice starker and more violent, explicit, and total. White supremacists are consumed by a desire to perpetrate violence on nonwhites, to "cleanse" the country of them, to destroy their communities through state and extrajudicial violence. But what underpins this fixation—the intellectual foundation of the white-supremacist movement—is a stalwart belief in the omnipresence of the cunning, world-controlling, whiteness-diluting Jew. Antisemitism is an attenuated force in modern American mainstream politics; engaging in it enables white supremacists to distinguish themselves from the other strata of a deeply racist society.

What follows is an examination of the history of anti-Semitism in America, in the interests of understanding the intellectual framework through which members of the white-supremacist movement justify their antiblackness, as well as a study of the phenomenon itself. The intellectual framework of the modern white-supremacist movement is built on a central principle of racist negation: Unwilling to believe that black people and other racial minorities are intellectually capable of organizing for their own betterment and producing positive social change, white supremacists pin any advance in racial equality on a cunning plot engendered by Jews. To the white supremacist, the Jew is most dangerous because of his adjacency to whiteness, and a desire to destroy it, with crafty malice, from within.

—

Anti-Semitism as we know it today is a phenomenon with roots extending back to medieval Europe—the first iteration of a putative Jewish conspiracy to dominate the world originated during the Black Death of the Middle Ages, in 1348 and 1349, when Jews were accused of systemically poisoning wells in order to kill off the Gentile population, and were slaughtered en masse from Spain to Strasbourg in a series of escalating pogroms. In the nineteenth century, as eugenics began to dominate mainstream thinking, a racialized view of anti-Semitism arose, in which Jews were a genetically distinct people who committed genetically predetermined acts of evil. In America, it is drawn in part from the European heritage of anti-Semitism, and in part from the modern pseudoscience of hatred. As the historian Leonard Dinnerstein put it, Jews in America until the late nineteenth century faced largely unaltered European stereotypes and bigotry— viewed as "cheats and blasphemers" who were outsiders in a Christian nation—but their population was so minuscule that they were simply "dots in a Protestant landscape."[2]

After the assassination of Russian Tsar Aleksandr II in 1881, a wave of pogroms washed over the Russian empire, due to suspicions that the murder had been committed by Jewish revolutionaries. Jewish communities from Kyiv to Yelizavetgrad suffered mass rapes, dozens of murders, and rampant destruction of property.[3] In 1882, Tsar Aleksandr III instituted a series of restrictive laws, some of which were known as the "May Laws," which harshly taxed Jewish communities, instituted enforced segregation between Jewish and non-Jewish rural communities, placed limitations on Jewish worship, and restricted Jewish movement through the Russian empire.[4] Further pogroms of increasing violence followed in 1903 and 1905. Between 1881 and 1924, when Congress enacted harsh restrictions on immigration, the Jewish population of the United States had swelled by some 2.5 million.[5]

The Jews who fled waves of pogroms in the Russian empire differed from the Jewish immigrants who preceded them. German-Jewish immigrants of prior generations had fanned out across the country, from the Far West to the Great Plains and the South, peddling wares in agricultural communities and establishing modest communities in cities like Cincinnati, Louisville, and New Orleans. The Reform Judaism that many German Jews observed encouraged assimilation into American culture. By contrast, their Eastern European counterparts tended to settle en masse in larger cities; many arrived in conditions of abject poverty; and their traditional dress and observance of the Sabbath and ritual dietary laws made them a large and visible minority. An efflorescence of Jewish cultural expression emerged in these new and vibrant communities. Jewish presses in New York were churning out fiery socialist tracts; Zionists were exhorting their people to take up Jewish nationalism; Yiddish plays drew large, raucous crowds in New York; and anarchists like Emma Goldman were spreading the revolutionary ideas they had brought with them across the sea. America suddenly had a sprawling, fractious immigrant Jewish community—primarily urban, and visibly and culturally distinct from their neighbors.

American Jews' new visibility and numbers attracted a new kind of prejudice. Since their arrival on American shores, Jews had faced what the political historian Michael Barkun defines as "ordinary anti-Semitism": "negative representations of Jews in popular culture; social, residential, and occupational discrimination; and random instances of physical and verbal harassment." Once the numbers of American Jews began to swell in the last decades of the nineteenth century, the country saw the emergence of "extraordinary" anti-Semitism—"explicitly anti-Semitic ideologies proposed as explanations for the problems of society, and the expression of these ideologies in political movements."[6] For centuries, Jews had lived in the United States, a small, oft-degraded, but largely unmolested minority; it took an influx of millions of Jews for "the Jew" to enter in full—the embodiment of all animus, the cause of all strife, obscenity, and suffering. Extraordinary anti-Semitism proved a useful tool for a country steeped in antiblackness from its inception: The two ideologies work in tandem, providing intellectual nourishment and moral justification each to the other, a poisonous wellspring that never runs dry.

The Progressive Era—a period of widespread, energetic social activism and reform in the United States lasting from the late 1800s until 1920—also coincided with the rise of eugenics and race science among the country's intelligentsia. While antiblack animus had shaped American society since its inception, race science and eugenics imbued prejudice with academic authority. Among the conclusions reached by the period's intellectuals was the notion that the Jew was a separate race, whose immutable traits—craftiness, cunning, money-lust—made him fundamentally different from, and unassimilable into, America's Anglo-Saxon stock. Progressive Era intellectuals like Burton J. Hendrick, writing in *McClure's* magazine in 1907, described the "Jewish invasion" of the United States, and condemned the restlessly acquisitional nature of the Jew. In Hendrick's view, every Russian Jew one saw was a "prospective landlord," eager to acquire land and choke out competition in the trades by any means, however underhanded.[7] Edward A. Ross, an intellectual at the forefront of the eugenics movement, matched Hendrick's vitriol toward Jews, but added a luster of scientific determinism. Writing in *The Century* magazine in 1914, he set forth a theory of the "Race Traits" of "Hebrews," which included "inborn love of money-making." "Their progress in studies is simply another manifestation of the acquisitiveness of the race," Ross quoted an anonymous school principal as saying. And: "With his clear brain sharpened in the American school, the egoistic, conscienceless young Hebrew constitutes a menace."[8]

Small wonder, given the rapaciousness and preternatural skill presented in Ross's view, that "the Gentile resents being obliged to engage in a humiliating and undignified scramble in order to keep his trade or his clients against the Jewish invader." Ross warned darkly that "should [the czar] succeed in driving the bulk of his six million Hebrews to the United States, we shall see the rise of a Jewish question here, perhaps riots and anti-Jewish legislation."[9]

As it happened, Ross would not have to wait very long for the "Jewish question" to be raised—famously—by none other than one of America's foremost industrialists: Henry Ford. By the time Ford acquired and began to publish the newspaper *The Dearborn Independent* in 1919, World War I had ended. But the war had fostered an environment of suspicion across the United States—suspicion of Bolsheviks, of antiwar agitators, of foreign agents and spies, of Jews as a proxy for all of them. Anticommunist fervor that arose after the Russian Revolution of 1917 contained intimations that Bolshevism was "Yiddish" in nature. While the source of Henry Ford's animus against Jews remains difficult to fully ascertain, employees recall him blaming Jewish financiers for World War I; E. G. Pipp, the *Independent*'s editor, recalled Ford talking about Jews "frequently, almost continuously" by 1918.[10]

On May 22, 1920, the *Dearborn Independent* published "The International Jew: The World's Problem." It was the first in a series of weekly screeds that ran until January 14, 1922. While some essays, such as "Jewish Copper Kings Reap Rich War-Profits," "Jewish Degradation of American Baseball," and "Jewish Jazz Becomes Our National Music," are distinctly of their time, other elements of the series remain central to the conspiracies of contemporary anti-Semitism. Among them are theories that Jews control the "world press"; start wars to enrich their own financial interests; and, above all, possess innate, racialized traits of cunning and exclusionary racial solidarity. *The International Jew* introduced a character to the American consciousness that would echo throughout the following century: the Jew as gray-faced éminence grise, controlling the puppet strings of power, utilizing wealth, ruthlessness, and lust for power to direct world events. To quote from the June 12, 1920, issue:

> The world-controlling Jew has riches, but he also has something much more powerful than that.
>
> The international Jew, as already defined, rules not because he is rich, but because in a most marked degree he possesses the commercial and masterful genius of his race, and avails himself of a racial loyalty and solidarity the like of which exists in no other human group. In other words, transfer today the world-control of the international Jew to the hands of the highest commercially talented group of Gentiles, and the whole fabric of world-control would eventually fall to pieces, because the Gentile lacks a certain quality, be it human or divine, be it natural or acquired, that the Jew possesses.

On July 24, 1920, the *Independent* published "An Introduction to the 'Jewish Protocols,'"—*The Protocols of the Elders of Zion*, a 1903 Russian forgery that had already been publicly debunked by the time Ford got his hands on it. The *Protocols* claimed to be meeting minutes of a nebulous Jewish leaders' council. It laid out an organized and diabolical plan to control the world through the systematic diminution, impoverishment, and discombobulation of Gentile populations. In doing so, it laid out a schematic for the "extraordinary" anti-Semitism that would have such fatal consequences in the twentieth century. Over the course of subsequent articles, the *Independent* introduced large swathes of the text in translation, disseminating the *Protocols* for the first time to hundreds of thousands of English-speaking readers. Criticism of the series by Jews and their allies were folded into its articles, posited as evidence of the censorship and control

Jews sought to nefariously exert over their fair-minded, clear-seeing critics. The Dearborn Publishing Co., of which the *Independent* was part, republished the articles in a four-volume series of books titled *The International Jew: The World's Foremost Problem* between 1920 and 1922. These books were delivered gratis to prominent individuals and distributed at Ford dealerships.

The International Jew was subsequently translated into German and circulated in Nazi Germany, where the book influenced Hitler's anti-Semitic propaganda campaign. Hitler himself was a vocal admirer of Ford and in 1938 awarded him the Grand Cross of the German Eagle, the highest honor of the Nazi regime for foreigners.[11] This ushered in an era in which anti-Semitism was a transatlantic export, as American racism and anti-Semitism influenced the rise and actions of the Third Reich, and Nazi ideology, in turn, was embraced by a minority of the US population.

In the 1920s and the 1930s, American anti-Semitism acquired new characteristics. The Christian anti-Semitism and social snobbery that had characterized Gentile-Jewish relations for the duration of the country's existence remained. But America now played host to "extraordinary anti-Semitism" as well: ideologies which, like those espoused in *The International Jew* and *The Protocols*, were predicated on the idea of nefarious Jewish world control, going well beyond the stereotypes of child-snatchers, greedy usurers, and Christ-killers that had pervaded Jewish-Christian relationships for centuries. From Ford's press and Hitler's propaganda machine came a vision of the Jew as world-encircling parasite, source and sustainer of the modern world's evils. This holistic worldview, built on an ancient prejudice, would saturate and shape white-supremacist ideologies for the remainder of the twentieth century—and into the present day. It's impossible to understand contemporary white supremacy without understanding its roots in the thoroughgoing anti-Semitic ideologies of the twentieth century. White supremacists trade these works by their intellectual forebears back and forth, rejuvenating these toxic, hateful texts over chat apps. They believe themselves to be drawing on a long and storied intellectual history. And, due to the depth and animosity of anti-Semitism in the twentieth century, they are not wrong: Their ideas have sources, old and powerful ones, a deep well of bitter water from which to drink and draw strength.

Instances of anti-Semitism in twentieth-century America are too numerous to count, and such detail is beyond the scope of this book. But there are a number of key figures who illustrate the potential of "extraordinary" anti-Semitism, and laid crucial groundwork for the ideological underpinnings of white supremacy as it currently manifests on the internet.

The rise of Hitler in Germany—partially buoyed, and undoubtedly inspired, by the anti-Semitic rhetoric of Henry Ford and the intricate web of racist laws that governed the Jim Crow South—prompted a number of American demagogues to embrace and proclaim the justness of eliminationist anti-Semitism. Conspiracy theories about Franklin Delano Roosevelt's government abounded; it was popularly speculated that Roosevelt's name was actually "Rosenfeld," and that a sinister cabal of the president's ostensible coreligionists were behind the "Jew Deal." Among them was William Dudley Pelley, founder of an esoteric Christian sect known as "Liberation," and creator of a short-lived university called Galahad College that taught courses in "Spiritual Eugenics."[12] On January 30, 1933, the day Hitler was elected chancellor of Germany, Pelley publicly announced the founding of the "Christian militia" he dubbed the Silver Legion of America—better known as the "Silver Shirts," in imitation of the Nazi Party's "brownshirt" thugs. Chapters of the Silver Shirts sprang up in twenty-two states, though its membership never passed fifteen thousand. Explicit in its ideology was the idea that Jews should be excluded from America. In 1936, Pelley ran for president on a platform of the registration and persecution of all American Jews and the reenslavement of African-Americans, managing to get on the ballot in Washington State. By 1938, Pelley began encouraging members of the Silver Shirts to carry sawed-off shotguns and stockpile two thousand rounds of ammunition in their houses to protect "white, Christian America"—a precursor to militia movements that would arise in subsequent decades.[13]

Historian Leonard Dinnerstein estimates that one hundred specifically anti-Semitic societies arose in the 1930s—compared to "perhaps a total of five" in the entirety of American history up to that decade.[14] Included among them was the Friends of New Germany, which later became the German American Bund, the largest explicitly fascist organization in the United States at the time; the Bund boasted some 20,000 members and claimed 100,000 sympathizers across the country. The organization catered to ethnic Germans in the United States, and was led by Fritz Kuhn, whose nickname was "America's Hitler." Throughout the 1930s, the Bund led Hitler Youth–style camps for children across the United States, enthusiastically embraced and disseminated Nazi anti-Semitic propaganda, and cultivated its own version of the storm troopers, who sported swastikas and SS-style uniforms.[15]

The Bund advocated strongly for nonintervention in the European conflict that would become World War II. In this, they were joined by another group predicated on violent anti-Semitism, the Christian Front, inspired by a charismatic Catholic priest named Father Charles Coughlin. From his pulpit at the National Shrine of the Little Flower Basilica in Royal Oak, Michigan, Coughlin was the spiritual leader of an anti-Semitic movement that would garner him followers throughout the country. He began broadcasting on the radio in 1926, trafficking in homiletics with a distinctly populist bent; by the 1930s, his weekly program, "The Hour of Power," was nationally syndicated and reached millions of listeners on dozens of radio stations. A 1979 obituary by the *Washington Post* estimated that the "lion of the airwaves" had built an audience of some forty million over the course of the 1930s,[16] and, as the decade wore on, he moved from decrying "modern Shylocks" and "the red fog of Communism"[17] to more extreme anti-Semitic, militant, and pro-fascist oratory. On the radio in 1938, Coughlin quoted extensively from the *Protocols of the Elders of Zion*; blamed Jewish bankers for the ravages of capitalism, and, simultaneously, denounced Bolshevism as a Jewish plot; and accused Jews of desiring "the subjugation of all nations to the naturalistic philosophy of race supremacy."[18] On November 9–10, 1938, *Kristallnacht*—the "night of broken glass"— shattered Jewish lives across Germany; Germans, directed by Hitler's government, burned synagogues, looted Jewish-owned stores, arrested 30,000 Jews, and murdered at least 91 throughout the country. Ten days later, Coughlin gave a radio address in which he falsely accused the "powerful" Jewish minority of making up 56 of 59 members of the Central Committee of the Communist Party in Russia—and added that "the three remaining non-Jews were married to Jewesses." He added, inaccurately, that the Russian Revolution had been funded by Jewish bankers. "It is my opinion," he said, "that Nazism, the effect of communism, cannot be liquidated . . . until the religious in high places, in synagogue and finance, radio and press, attack the cause, attack it forthright, and the errors and spread of communism."[19]

Red-baiting anti-Semitism—the notion that Jews spread communism and are directly and solely responsible for the atrocities of Stalin, Lenin, and other communist leaders—remains in currency among white supremacists today.

In the same year, 1938, Coughlin began to call for the formation of anticommunist militias, on air and in his magazine, *Social Justice*. His followers were eager to answer his call, and formed the Christian Front, a militia organization that was explicitly anti-Semitic in nature. At Christian Front rallies, attendees gave Heil Hitler salutes and advocated for the "liquidation of Jews in America," according to Dinnerstein. From 1939 to 1942, Christian Front members physically assaulted Jews, desecrated synagogues, and placed yellow stars on Jewish businesses around the country. While these groups were overtly militant in their organizing and rhetoric, they reflected a broader anti-Semitic sentiment in the American population; polls from the period consistently showed strong support for the view that the Jews held "too much power" in America.[20]

When the United States entered World War II after the bombing of Pearl Harbor on December 7, 1941, the wartime government cracked down on members of America's growing fascist movement. The late 1940s and early 1950s saw a dramatic reduction in overt anti-Semitism nationwide; after the war, public opinion shifted against open Jew hatred, and legal challenges made headway against institutional religious discrimination. But at the same time, anticommunist fervor, and the growing civil rights movement, gave rise to a new generation of "extraordinary" anti-Semites—and reinvigorated Hitler's and Ford's ideas of Jewish scheming to fit the political conflicts of the day.

Anti-Semitism in the mid-twentieth century served—as it serves today—as an ideological underpinning for other, older, and more visceral prejudices: Most notably, anti-Semitism and antiblack racism became irrevocably intertwined with the dissolution of the Jim Crow legal order and the rise of the civil rights movement. In 1954, Jim Crow was dealt a harsh blow with the Supreme Court's *Brown v. Board of Education* decision, which declared segregated schools unconstitutional. The decision—and initial attempts at implementation—provoked a reaction known as "massive resistance," a euphemistic term for a brutally violent retaliatory backlash among white Southerners. Southerners formed "White Citizens Councils" to combat the burgeoning civil rights movement; as Dinnerstein puts it, "Many of the most fervent segregationists were also anti-semitic and associated Jews with racial integration." Southern Jews were, for the most part, timid and cautious in airing antisegregation views, aware that for many of their Christian neighbors, suspicion ran high that, as a 1948 Confederate Daughters of America circular put it, "Most of the funds and agitators used in stirring up your southern Negroes are Jewish in origin." But Northern Jews showed no such compunction and formed a significant part of the antiracist coalition pushing for the dismantling of de jure racial discrimination in the South. The National Association for the Advancement of Colored People, the NAACP, which had led the legal charge that precipitated the *Brown* decision, was at the time of the Supreme Court's decision headed by Arthur Spingarn—a Jewish man.

White supremacist agitators such as J. B. Stoner—a member of the Ku Klux Klan since his teens who was later convicted of the 1958 bombing of a black church in Alabama—utilized Spingarn in potent racist rhetoric that sought to draw virulent, conspiratorial links between Jews and "race-mixing." Stoner had founded the Christian Anti-Jewish Party in 1945; a 1955 pamphlet from the party,[21] titled "DEFEND THE WHITE RACE," sought to draw links between Jews, "race-mixing" and communism. "The Jews have destroyed Racial

Segregation," the pamphlet reads. "It has amazed some people to discover that the President of the NAACP is NOT a Negro but the JEW Arthur Spingarn. . . . The Jew plan of mongrelization [intermixing] would end the African race as well as the white." This nefarious program was attributed to "Jewish communists."

Such agitation, by Stoner and others, led to a campaign of attempted and actualized white-supremacist bombings of Southern Jewish properties in 1957 and 1958, with synagogue-bombing attempts taking place in Charlotte, North Carolina; Gastonia, North Carolina; Birmingham, Alabama; and Jacksonville, Florida. A Jewish school annex in Miami, Florida, and a Jewish community center in Nashville were successfully bombed in 1958, and the historic Hebrew Benevolent Congregation in Atlanta, Georgia, was firebombed and its building severely damaged.[22]

The same year—1958—saw the political emergence of George Lincoln Rockwell, whose short activist career spanned only nine years, but who has left a lasting imprint on the ideology and tactics of the American far right. Three years after the onset of "massive resistance," Rockwell founded the World Union of Free Enterprise National Socialists, later to become the American Nazi Party, in Arlington, Virginia. Rockwell's virulent anti-Semitism formed the cornerstone of his politics, and while his organization was never enormous—the embrace of the swastika and storm-trooper uniform rendered him a fringe radical—his cunning courting of the press, stage management of agitating actions, and ability to rally financial support from sympathizers across the country would reverberate for decades. Rockwell's passionate, eliminationist anti-Semitism— he sought to destroy "kikes," who he believed were "traitors"— was commingled with the racism and anticommunism of the era. Frequently stating that he and his storm troopers were merely against "communism and race-mixing"—both of which were, incidentally, plots orchestrated by Jews—Rockwell was a master of political theater who obscured the meager numbers of his movement. His storm troopers picketed the hit movie *Exodus*, a romantic narrative of the early years of the State of Israel, drawing massive counterprotests—and equally massive press coverage. He drove a "Hate Bus" across the country to coincide with the integrated Freedom Rides antiracist activists undertook in the South in the early 1960s. And he repeatedly utilized the First Amendment to ensure that he could speak in unfriendly territory, including New York City, with the law—and state power, by way of police protection—on his side. He pioneered Holocaust denialism, calling Nazi atrocities a "hoax"—a technique that would prove irresistible for racists from that moment onward, up to the present day. By the time of his assassination, by a disgruntled ex-storm trooper, in 1967, Rockwell had pioneered a white-supremacist vision that commingled anti-Semitism, racism, and conspiracy theories, and took full advantage of the press as a means to spread racist propaganda.

After Rockwell's death, one of his disciples took up the mantle of American extremist ideology. In the 1970s, a young neo-Nazi named William Luther Pierce produced a work that would go on to inspire an extraordinary amount of violence. The novel was called *The Turner Diaries*. Published in 1978, it was a futuristic description of the violent struggle for a white utopia in the United States. While it was disseminated as a work of fiction, some of its devoted readers did whatever they could to make the racist fantasy it depicted reality—up to and including murder.

The Turner Diaries proved a remarkably resilient and compelling narrative for white supremacists and conspiracists across the country; it was sold at gun shows and by mail order. Its prose is simple and unadorned, consisting of a series of diary entries by the book's white hero, Earl Turner, a terrorist in a cell called the Order, engaged in violent revolution against a multicultural United States government called the System. His hero wrote about "swarthy, kinky-haired little Jewboys" who paid off African-Americans to oppose white racism, and cast a "Jewish spell" over the majority of white Americans, lulling them into materialism and complacency.

The Turner Diaries would go on to inspire a white-supremacist terrorist gang called the Order, directly named after the group in the book, to rob banks and armored cars, and ultimately shoot to death Jewish radio host Alan Berg in Colorado in 1984. Most famously, the book was the ideological lodestar of mass murderer Timothy McVeigh, who bombed the Alfred P. Murrah Federal Building in 1995, killing 168 people, including children. The FBI has labeled it the "Bible of the racist right."

If so, a devotee of the *Turner Diaries* subsequently produced the movement's catechism. David Lane, a member of the terror cell the Order, wrote a tract while imprisoned for Berg's murder that came to be known as the "white genocide manifesto"—echoing alarms about white "racial suicide" dating back to the era of eugenics. He subsequently distilled the manifesto to a nostrum that has become ubiquitous across the world of white supremacy ever since. The "14 words" are simple: "We must secure the existence of our people and a future for white children." But the road that led to its creation draws back through the past of ideological racism—and into the present.

The Jewish-led plot to dilute the white race is multifaceted, according to the contemporary far right, and presents itself not only as an attack on "traditional" (i.e., heterosexual and stereotypically virile) masculinity, but also as a plot to deliberately shift demographics within the United States to dilute the white share of the population.

Lane's White Genocide Manifesto lays out the connection between racism and antisemitism baldly, asserting that "all Western nations are ruled by a Zionist conspiracy to mix, overrun and exterminate the White race." The idea of the plot is premised just as much on a bone-deep and visceral antiblackness as it is premised on anti-Semitism. Over and over again, the notion that Jews are organizing a cunning genetic experiment to dull the natural insubordination and heroism of whiteness through demographic dilution recurs in white supremacist rhetoric. The general theme is that Jews encourage race mixing within predominantly white countries to create "standard citizens" of mixed race—who would be stupid, docile, and savage because non-white people are inherently stupid, docile, and savage, and thus more malleable—the perfect subjects for Jewish world domination.

It tells you about the nature of far-right anti-Semitism that its targets tend to be random Jews—not powerful ones or ones even close to power. That's why recent high-profile white supremacist attacks on Jews have targeted essentially random synagogues. Those who celebrated Donald Trump's election by toppling graves in Jewish cemeteries in Brooklyn and Philadelphia and St. Louis have never been caught—but their targets were dead, beyond the ability to manipulate anything at all. The notion of a nefarious plot by Jews is not limited merely to Jews who are proximal to power and wealth; the key to far-right anti-Semitism, and the reason it endures as a fatal threat, is the belief that *every* Jew is engaged in the machinations of evil. Old or young, rich or poor, every Jew is a soldier in a war against whiteness. John Earnest, a teenage white supremacist who allegedly murdered sixty-year-old Lori Gilbert-Kaye in the Chabad of Poway synagogue in southern California in April 2019, made that clear in the manifesto he wrote before the shooting: "Every Jew is responsible for the meticulously planned genocide of the European race. They act as a unit, and every Jew plays his part to enslave the other races around him—whether consciously or subconsciously."

The notion of the cunning, enslaving Jew shows up in the ways white-supremacist vocabulary incorporates terms drawn from Hebrew and Yiddish. White supremacists, especially those operating online, frequently deploy terms drawn from the Jewish vernacular, in particular the term *goyim*—a word for "Gentile" or "non-Jew" that, in some contexts, can be derogatory, though its literal meaning is simply "nations," and it is usually used as a simple term differentiating ingroup from outgroup in Jewish settings. White supremacists proudly employ this bit of ingroup Jewish vocabulary to convey the impression that they have cottoned on to some elemental bit of Jewish nature, and display supposedly insider knowledge of Jewish culture. The phrase "the Goyim know"—i.e., we, the Gentiles, have noticed your nefarious conduct, Jew—is a favorite of white supremacists all across the internet, particularly when harassing Jewish targets. White supremacists use the term *Oy vey*—"Woe is me" in Yiddish and a stereotypical part of Jewish vocabulary—exclusively to mock Jewish pain. Similarly, the most common white-supremacist term for the Holocaust, particularly in the context of Holocaust denial, is the Hebrew word for it: *Shoah*. When Jews speak out about anti-Semitic sentiments, incidents, or the memory of the Holocaust as forewarning for other genocidal events, a common white-supremacist rejoinder is the grossly demeaning phrase, *Oy vey, anuddah shoah!*—simultaneously mocking Jewish pain and worry while also telegraphing a sense of insider knowledge of Jewish culture. They refer to money, when related in any way to Jews, as "shekels," the national currency of Israel. White supremacists also like to quote certain passages of the Talmud—one of which features a hypothetical about pedophilia—with the goal of tarring the entire six-thousand-page document as a nefarious ode to child abuse and degeneracy, as well as to convey the idea that they are intimately familiar with sacred Jewish texts and the supposed essentially evil nature of the entire "Jewish race."

The online rhetoric that works to stoke violence against Jews targets all Jews, regardless of social status. On multiple occasions, I observed white supremacists going out of their way to terrorize not just outspoken or prominent political foes, but simply random Jews, to remind them that they are unsafe precisely because they are Jews. One particularly horrifying example came in the form of a public channel on the encrypted chat app Telegram called The Noticer, which gathered screenshots from Twitter accounts of people who mentioned that they were Jewish, and blasted these screenshots out to an audience of thousands of avid anti-Semites. As of May 2020, The Noticer channel had eleven thousand members, and was open to any Telegram user. Its administrator or administrators had posted screenshots of more than sixteen hundred Jews.

The goal of The Noticer—and the reason behind its name—was the idea that it was a channel that targeted Jewish people who were ostensibly trying to pass as white. Having grown up keenly aware of not being a Christian in America—a country whose political and cultural spheres are dominated by the values and implicit cultural assumptions of Christianity—I knew myself to be white but with an asterisk. The asterisk of the Jewish star. While we may have assimilated into whiteness in the decades following World War II, a gradual cultural shift that enabled Jews to rise in social status, white supremacists consider this demographic shift a plot engineered by us to poison and destroy whiteness from within. It is, to them, the greatest transgression of the Jews, and what must be punished most. The administrator of the channel had noticed that these Jews were trying to blend in with whiteness, and discuss the condition of being a white person in America. Posts on The Noticer each followed the same general format: a photo of the targeted individual, followed by a collage of his or her tweets, one of which always included the revelation that the Twitter user was Jewish. The phrase *fellow white people* was often utilized by the targets; the phrase has become something of a white-supremacist meme, specifically referencing the idea that Jews are trying to pass as white. (For me, a white-skinned Jewish woman, the experience of whiteness has always been conditional; that is to say, I passed as white with cops and in job interviews, but I knew my grandparents had been citizens until they weren't, and I knew that synagogues had guards for a reason, and I knew you could be white until you were a Jew, and that was something else.) The point of The Noticer and similar endeavors was to specifically point out that Jews should be excluded from whiteness—and Jews' ambiguous status was due to deliberate cunning, a plan that could be thwarted by the careful attentions of white supremacists.

Individuals targeted by The Noticer were generally people who were vocal and erudite on Twitter—lawyers, professors, tech consultants, producers, journalists, authors. People who were innocent of anything but being Jews and daring to voice their opinions. Most, however, were not actively reporting on or engaging with the far right, and found the fact that they were suddenly being targeted for harassment by neo-Nazis startling and terrifying. That was the goal of the channel in the first place: to let all Jews on social media know that they were and are unsafe.

In a similar incident in June and July of 2018, students at Yeshiva University, an Orthodox Jewish university in New York City, were horrified to find that thousands of their photos had been harvested from YU's Flickr page and other public sources and posted on the neo-Nazi site Vanguard News Network. In sprawling threads, commenters on the Vanguard News Network sought to determine the "phenotype" of the Jew, used racially disparaging terms like *Juden*, and added pictures of students from Yeshiva University–affiliated high schools. According to the *YU Commentator*, the university's student paper, "There are countless photos of babies, couples and the elderly on the thread." One female student at Stern College, Yeshiva University's all-women sister school, told the *Commentator* that finding her photo being mocked by neo-Nazis made her feel targeted, unsafe, and small—a feeling I knew well. Other students reported feeling terrorized to be targeted merely for their affiliation with a Jewish institution. The fear inculcated by this rhetoric was intentional. In the white-supremacist worldview, it is the innate racial predestination of every Jew to fight against and subvert the natural order of the world—a world order in which white men retain unquestioned dominance.

The radical right's obsession with Jews has led to fatal consequences in the past and present, but that fixation serves another purpose beyond the blind accumulation of hatreds. It knits together disparate ideological influences, political philosophies, and fractious subgroups under the banner of anti-Semitism. Racial animus in and of itself, while a powerful and fatal force, demands a broader intellectual framework in which to flourish; the white supremacist requires the Jew to create a holistic system of depravity, against which he is engaged in brave and suppressed struggle. The taboo of the swastika lures in young men who often fit the profile sociologists utilized to describe youth who committed acts of anti-Semitic vandalism in the years following World War II: "emotionally disturbed youths between the ages of 10 and 18."[23] The glee of cruelty gels into an ideology; a century of anti-Semitic propaganda serves as proof texts for the willing, who already crave an enemy. On these dubious foundations, a worldview is built: one in which everything from gay marriage to immigration to social-justice movements can be blamed on the machinations of a sinister, cunning, and infinitely resourceful enemy. To the hammer, everything looks like a nail; to the white supremacist, every evil looks like a Jew.

CHAPTER 3

BOOTS ON FOR THE BOOGALOO

In the summer of 2019, white supremacists felt constrained by widely publicized—if in practice halfhearted—attempts to curb the spread of racist and conspiratorial rhetoric on mainstream social-media sites like Twitter, Facebook, and YouTube. While white-supremacist foot soldiers continued to maintain a robust presence on mainstream social media, they also began to seek alternatives. They started casting doubt on long-established hubs, like the anonymous message boards 4chan and 8chan. The chatting app Discord—popular among video-game enthusiasts—had previously served as a key hub for far-right discussion online, including much of the planning of the fatal "Unite the Right" white-supremacist rally in Charlottesville, Virginia, in August 2017. But a mere two days after the attack in which Heather Heyer died and dozens more were severely injured, an antifascist media organization called "Unicorn Riot" began to release an enormous cache of Discord chats between members of the far right. Unicorn Riot eventually set up a publicly searchable database of far-right Discord messages; "Unicorn Riot Discord Leaks opens far-right activity centers to public scrutiny through data journalism,"

46

the organization wrote in its description. This proved true: The chats, which had been conducted with the presumption of privacy and thus contained free-wheeling far-right discourse, led to the identification and outing of dozens of white supremacists around the country, both by antifascist activists and by journalists reporting on hate movements in the United States.

In June 2019, I stumbled across a thread on 8chan in which users expressed their concern about the number of "shills" who had begun to surveil the anonymous board after it served as a platform for Brenton Tarrant, a mass shooter who murdered over fifty Muslims at prayer in Christchurch, New Zealand, to post his manifesto. As a result, 8channers were looking for other options to express their opinions online and reach one another; Discord had proved too easy to infiltrate. (After the third mass shooter in several months uploaded a manifesto and livestream of his acts to 8chan, the message board was pushed offline by its internet service provider.)

Ultimately, some users settled on the encrypted messaging app Telegram. The app was launched in 2013, and rose to prominence as a platform for political expression in Russia; it battled Russian authorities in court over its refusal to hand over its encryption keys to Russian authorities. (As a fact checker for the *New Yorker*, I spoke to numerous Russian dissident sources on Telegram, including a Chechen fixer who had to flee the country after our article, critical of local dictator Ramzan Kadyrov, was published.) But such a staunch commitment to privacy has its downsides: In 2019, Telegram became a prominent gathering place for far-right extremists who faced or feared censorship on social media. On the 8chan thread, users listed Telegram channels in which they sought to gather.

Altogether, beginning on June 1, 2019, I joined more than ninety far-right groups on Telegram, a plurality of the English-language channels listed on the 8chan thread, as well as groups I found through groups I joined. I also found a number of these chats through a channel called "Procurement," which offered lists of far-right channels and dubbed itself a "free speech platform." My intent in joining these groups was to gain a fly-on-the-wall view of far-right rhetoric, surveilling its violence, racial animus, and anti-Semitism in an environment in which contributors felt safe to speak freely, embracing the new platform on which they found themselves and connecting enthusiastically with one another. I didn't participate in these ever-moving conversations, just lurked as "Tommy," an anonymous fellow with a picture of a banana as his avatar. The vast majority of participants in the chats and subscribers to the channels were similarly anonymous, so such an obscured identity did not attract undue attention. I utilized a fake phone number generated by an app to obscure my own identity still further.

A Southern Poverty Law Center report, published on June 27, 2019, revealed that the neo-Nazi website the Daily Stormer had warned its fans in August 2018 that the "SPLC Is Monitoring You" on the chat app Discord, and lauded Telegram's end-to-end encryption as an alternative for white nationalists. The SPLC report added that Telegram posed particular dangers, compared to message boards like 8chan: On the app, "extremists can connect in channels that post publicly facing propaganda and then organize privately on the same app by using its encrypted chat feature, where plans to commit acts of terror can go undetected by law enforcement agencies." In my experience, a chaotic mix of memes, calls for violence, and detailed dossiers on prospective "enemies" were characteristic of far-right Telegram channels.

The channels' names were evocative, and many of them focused purely on spreading anti-Semitic propaganda. On 8chan, a graphic surfaced listing fifteen Telegram channels, grouped under the label "Guild of Counter-Semitism." Another graphic mapped out a network meant to guide Telegram users through an ideological journey of radicalization, starting from "entry-level redpills" and advancing to channels about the "gay trans agenda" and "based screencaps and good reads" (*based* being a frequently used far-right term for "ideologically far-right"). I also encountered a channel run by Paul Nehlen, once a congressional primary challenger to Paul Ryan endorsed by Donald Trump, whose virulent anti-Semitism saw him banned from Twitter and the Wisconsin Republican Party. I joined Gen Z Y K L O N; K i K e S C e N T R a L; Jewish Ritual Murder Abortion Satanism Pizzagate; Judenpresse Monitor/Archive; Holohoax Memes & Info; Jews Own USA (Wars Media Banks). A chat called "MakeAmerica110" was named after a frequently floated white-supremacist statistic—that Jews had been expelled from 109 countries. They wanted to make America the next.

The chats varied in membership, with some as small as twenty-two members and others as large as five thousand members. Some were open chats, where users could converse with one another. Others operated as feeds, with memes, news links, videos, social-media posts, and rants spread to subscribers by an individual channel operator. Altogether, as of June 5, 2019, the chats I'd joined collectively had 32,380 members. A study by the reporter Tess Owen of Vice News, published in October 2019, did a sweeping analysis that proved Telegram was growing exponentially in 2019 as a platform for the far right, as extremists were pushed off mainstream social-media platforms like Facebook and Twitter. One channel Owen observed had ten thousand members that it reached multiple times a day. Over two-thirds of 150 far-right channels Owen examined had been created in 2019; 22 were created in the month after the

Christchurch, New Zealand, white-nationalist massacre perpetrated by Brenton Tarrant. Eighty-two of the 150 channels examined in total had appeared after Christchurch, and as such were focused on preparing for violent action—disseminating instructions for how to build pipe bombs and homemade guns, survivalist manuals for the coming race war, and, Owen writes, guides to prepare for committing a mass shooting.

The channels I observed had putatively distinct focuses—Gen Z Y K L O N was meant to appeal to younger people, who were members of "Generation Z," a term coined by demographers that refers to the postmillennial generation; other channels focused on Jewish perfidy or racist memes. In practice, though, messages that originated in one chat room were frequently forwarded to others, so it wasn't unusual to see the same anti-Semitic or racist meme surface multiple times, reaching overlapping but distinct audiences.

Videos of grisly violence against black and brown people were circulated without context, so that, opening a chat room, a user might see a video of a black man's hands being cut off—a continual desensitization to violence against nonwhite people. The tone of conversation ranged from the deadly earnest to the deeply juvenile. There was frequent infighting between far-right factions—users accusing one another of being "faggots" and "kikes" at the least offense, "raiding" other groups to spam them with gay and furry porn. The nearly-all-male members of the chats reveled in homoerotic humor even as they espoused violent homophobia. But these puerile jokes were undercut with deadly serious rants about their cause: There were screeds asserting that US electoral politics had reached its limit and needed to be replaced with violent revolutionary activities, and a seemingly endless well of earnest vitriol against minorities and Jews. The two cadences of conversation overlapped indistinguishably, forming an endless, roiling soup of incitement and gloating camaraderie.

Users swapped texts like Brenton Tarrant's manifesto about "white genocide," PDFs of *The Turner Diaries*, the neo-Nazi book *Siege* by James Mason, Holocaust-denial manifestos, and quotes about Adolf Hitler. They also voiced their discomfort and frustration with the Republican Party's open embrace of Israel, and shared memes about Jewish "decadence," world control, and degeneracy—themes Hitler and Henry Ford might have been proud of. They shared memes featuring Pepe, a cartoon frog commandeered by the alt-right; swastika banners; and images of pristine white families, often with slogans like "Remember what they took from you." They followed mainstream news closely, seizing on elements of contemporary news reports that fed racial animus. In May 2020, a viral video of an unarmed twenty-five-year-old black man in Georgia, named Ahmaud Arbery, being chased down and shot to death by white vigilantes flooded the internet, generating commentary from mainstream news outlets as well as politicians on both sides of the aisle. Arbery had been out jogging in Brunswick, Georgia, his native city, before he was chased down in a pickup truck by thirty-four-year-old Travis McMichael and sixty-four-year-old Gregory McMichael, a recently retired police officer, and shot repeatedly. After seventy-four days of inaction by law enforcement, the McMichaels were arrested and charged with Arbery's murder. They have denied criminal behavior and are awaiting trial at the time of this writing. Far-right channels reveled in Arbery's death, calling him a "n— criminal," and nicknaming him "Armed Robbery." As a wave of thoughtful essays and analysis by black runners delineated the danger they felt while engaging in their hobby, far-right Telegram users began utilizing the term "jogger" as a pseudonym for the n-word. "They listen to jogger music. They elect a jogger as their president. . . . America is a nation of jogger-loving joggers," wrote the anonymous administrator of the channel The Bureau of Memetic Warfare on May 8, 2020.

They also routinely shared videos of physical assaults on Jews. They frequently appealed to an ur-Jew named "Shlomo": one user in Gen Z Y K L O N lamented his own habit of sleeping in by saying he was behaving "like a minority" and vowed to do better. "Not today shlomo [*sic*]," he wrote, "not today. Time to get up and prepare for the coming race war."

The topic of an impending "race war"—an event variously referred to as "Minecraft," "The Hootenanny," "All Saints' Day," "the collapse," and the "Day of the Rope"—was a consistent obsession across myriad chats. One channel, "Sminem's Siege Shack," with nearly four thousand subscribers, dispensed survivalist advice along with a steady stream of racist, anti-immigrant, and anti-Semitic propaganda. Subscribers were advised to learn how to make wood gas; to learn Morse code and how to make geocaches; how to make charcoal. "If the hootenanny catches you outside and you're somehow cut off from your house or base of operations, you better have important survival items concealed and mapped," wrote the channel's owner. The "race war"—an apocalyptic social breakdown in which white supremacists carry out their most violent fantasies against American minorities—is a persistent, Rag-narokian presence in extremist discourse, discussed with both irony and genuine longing. The most popular name for it is "the Boogaloo," a reference to a widely panned 1984 sequel to a breakdancing movie, *Breakin' 2: Electric Boogaloo*, only the sequel in question here is to the Civil War. In the late spring of 2020, the term *Boogaloo* experienced an explosion of popularity, as a series of far-right protests against coronavirus quarantine and lockdown orders by state governments spread across the United States. The protesters were a loose coalition of heavily armed white nationalists, antivaccine activists, conspiracy theorists, and members of the antigovernment militia movement. As the watchdog group the Tech Transparency Project reported, a large network of Facebook pages dedicated to the Boogaloo—and variants like "big luau," "boog," and "big igloo," designed to evade moderators—shared extremist content, including a report on how to disrupt US government supply lines and assassinate government officials. The Facebook groups contained numerous white-nationalist members, with profiles that celebrated Adolf Hitler, the TTP found. At the protests themselves, far-right activists displayed AR-15s alongside Confederate flags and signs with slogans like LIBERTY OR BOOGALOO. In Columbus, Ohio, a man the Anti-Defamation League identified as a member of the National Socialist movement attended a protest, bearing a sign with a Jewish star, a caricature of a Jew, and the slogan THE REAL PLAGUE. Weeks later, during a national uprising over police brutality in June 2020, "Boogaloo" proponents nimbly shifted to menacing protesters with the Black Lives Matter movement. These often-armed incursions were an overt attempt to escalate protest into war.

The name *Boogaloo* is a prime example of the way extremist rhetoric works online, and in its spillover into real-life rallies: Naked desire for violence buried in tongue-in-cheek, memeified rhetoric, spreading among irony-saturated young men. The corpses they long to create are buried under slick layers of euphemism and crude humor.

Explicit anti-Semitism of the coarsest kind was coupled with exhortations to violence. These were rarely explicit, but were rather oblique calls for revolution, to get armed, to be ready to fight for one's ideals.

One user in a chat room called "End Cultural Marxism" described America's imminent death by immigration—a "bullet" that would put an end to cultural and social cohesion. The GOP, he said, was holding a gun to the heads of those who opposed immigration. "The entire system is rigged," he wrote. "The only way to win is to flip the table." One popular, forwarded message that appeared in a number of channels featured an array of long guns, laid out on a picnic table of weathered wood. "You may not be able to choose the perfect weapon when the time comes," wrote user The Way Down, "but by god you can choose to fight." There were channels like "Terrorwave," "Hans' Right Wing Terror Center," and "VetWar" that actively embraced a philosophy of far-right accelerationism—the notion that a white-supremacist revolution can be attained only through violence, not politics or rhetoric, and that the best time to begin such violent acts is right now. In "Rey's Cowboy Saloon," roughly twelve hundred sub-scribers were reminded that flamethrowers are legal in all fifty states without requiring registration. "And yes, you can legally buy the mix to create napalm," the anonymous channel runner added, including a link to a site selling flamethrowers.

While many commentators are eager to pin the rise of white supremacy in the United States on Trump exclusively—and it is true that he has played an undeniable role in fanning its flames—the chat rooms were a good place to note the precise ways in which far-right rhetoric is distinct from the policy platform of the Republican Party, even in an era in which the Republican Party is drifting further and further to the right. A persistent low-grade resentment of capitalism—as opposed to the big-business embrace of conservative social policy—pervaded the chats. Corporations were dominated by Jews, and any corporation's halfhearted, brand-boosting stab at social conscience in an ad campaign or tweet was greeted as further evidence of corporate degeneracy. Discussions of foreign policy were entirely dominated by the conviction that Donald Trump was acting as a puppet of Israel; resentment of the US-Israel alliance; and asserting that all foreign wars, including the rumbles of conflict with Iran, are designed to satiate Israel's thirst for blood.

This attitude summed up much of the far right's stance toward Trump: He was ideologically aligned with them but not extreme enough, too surrounded by Jews, too willing to make mealy-mouthed concessions to the social norms of pluralism they abhor. To these extremists, the fact that there wasn't an Einsatzgruppen shooting minorities and Jews in the streets, and they hadn't been invited to join, was reason enough to abandon their electoral hopes in Trump as savior of their movement. Trump's overtly racist campaign, election, and inauguration reinvigorated white-supremacist activity in the United States, both bolstering and expanding extant groups and resulting in a proliferation of new fascist groups. It didn't hurt that Steve Bannon, an ideologue openly friendly to the alt-right, managed Trump's campaign in its final days. Yet over the ensuing years, the tenor of fascist rhetoric with regard to the Oval Office has changed from triumphant to disillusioned.

While Trumpism awakened and emboldened the movement—enabling white nationalists to feel that they were going to be electorally represented at a federal level—their own impatience, and the ways Trump himself has made peace with the mores of the conservative elite he had once promised to defeat, have steadily chipped away at that hope.

The 2016 presidential election proved a high-water mark for many white supremacists, a jolt of hope that rejuvenated an ideology that had been thoroughly isolated from mainstream political conversation during the Obama era. (Media discussion of the Tea Party movement largely papered over its overt and persistent racism, a myopia that would unfortunately persist throughout Trump's rise and in mainstream analysis of his supporters' motivations.) It's difficult to overstate just how excited white supremacists were at the moment of Trump's election. It was a white-hot shot of adrenaline into the arm of white nationalists nationwide. In November 2016, the neo-Nazi site Daily Stormer praised Trump's election in ecstatic terms. "We Won," site founder Andrew Anglin wrote on November 9, 2016. "All of our work. It has paid off. Our Glorious Leader has ascended to God Emperor."[1] Ten days after Trump's election, the National Policy Institute, the generically named but emphatically white-nationalist think tank led by professional racist Richard Spencer, held a conference that became infamous for its climactic speech. Speaking to an audience of two hundred, Spencer shouted, "Heil Trump! Heil our people! Heil victory!" to a crowd, who responded with Nazi Seig Heil salutes. The evening before, Spencer had told his followers that it was "time to party like it's 1933"—the year Adolf Hitler was appointed chancellor of Germany. "Let's party like it's *2016!*" he added to cheers.[2]

In 2017, at the Unite the Right rally in Charlottesville, Virginia, the far right hoped to demonstrate their newly prominent place in the American polity—and their representation by a sympathetic president—with a show of force that would demonstrate not just their numbers, but the new endorsement of their tenets they believed Trump's election and inauguration signified in American society. Trump infamously made a series of statements in support of the fascist marchers, even after the murder of Heather Heyer, though he was met by a furious backlash that spanned nearly the entirety of the American political spectrum. By 2019, fascists' hopes for a "God-Emperor" who would heed their wishes and fulfill their most violent fantasies had largely soured. The conservative establishment had made its peace with Trumpism, and for all the chatter of the Republican Party being coopted and corrupted by Trump, the influence was decidedly mutual. Trump's pandering was more oriented toward the Republican elected officials whom he needed to accomplish his goals—following their lead on Israel, on tax cuts, on judgeships—than toward the white-nationalist fringe that had invested so much of their hope in him. Trump's decision in December 2017, widely hailed by conservative evangelicals, to move the American embassy in Israel from Tel Aviv to Jerusalem was considered, on the far right, to be the final straw in their disillusionment. Brad Griffin, chief of PR for the rabidly anti-Semitic neoconfederate group League of the South, worded his objections succinctly in a blog post objecting to the embassy move that month:

> In the end, [right-wing Jewish megadonor] Sheldon Adelson and Organized Jewry got what it wanted from Trump and the GOP. It has gotten everything it wanted this year with the exception of a ground war in Syria to oust Assad. Wall Street is roaring. The massive tax cuts are on the way. The Charlottesville resolution [condemning the Unite the Right rally, white supremacists, and the KKK] was unanimously passed by Congress and signed by Trump. The Iran deal was decertified. Tomorrow, Trump is huddling with top Jewish donors to celebrate Hanukkah at the White House.

The perception that Trump was enslaved to the Jewish agenda grew in intensity in 2017 and 2018, and white supremacists began to portray Trump's Jewish advisers—particularly his son-in-law Jared Kushner, who was perceived as taking and corrupting the pure-white femininity of the president's daughter Ivanka Trump through interbreeding—as pernicious, crooked influences. By early December 2017, just over a year after ecstatically celebrating Trump's election, the Daily Stormer had taken to calling the White House the "Jew

House," infuriated at the presence of Jared Kushner and Gary Cohn, then the president's chief economic adviser.

Trump's extremist rhetoric, embrace of violence, and propensity to engage in public racism—and succeed precisely because of his willingness to do these things—led white supremacists to hope for the first time, in most of their lifetimes, that they might see a government ready to purge the country of nonwhite people and create the white ethnostate they dreamed of. Trump's policies have trended strongly in that direction. His administration has sharply curbed legal immigration, and enacted mass-scale cruelties on the Southern border in the form of its family separation policy, which started in the spring of 2017, though it became official administration policy only the following year.[3] Stephen Miller, the president's chief immigration adviser, has documented sympathies with white-nationalist sentiments, sharing content from extremist sites and expressing a desire to completely cease legal immigration to the United States. Trump's racist and xenophobic rhetoric has hardly ceased in office; it has only continued with the aid of the megaphone of the presidency, as he systematically targets opponents of color to publicly pillory. He has advocated for police brutality against protesters repeatedly, and attacked Black individuals who criticize him with particular rancor.

These policies and statements have—rightly—horrified an enormous segment of the American voting public, and inserted a frantic urgency into progressive organizing, resulting in substantive electoral gains. Trump's open hostility toward immigrants and people of color has led progressives to justly decry his administration's racism. But for the white-nationalist fringe, not only has Trump failed to oust Jews from government, he has not been racist or anti-immigrant *enough*—not nearly.

Trump's rhetoric during the 2018 congressional midterm elections was extreme and centered around racist xenophobia almost entirely. In the weeks preceding the election, the specter of a "caravan" of migrants snaking its slow way up from Central America was the chief subject on which he campaigned. A steady stream of conservative media hysteria—and increasingly unhinged conspiracy rhetoric, which posited that members of ISIS had somehow joined the ragged group—both fed, and fed off of, the president's fixation. Yet a strong current within the white-nationalist movement viewed this as cynical pandering, unlikely to be backed up with the violent and genocidal policies they yearned for. Brad Griffin, of the League of the South, summed up this disillusionment succinctly five days before the midterm elections, inspired by Trump's publication of an astonishingly racist anti-immigrant video ad on October 31. In a blog post, he wrote:

> The GOP ran on immigration in the 2012, 2014 and 2016 elections, but hasn't done shit about the issue. Amazingly, the GOP under Trump is somehow deporting fewer illegal aliens than Barack Obama.
>
> The GOP was given the White House, Congress and the Supreme Court. They had the chance to Build The Wall which was the #1. issue in 2016. The problem is that they didn't want to Build The Wall. They don't want to end birthright citizenship either. After running against DACA and holding multiple failure theater votes against it since 2012, the GOP has tried to give amnesty to the DREAMers. They haven't passed Kate's Law, an e-Verify bill or done anything about sanctuary cities either.
>
> . . . The GOP is campaigning on White Nationalism, but governing on mainstream conservatism. They're not campaigning on the tax cuts or banking deregulation or Jerusalem because no

one cares about that shit. Instead, they are cynically campaigning on the one issue they refuse to do anything about.

Satisfying extremists is notoriously difficult. Trump has been constrained by the United States legal system, by members of his own party, and by an opposition that gained control of one of the branches of government in 2018. Anything short of a Reichstag Fire–type abrogation of any façade of normal order, or government-sanctioned fascist armed gangs shooting migrants down in broad daylight, might fail to appease the far-right fringe.

The far right will likely still vote for Trump in 2020, if they bother to vote at all. But their numbers, while difficult to track, seem insufficient to sway an election; their power chiefly lies in the ability to perpetrate violence and terror, and that requires comparatively few people.

There remains an electoralist element within the white-nationalist movement—a strain that hopes to achieve its goals by gaining influence and power, chiefly within the Republican Party. For the most part, this has entailed calculated runs for local government—for example, a twenty-year-old white supremacist and hate group member ran for school board in Killingly, Connecticut, in 2019. The white supremacist YouTuber James Allsup, a former campus ambassador for Donald Trump at Washington State University and an open devotee of Richard Spencer and other white-nationalist ideologues, was elected precinct committee officer of the local GOP in Whitman County, Washington, in 2018.[4]

The leader of the white-nationalist hate group Identity Evropa, Patrick Casey, laid out a clear plan to infiltrate local Republican parties around the country. "Identity Evropa leadership strongly encourages our members to get involved in local politics. We've been pushing this for a while, but haven't seen much of it happening," Casey wrote in an October 2017 message to the group's Discord chat. "The GOP is essentially the White man's party at this point (it gets Whiter every election cycle), so it makes far more sense for us to subvert it than to create our own party."

Yet for the most part, figures like Casey, who retain hope that the GOP remains a viable route for open white nationalists to gain power, have become a minority on the far right. Those who sought to broaden the Overton window of American discourse through an outward appearance of respectability, like Richard Spencer, have largely found themselves disgraced as the American left grows more and more vocal about the need to stamp out organized racism. Disillusionment with Trumpism—as well as the innate violence of the white-supremacist movement's culture, which disdains such slow and unthrilling measures as voting and committee meetings—has led to a distancing from their brief embrace of electoral politics. A much larger faction has embraced a philosophy known as "accelerationism"—the notion that things must get much, much worse as fast as possible and that this will eventually bring about a hoped-for race war, ending in a purge of *untermenschen* (subhumans)—Jews, people of color—and a snow-white, ethnically cleansed republic.

I gleaned all this from a combination of reading extremist publications, surfing far-right forums, and, above all, spending my days immersed in the murk of far-right chat rooms on Telegram. I muted cell-phone notifications on the chats, choosing to dip in when I wanted to, rather than being constantly bombarded with racial slurs and white-supremacist rhetoric from chats like the "White World Union for National Socialism."

The actual ideology of these linked networks was difficult to pin down precisely, amid a thicket of memes, irony, and racial slurs.

White supremacy was latent in every word and meme—the idolization of "Saint" Dylann Roof, the hail of "Heils," the endless rhetorical scourging of kikes and n—s. But one term that began surfacing over and over was *globohomo*, or *globohomoism*—the most abstract term I'd found, and one that seemed to act as a galvanizing force. The term cropped up in neo-Nazi and racist channels of all kinds, accompanied by fascist symbols like the *Sonnenrad* or "Black Sun," in long ideological screeds, and in passing banter. Taken in context, *globohomo* was the closest thing I found to a unifying ideology—a ubiquitous state of affairs deplored by the membership of dozens of channels, with an audience of thousands.

I wanted to understand what *globohomo* meant for the same reason I wanted to dive deeper and deeper into understanding the white-supremacist movement. Because treating it as an unreasoning and terrible threat without its own internal logic gave it power. I wanted to understand the collective ideology these disparate groups ascribed to in order to be able to counter it nimbly and without stumbling—and to understand its appeal to the people it was radicalizing every day.

In a number of posts about *globohomo*, it seemed like a generalized reference to contemporary economic life—there were references to "globohomo megacorporations," "globohomo materialism," and a longing for "the upcoming post-globohomo, techno-feudalistic ages of revenge and strife." The term *homo* is usually used as derogatory shorthand for homosexuals, but in this context it served two purposes: It also meant "homogenization," the increasing sameness of everything worldwide. Some references directly appealed to homophobic prejudice. When a gay-pride-themed "Make America Great Again" hat appeared in Donald Trump's official shop in June 2019—with the caption "Show your support for the LGBT community and the

45th President with this exclusive Make America Great Again Pride Hat"—it enraged numerous users in the chat rooms I monitored. A post originating in "Alt-right Shitlords Inc." with a picture of the hat and the slogan "Be sure to get your globohomo MAGA hat before 2020" circulated through four different channels. A similarly vitriolic response greeted Donald Trump's May 31, 2019, tweets in support of LGBT Pride Month. "Hey, maybe him going full globohomo will wake his religious followers up . . ." wrote one user under a screenshot of the tweets.

But what, precisely, was *globohomo*? In context, it seemed like an expansive, flexible term that encompassed racism, anti-Semitism, homophobia, and a critique of capitalism and corporate power into a single word.

In an essay published in November 2018, an eclectic New Zealand website attempted to provide a full definition of the term. VJM Publishing is a site that hosts a blog, publishes books, and sells merchandise through an online hub called TradeMe. The site's profile on Minds, an alternative social-media network popular on the far right, adds that it offers readers "suppressed political philosophy." Such "suppressed" viewpoints include posts titled "How a New Zealand Nazi Party Could Eliminate All Competition through Existing Mechanisms," "What New Zealand Could Afford If We Didn't Take in Refugees," "The Holocaust Religion," "Are You Suffering from Retard Fatigue?" and "The Negrification of the New Zealand Maori." The site published a post in November 2018 titled "What is Globohomo?"

Below the header was a grotesque cartoon of a monster whose legs are those of a spider and whose face is that of a Jew, with a hook nose, a massive crooked-toothed grin, and a Star of David hovering above its head. The Jew-spider presided over a throng penciled in thick, repulsive-looking chiaroscuro: A feminist was represented as a nude woman screaming, carrying a cross and a sign that read "i am god." A racist caricature of a black "thug" stood beside her, grabbing his crotch; next to him marched a tattooed, switchblade-wielding man with the word *LOCO* tattooed on his forehead, meant to represent Latinos as dangerous criminals. Communists, gay-rights advocates, and hippies marched under signs that read "end white pride," "stop white oppression" and "black lives matter." At the front of the crowd a hairy woman in a gimp mask with tape-covered nipples bore the words "punish me" on her sagging belly; an obese man chomped on a hamburger; and an antifa flag soared beside a sign that read, "open borders 4 everyone." Over all this presided the spidery Jew—the architect of what was represented as a scene of chaos, degeneracy, and social disorder. A reverse Google-image search of the photo traced it back to an artist named "edelhert89" on the art website Deviantart, where it was titled "American Progress"; the image had been used to illustrate posts on several white-supremacist publications. (Other cartoons by the artist included "Lolocaust"—a caricature of a scream-ing Jew with the words "MUH HOLOCAUST" used as a caption—and "Scum," a photocollage of mostly black protestors.)

"Internet dwellers will have found themselves more and more frequently encountering the word 'globohomo.' It's always used derisively, usually by members of the alt-right," the essay began. "Globohomo is very much a world-wide phenomenon, in the sense that it seeks to expand its reach into every corner of the planet. It intends to destroy all local cultures, whether they be national, provincial, city, town, village or family. These local cultures must be destroyed so that people have no resistance to the propaganda of the globalists."

In case the anti-Semitic dog whistle *globalists* wasn't clear—or the accompanying cartoon was somehow too subtle—the anonymous author added that the "globalist element" consisted of "international bankers," a euphemism ripped straight from Henry Ford. There followed a curious, halfhearted indictment of global capitalism: "What they desire is the destruction of all national cultures, so as to pave the way for a world of McDonald's-eating, Coke-drinking, television-watching mass consumers."

The author claims that globohomo is expanding into cultural spaces like a cancer, "for the sake of maximising profits and control, both of which are held by an international class with loyalties to no land and to no people"—the Jews.

Globohomo takes ideas from prior generations of ideologues and extremists: Its hatred of sexual "degeneracy" in the form of homosexuality, transgender identity, and sexual promiscuity has clear connections to Nazi ideology. Its contention that Jews are the fundamental cause of all ills and malcontent hearkens back to Hitler, and Henry Ford before him. The notion of a globalized program, run by Jews, dates back to the *Protocols of the Elders of Zion*—with its claims that Jews were attempting to establish a "Super-Government" and a "Jewish Super-State." That the mechanism of such a conquest would be by means of sly cultural subversion is referenced in the *Protocols* also, in which the sneering Elders state that "the art of directing masses and individuals by means of cleverly manipulated theory and verbiage, by regulations of life in common and all sorts of other quirks, in all which the GOYIM understand nothing, belongs likewise to the specialists of our administrative brain." Notions of a cunning Jewish plan specifically to dilute the white race echo segregationist fulminations against Jewish-masterminded "mongrelization" and George Lincoln Rockwell's anti-Semitic screeds against "communism and race-mixing." And the odium toward both trans people and Jews evinced by the far right is an echo of Nazi ideology; among the first acts of oppression by the far right was to crush the nascent Weimar community of trans and gender-nonconforming people, and to destroy scientific studies into divergent gender presentation.

Far-right publications and chats—which tend to strike a toxically masculine, puerile, and violent tone—are particularly fertile ground for users to marinate in homophobia and transphobia, two breeds of hatred that have deep roots in American culture writ large. Transphobia, in particular, is a useful tool for the far right; the transphobia evinced in American society in general and especially on its right flank means that antitrans animus is never far out of reach for the far-right's propagandists, either. While most Americans are generally not raised with a visceral disgust toward Jews, transphobia is often presented in general discussions as a "natural" or "visceral" phenomenon, with disgust toward trans people and frustration at the notion of accommodating them a common and mostly socially acceptable view to express. As a result, white nationalists and far-right anti-Semites, positing that trans rights (and transness in general) are a Jewish plot to dilute the white race, makes use of the potency, broad reach, and visceral nature of American transphobic sentiment to deepen anti-Semitism and transfer those same qualities from trans people to Jews.

Antitrans rhetoric from politicians and right-wing news outlets—the perennial panic over trans women using women's bathrooms; baseless fearmongering about gender-affirming care for trans children—is frequently utilized and repurposed by far-right polemicists. It's yet another example of an all-too-common phenomenon. The open prejudice that has become the driving force of the mainstream Republican party serves to feed the violent, extremist fringe; the more vicious mainline Republican rhetoric becomes, the more the radical right bays for violence, for strife, for war. Having enabled Trumpism and thoroughly condoned—or joined in on—white-nationalist campaign rhetoric, the GOP finds itself uniquely unable to fend off the incursion; it is akin to someone who starves a hound, lets it loose to savage the neighbors, then finds himself surprised when the red-jawed hound turns at last on its owner.

———

In the summer of 1348, the Black Death was beginning its ravages through northern France, and it started in the Duchy of Normandy. The towns of the province were devastated by the swift-raging infection, and throughout the region's worst-struck villages, desperate citizens began to fly black flags of warning and of sorrow from their churches. The spread of the plague to other provinces was stopped by winter, and Picardy, to the northeast, was unaffected. A monk in the abbey of Fourcarment recorded at the time that "the mortality in Normandy was so great among the people of Normandy that those in Picardy mocked them." By the summer of 1349, however, the plague, transmitted easily among a populace that believed bathing to be dangerous to their health, made its way onward. The inhabitants of Picardy, forewarned by the black flags of Normandy, but believing themselves to be immune to the misfortune of their neighbors, were struck so badly that, according to the same contemporary account, "No one could be found even to carry the corpses to the tomb."[5]

In the United States in 2019, nearly seven hundred years later, the Picardy faction of the Republican Party has awoken at last to the plague in its midst. Throughout November, events sponsored by the corporate wing of the Republican establishment—most notably various stops on Turning Point USA's "Culture War" tour—were struck by an incursion of youthful white nationalists, who took the events' Q&A portions as opportunities to push their political agenda with increasing stridency. These young white nationalists called themselves the Groyper movement—a moniker based on an obscure Pepe the Frog meme. Their agenda had three major points: advocating for anti-Semitism; advancing the theory that white Americans are being "replaced" by immigrants, including legal ones; and asserting the necessity of explicit homophobia.[6] Their greater goal is a calculated shattering of the Overton window, drawing the GOP closer and closer to the white-nationalist movement until their goals and public rhetoric are fundamentally indistinguishable.

Throughout his tour of various colleges all over the United States, Charlie Kirk, Turning Point USA's twenty-six-year-old spokesman, struggled to answer questions from smirking young men in MAGA hats, like "Can you prove that our white European ideals will be maintained if the country is no longer made up of white European descendants?" Success and press coverage emboldened the insurgent faction: In November 2019, Donald Trump Jr. faced a humiliatingly abbreviated book launch, scampering offstage a mere twenty minutes after his event began as he was beset by demands for a Q&A. That same month, Kirk was chased bodily from an event at the University of Houston by a massive, hostile crowd, chanting, "America First!"

The insurgent faction is led, tactically and spiritually, by a twenty-one-year-old named Nicholas Fuentes. Based on his YouTube streams and Telegram channel, whose audiences have grown exponentially, he is delighted by the attention his stunts have garnered. Fuentes has also received support from the hate group Identity Evropa, whose leader, Patrick Casey, has declared himself affiliated with Fuentes's "army" of insurgent youth. Although Fuentes is frequently described as a "Trump supporter," the principal objections he and his faction hold toward the Trump administration are their insufficient cruelty to nonwhites and their coziness with Jews. Prior to these events (and no doubt again after the furor around them has died down), Fuentes has been neither a particularly significant nor a particularly popular figure on the white-nationalist right; he was a minor participant in the deadly Unite the Right rally at Charlottesville in 2017, and has languished in middle-tier obscurity ever since. His strategy, while effective, did not require any significant cunning: Pointing out the hypocrisy of establishment conservatism in the age of Trump is a fantastically easy task, fruit hanging so low it brushes muck.

The scramble to repudiate white nationalism on the part of Republicans heckled by its representatives has been a tragicomedy in tweet form. Benny Johnson, accused serial plagiarist and current chief creative officer of TPUSA, laid out a long thread, establishing Fuentes's history of public bigotry, from advocating the return of Jim Crow laws to "Unabashedly Sexist" (*sic*) commentary. Johnson ended with a passionate plea to fellow conservatives to "disavow hatred, racism, identity politics and open anti-Semitism." The addition of *open* is curious: Is hidden anti-Semitism A-OK? Is white nationalism, a scourge on America, with a death toll in the millions from slavery to civil war to terrorist bombings, simply another form of "identity politics"? At any rate, Johnson spent the following day live-tweeting the House impeachment inquiry, manically defending a president who has predicated his entire rule on racism, and who is credibly accused of multiple sexual assaults. Later, during protests in D.C. against police brutality, Johnson posed, grinning, with a cadre of armed men in Hawaiian shirts—"boogaloo" proponents—who had come to "defend the city" against antifascists.

Dan Crenshaw, a Republican representative from Texas who was heckled by Fuentes's acolytes no fewer than three times, took to Twitter to clarify that "conservatives are 100 percent different" from these "vehement racists, anti-semites & ethnic-nationalists." The irony was palpable, though Crenshaw appeared to be serious—unbelievable, given his slavering adulation of an openly white-nationalist president. Crenshaw is an avid supporter of Trump and his policies, particularly those surrounding immigration; he has advocated ending visa lotteries and policies that make it easier for immigrants' family members to immigrate, and has militated repeatedly for Trump's signature border wall, a concrete symbol of xenophobia. In other words, it seems as if he would like to embrace ethnonationalism and prop up anti-Semitic ideologies without having embarrassingly open ethnonationalist anti-Semites show up and ruin his good time.

Trump's own statements, coupled with his policies, form the strongest argument white nationalists can make that their militancy most authentically represents his vision. One wonders what, precisely, someone like Charlie Kirk could have said had an audience member taken up one of Fuentes's suggestions: asking Kirk "to defend the President's preference for immigrants from Norway versus Haiti."

While the litany of Trump's acts cozening and encouraging a once-fringe, white-nationalist element of the American polity would happily fill another book or a dozen, it's worth considering the architect of the immigration policies that establishment Republicans like Dan Crenshaw champion.

A series of articles by the Southern Poverty Law Center's Michael E. Hayden, drawing on some nine hundred emails sent by Stephen Miller to editors at the far-right website Breitbart, have laid out precisely the ideological affiliations of the administration's immigration czar. From championing the Confederate flag to repeatedly linking to openly white-nationalist sites like VDARE and American Renaissance, Miller stridently supported the tenets and ideologues of white supremacy; and, like the Fuentes faction, he also advocated a complete cessation of legal immigration of any kind.

After years of measures to torment migrants—such as the administration's "Remain in Mexico" policy, which stranded tens of thousands of asylum seekers in squalid and dangerous refugee camps on the Mexican side of the US border—and slash legal immigration, Miller quietly took advantage of the uncertainty and fear of the coronavirus pandemic of 2020 to enact the most ambitious anti-immigration actions of the Trump administration. While the justification for new anti-immigrant policies was putatively economic, Miller helped to ensconce in federal policy the long-held white-supremacist belief that immigrants bring disease. On April 22, 2020, Trump signed a Miller-engineered executive order barring new green cards from being issued. "The first and most important thing is to turn off the faucet of new immigrant labor—mission accomplished—with signing that executive order," Miller told staunch Trump supporters on a phone call leaked to the *New York Times*.[7]

Miller's emails show a familiarity with—and advocacy of—the "great replacement" conspiracy theory, which posits a plot by elites to replace the white population of America and Europe with nonwhite immigrants. Miller stops short of promoting a crucial tenet of "great replacement" theory embraced by most of the white-nationalist right: that this replacement is being orchestrated by Jews. (That precise theorem is what motivated the Pittsburgh synagogue shooter to murder eleven Jews in 2018.) Perhaps this is because Miller is Jewish, a fact that the White House has belabored in its increasingly mendacious defenses of the staffer, going so far as to accuse the Southern Poverty Law Center of an anti-Semitic campaign against Miller.

Yet it is impossible to encourage and implement white nationalism, as Miller has relentlessly and without pause, without elevating anti-Semitism at the same time; they are one and the same for most of the ideology's proponents. This is why an administration awash in anti-immigrant sentiment, slashing rights for asylum seekers and refugees, governed during the worst pogrom in American history. It is not a coincidence. It never was.

None of the Republican figures so quick to disavow Fuentes did the same for Miller; indeed, there has been a profound, impenetrable closing of the ranks around him on the right. The chief difference at play is that Miller advocates for the end of legal immigration from the White House, while the insurgent faction does so on Telegram, and lined up in the audience section at events, like plebes. It's difficult to avoid the conclusion that the differences are not primarily ideological; principally, they are about an aversion to heckling.

The sudden, awkward repudiation of white nationalism by conservative ideologues subjected to its unruly minions may be comical, but it is a small part of the story of a national plague. Begrimed in the filth of racist invective and nativist sentiment that groups like TPUSA have eagerly whipped up in their own right, the Republican establishment finds itself unable to ward off the full bloom of pestilence, even when it finally turns against them.

All across America, the black flags of mourning and warning have been waving for a long time. There are thousands of children who have been separated from their families by Stephen Miller's policies; there are dozens of dead, murdered in an El Paso Walmart and in a Pittsburgh synagogue and on a Charlottesville street and by inadequate medical care in migration facilities. Through these years, as racial minorities and Jews and feminists and trans people and gay people have cried out in pain and alarm, the Picardy faction of the GOP laughed. They turned a profit on "triggering the libs"; they called opposition to the tide of rising white nationalism "Trump

Derangement Syndrome." Now that, at last, the buboes have begun to rise, odorous and pustulent, on their own white skins, they have begun to call out. Now, at this late hour, and covered in filth of their own making, they have begun to feebly ring the bells of warning. They are telling us what we already knew: There is a plague among us, with death written on its pale countenance, advancing through each city, each street of this country.

CHAPTER 4

OPERATION ASHLYNN

WhiteDate.net looks innocuous at first: Its home page could be cribbed from Ashley Madison, or FarmersOnly, or any number of niche dating sites that have cropped up across the web to lure in the lonely would-be suitors of the world. A stock-photo, glossy-lipped blonde smiles into her beau's suited shoulder, lowering her lashes demurely; a typed slogan reads, "We know where we come from, and where we belong, and wish to share the feeling with like-minded partners." Beside a saccharine pink heart, the words *for European Singles* clarify WhiteDate's purpose: to connect white supremacists seeking to preserve the future of the white race through love, and a little strictly procreative nookie.

European is a broadly conceived, and euphemistic, term for those WhiteDate seeks to connect, and certainly its clientele bears little resemblance to the varicolored crowds of Paris or Seville. A cursory scan of the would-be suitors on offer ranges from the heavily bearded to the skinhead-shaven, from light summer tan to downright sickly pallor—and, almost entirely, male. The disparity is so profound that WhiteDate has an obliquely titled page called "Mini

Flyer," containing an astonishing strategy for attracting women to the site.

"Men are vanguards and it is reflected in the ratio between men and women on WhiteDate," the page begins. "So gentlemen, don't be shy and invite white ladies in real life who display trad potential." *Trad* is short for "traditional"—meaning someone willing to hew to the antiquated gender roles beloved of white supremacists.

Users of the site are encouraged to print out a mini-flyer that says:

You look like one of us.
    Join us on WHITEDATE.NET.
    Our survival is as important as the survival of the Siberian Tiger.
    "We have started to present this mini-flyer with a 'Hi!' and a smile, letting the ladies read and memorize it, then taking it back," write the anonymous founders of the site. "Walk away and present the same flyer to the next one that crosses our way. Even if she is not the ideal woman for you, she might be for one of your white brethren."

The landing page, adorned with stylish white couples, coyly advertises its commitment to an anachronistic, ossified view of gender: "We follow classic roles where strong men take the lead and graceful women play the game. Wisely."

I was about to play my own part in this dubious game, and without much grace at all. As a mouthy, antiracist feminist with a Twitter account, I've experienced some of the violent rhetoric employed by white supremacists firsthand. Of course, after the fiftieth, or hundredth, or thousandth time someone points out that I'm Jewish, or fat, or a bitch, I struggle with the urge to point out that I know all these things about myself already, and it's really not much of a revelation. Still, it's a bummer, and sometimes a struggle to retain a voice that can be passionate or humorous or carefree, knowing that every comment I make or selfie I post will be adorned with a gush of deeply creative comments, like "You're ugly," or "You're fat," or "You're a Jew," or "You're a fat, ugly Jew." At times, the harassment has become somewhat more concerning—having my home address and family members' names posted to the extremist social media site Gab; my parents receiving a letter addressed to me from the racist group Patriot Front; and the occasional violent comment. ("We know where you live, your family members, EVERYTHING. What you give, you're going to get, ten fold," one email read.)

But the counterpoint to the harassment of feminists and the violently sexualized degradation of women deemed to be sexually wanton, careerist, and traitorous to their race is a veneration of the pure, submissive white wife, a hyper-Aryan, time-hopping combination of 1859 and 1950. I had seen the harassment firsthand, but as a fat, ugly, scheming feminist Jew (with a reputation for leftist journalism), the machinery of Aryan courtship was closed to me.

Enter WhiteDate.

I found WhiteDate via a blog post on the racist publishing house Counter-Currents' website, titled "A New White Dating Site." Ever since the events of August 12, 2017, in Charlottesville, my horrified interest in online hate had sharpened. I'd trawled white-supremacist publications, forums, and message boards, learning the jargon of fear and loathing, trawling for answers. But when I saw the mini-flyer on WhiteDate.net, I knew I had a chance to go further. Here was a network of white supremacists, itching to open up to a sympathetic woman, if one ever breached their sausage party. Had there ever been riper grounds for catfishing? And what might they reveal for the chance to meet the demure white woman of their dreams? The site was created in February 2017, and cofounded by "Liv Heide," who claims to be a woman from northern Germany living in Paris. In interviews on fascist-sympathetic YouTube channels, she describes the site as a way for "woke white men and woke white women to find each other," because, she says, "we are dying out." Videos on the WhiteDate.net YouTube channel, before it was suspended in 2019, had titles like "Communities Uber Alles," "Eugenics is Everywhere" and "Hail our White Men!" Heide does not feature in any of the videos, and never appears on camera when interviewed by other channels, but her voice—a feminine monotone with a heavy German accent—serves as narration over sequences of stock photos depicting idyllic white couples in WhiteDate.net advertisements. Their pitches are urgent—your date might avert a genocide!—coupled with the paucity of women among the "Siberian tigers."

My initial goal was to nudge as many men on WhiteDate as possible to reveal as many personal details as possible, so that I could, ultimately, out them as white supremacists. I'd funnel their information to antifascist groups that sought to let neighbors and coworkers know about the reactionary and violent politics going on in their midst, perhaps unbeknownst to them. Even a cursory scan of the website revealed numerous men claiming to be members of the military, or of police forces. The idea that avowed white supremacists were serving as armed agents of the state was alarming; nearly a dozen members of the military had been outed by journalists and were under investigation by the military for belonging to Identity Evropa, an explicitly white-supremacist identitarian group with ties to international far-right movements. I wanted to have the opportunity to engage these men—and perhaps get them to drop their guard enough to reveal exactly who they were.

So Ashlynn was born.

She was a figment of my imagination, everything a white supremacist of any stripe could want, with the whitest name I could think
of. I thought about "Ashley"—"Ashleigh"—"Ashlee"—but the "lynn"
felt heavy with both consonants and promise. I closed my eyes and
thought about the ideal mate of a male Fox News viewer, then twisted
her twenty degrees to the right and plopped her in the Midwest.
The result was a crudely drawn caricature, a sort of hideous mash-
up of all those parachute-journalism Trump-voter features that had
blossomed so absurdly since the election. Blonde, gun-toting, based
on a farm-slash-compound just outside Amber, Iowa, and totally
fictional—she was a New Yorker's idea of an Iowan, imbued with all
the parochial narrow-mindedness of my own urban life.

To create an image to match the name, I found a social-media
account belonging to a European hunting enthusiast with long,
strawberry-blond hair, almond-shaped blue eyes, and a hint of
world-weariness around her thin mouth that made her look less like
a pin-up. She wore camo, a girlish smile, and a long gun at her shoulder. She had photos of herself in Tyrolean hats and adorned with
deer blood—but also had a sizable number posed attractively against
wheat fields and forests, which were anonymous in the way fields are,
so country-less they could help me create an American country girl.
I cropped the photos carefully to make sure they weren't reverse-
searchable on Google—so no one could find her and pester her due
to my machinations. Then I set out to seduce some lonely bigots.
After all, I was at war with white supremacy. And seduction has been
part of warfare since at least as far back as the Bible, when Jael the
Israelite hammered a tent peg into the sleeping skull of Sisera.

On WhiteDate.net, there were thousands of men for the picking. Dozens of them sent messages to ashlyn1488. I'd crafted the

username from well-known neo-Nazi symbology. *14* was for a white-supremacist credo called the "14 words," composed by convicted white-nationalist terrorist David Lane: "We must secure the existence of our people and a future for white children." *88* stood for "Heil Hitler," because H is the eighth letter of the alphabet. Ashlynn was a fascist through and through.

I set up a backup email account that similarly drew on white-supremacist sloganeering: itsoktobeashlynn@gmail.com, a play on the semi-ironic white-pride slogan "It's OK to Be White." I invented a backstory about a father deep into white supremacy, an eager daughter embracing his ideas while working as a waitress at a diner (I researched the diner near the small, unincorporated town I picked) and shooting deer on the weekends. It was necessary to invent these specifics ahead of time; I wanted Ashlynn to have ready answers for any small talk, to seem like a real flesh-and-blood woman eager for white seed.

You might be surprised by the sheer ordinariness of the men who messaged Ashlynn, seeking amorously to prove their bona fides by means of ugly rants about minorities. These men had signed up for a white-supremacist dating site, whose slogan, written in black and white at the bottom of the home page, was "We have woken up!"—and whose supportive press clips came exclusively from white-supremacist sources, like NoWhiteGuilt and Amerika.org: "Furthest Right."

In the sheer plenitude of communications from men, it wasn't that dissimilar from my experiences on, say, Tinder, or OkCupid, as a veteran of the grim world of online dating. In fact, one of the things that unnerved me was the sheer banality of it—just another online marketplace for love, a clumsy interface for tech-assisted tenderness. After a while, overwhelmed by the number of suitors Ashlynn had attracted, I asked a few like-minded online friends to help me respond to the messages. Ashlynn became a compound personality for a time, with each of us assigned to chat up different men. But the paranoia of such a space made soliciting last names and precise locations difficult—more often than not, fishing for more information, no matter how subtly, ended conversations entirely. One by one, the others dropped out, until only I was left, embodying a woman who'd never existed, a siren who wanted to lure fascists to dash themselves against the rocks.

Eventually, I began to think of the account, which was by now nearly a year old, as an exercise in anthropology. There are a few leaders in the white-supremacist movement who are carefully trained in how to talk to the press in order to amplify their movement—ones who might even willingly talk to a Jewish reporter like me. Those men, like Richard Spencer—dubbed the "dapper white supremacist," who had burst onto the media scene in 2016—and Matthew Heimbach, once head of the white nationalist Traditionalist Youth Network, knew how to carefully spin credulous reporters into printing their claims about wanting a "peaceful ethnostate," or "separation between the races," without too much pushback.

Spokespeople for the white-supremacist movement are known to pick their words carefully, with the same figures cropping up over and over again in national news articles about the far right's ascension in the Trump era. While getting comment from a group is standard journalistic protocol—both to immunize from lawsuits and to retain a stance of fair-mindedness—and spokespeople are the easiest to reach, I couldn't help but feel that these smooth-talking spokespeople had obscured the real violence at the heart of white-supremacist organizations. I wanted to take the chance to dig deeper. And I wasn't particularly inclined to be charitable.

I wanted to talk to the rank and file, ordinary men who just so happened to be drawn to a whites-only dating site—who would never, ever encounter someone like me without a carefully drawn layer of subterfuge. Given white-supremacist beliefs in the "degeneracy" of pornography, the evils of homosexuality, and the retrograde gender roles the movement espouses, users seemed to be seeking a white woman to put on a pedestal when they approached Ashlynn. Their approaches were rarely overtly sexual. Instead, they were reverential, seeking a white mate to propagate the race.

"I wish you the best of luck finding a white husband to have kids with. What's your favorite kind of gun?" wrote "geneticMessiah," who admitted in his profile that he was "a little overweight but working on it."

"People like us are few, it was a surprise to find someone like you not too far away," wrote "Vulcan," based in Sioux Falls, South Dakota.

"There is nothing more Noble then to dedicate/devote/forge the future of your soon to be children and then grandchildren," wrote "Molten Runes." "I should have you come and visit me for an adventure in the Scandinavian Nature, fishing is a given, maybe get a hunting pass for moose season if you're interested in that."

There were a large number of men like Molten Runes, writing to me from Europe. I spoke with Rafael, a Swiss assistant professor who complained about the black students in his classes—though his phrasing was considerably less polite. There was a British security guard, a German from Hamburg who was studying tourist management (but didn't want to follow "most of the Wests interracial footsteps"). From another German, I received *freundliche Grüsse*—friendly greetings; all were complimentary of my Aryan appearance. "Do you hunt your own food? If yes then come to my village, marry me, bear my children and hunt down those damn foxes that keep killing my roosters," wrote "Wizard," from Croatia.

Most of them, though, were from the United States—Utah, Oregon, Texas, New Jersey, New York, Louisiana, Ohio, California, Massachusetts. They were from Akron and Cedar Rapids; Tucson, Arizona; and Boulder, Colorado. One was even from the tiny, hippy-dippy college town of New Paltz, New York, where I'd been a few weeks earlier, purchasing fair-trade coffee and socialist books. My paramours came from all over the country, and the sheer geographic variation was a powerful argument against any notion that white supremacy is confined to the American South, or even to red states; if anything, the New Yorkers and Californians, feeling themselves to be warriors of a valiant counterculture, were even more vociferous in their hatreds.

Many of the avatars the men of WhiteDate used were drawn from the iconography of white supremacy—pagan runes were the most popular—but the vast majority were simply photos of white men. White men with beards and without; thin and muscular and fat; bespectacled or green-eyed or brown-eyed or blue-eyed. It was like selecting a swatch for a white wall: beige, ivory, alabaster, eggshell, bone, porcelain. (The drop-down menu for "Ancestry" on WhiteDate allows you to pick your type of whiteness—or desired type in a partner—with similar precision: Afrikaner, Belgian, Croatian, English, German, Italian, Manx, Romanian, Swedish.)

They were hiding in plain sight, these whiteness-loving men, working in warehouses and on farms, on army bases and construction sites; a large number were software developers. And the variation in the jobs they claimed to have, likewise, argued against the idea that extremists are unemployed, or incompetent, or lurking in their mothers' basements. These men had jobs, homes, cars, full lives—and were drawn to, and animated by, white supremacy.

Many of them cited YouTube personalities like Stefan Molyneux and Jean-Francois Gariépy as the forces that led them to join the white-supremacist movement; others mentioned divorces—so many divorced men—or the 2016 election. "We have been lied to about everything, from our origins to the people who fight for us today," wrote "John," a long-haired North Carolinian with an avowed passion for blacksmithing. "Needless to say, my slide down the pipeline happened very fast."

Surfing profiles showed me different explanations for what had led men to the "red pill"—a term that's a reference to the movie *The Matrix*. There's a scene in which Neo, the hero, must choose between the blue pill, which will allow him to continue to live in a world of comforting lies, and the red pill, which will expose him to difficult truths. For white supremacists, the red pill was racism—the "difficult truth" that society was conspiring to keep the white man down, through the media, "cultural Marxism," and other shady, Jew-tinged operations. One man described being radicalized by his ex-wife's support for the Greek fascist Golden Dawn party. Another simply blamed the "Jew and neger [*sic*] infestation" that surrounded him. But over and over again, the internet had proved the key to radicalization. Most euphemistically called themselves "red-pilled" or "race realists," but one suitor wrote to me: "I also don't mind getting called racist, because that is just some made up word by the false prophet MLK. To me, it just means that I think black people are annoying and I don't want to be around them and if that makes me 'racist' then so be it."

More representative was this profile: "I've been red pilled. Let's just get that out of the way from the very beginning. I'm retired military, and spent all of my life asleep to what was really going on. After I retired, I spent 2 years researching and going down rabbit holes to find the answers . . . and when I did, it changed my life. Once you know, you can't go back to living the way you did before, because everywhere you look you understand why things are the way they are. I'm pro White and pro European."

In my conversations with my suitors, it was psychologically easier to stress anti-Semitism than other hatreds; it felt less ugly to condemn my own kind than others, while exhibiting enough hatred to gain their trust. So I wrote about aching feet, dull customers, and how much I hated Jews. They asked Ashlynn questions that stumped me until I googled turkey season in Iowa, wild boar populations, and, especially, guns. I reverse-engineered knowledge I'd never had. They wanted "their woman," one to own, and I tried to make myself that woman as best I could. ("Rather than spending hours in a car chasing a paycheck, my woman would rather be with me," explained one man in his profile.) Ashlynn wasn't very serious about her job. Ashlynn wanted a husband to bear white children with, who would support her in her submissive, feminine motherhood.

When they wrote to me, they wrote about their cats, about their dinners of pinto beans and pork, about their love of Xbox gaming, about gas prices, the motorcycles they owned. They wrote about guns. They wrote a *lot* about guns. And just as often they wrote about their desire to maintain the purity of whiteness; about the white children they hoped I or some other willing woman would bear them; and about the sinister Jews controlling the world, about the "cucks" (cuckolds) running the government, about the "Marxists" brainwashing kids, about "white genocide," and their favorite fascist YouTube channels.

"I used to work out a lot and am getting back into it; I love watching—mostly 80s—movies at home; I like socializing at the pub but mainly because I don't have a family," wrote one suitor, named

"Marty." "And by the way you became the most beautiful woman in the world when you said 'kikes.'"

That was me. The most beautiful, kike-deploring woman in the world.

Here's the truth that emerged for me out of a whole lot of deception, out of becoming Ashlynn and courting her suitors. The worst people are still people; their humanity is impossible to disregard, but it does not absolve them. If anything, it makes their choices more abhorrent, surrounded, as they are, by the banality of a life indistinguishable from other lives. Even a self-described Nazi eats dinner, and chances are it's pork and pinto beans, and would you like the recipe? ("I eat only beef and eggs with bouts of pineapples from a can. But on dates, I expand that diet so as to not be 'weird,'" explained "Karamazov," candidly.)

Some WhiteDate.net users declined to get more intimate—refusing to send emails or text, even on encrypted chat apps like Telegram. Mostly, they cited fears of Marxist infiltration. Others rejected Ashlynn for unpredictable reasons, like the racist pagan who couldn't abide a woman who hunted for sport. All of them were delighted at the prospect of a Nazi girlfriend—just one that met their specifications.

Eventually, I began asking them to write love letters: Since they viewed themselves as romantics—heirs to a noble European heritage—I thought this would be the purest way to find out what they wanted, a shortcut to figuring out how racism, misogyny, and desire commingle. I asked them a simple question, tantalizingly phrased: "If you could write a love letter to your future white wife, what would it be like? I would love to see what you write . . ."

The results were like a car crash between Nicholas Sparks and *Mein Kampf*.

Here's a typical example:

Dear Ashlynn,

I was really happy to hear back from you and to receive the photo that you sent. It's real pretty. I will tell you that you have quite a nice figure to my liking. It also reminds me of where I lived in Iowa. It's nice to see fields and trees and hills and things where everything is green. Out here we've just got basically desert and then the giant mountains scattered about.

To answer your question, well I'd have to think about that. It's kind of hard to imagine being married at last, I think it would be an incredible feeling to be finally married. Well, are you looking to get married? I think for me I am because well there is only so much dating to be done in life. It would just be nice to live with a great woman and see her every day. And especially one that is a race realist, because I want my wife to teach our kids to keep away from the darkies and to marry white people when they grow up, because that is the how we continue our way of life, and to teach them about the ethnostate that our people will someday create.

When I look at the picture you sent I think to myself in my mind that I would like to just walk up to you and give you a big hug, and pick you up off the ground a bit and twirl you around. And I would like to see the look in your eyes and gaze upon your face and then I imagine kissing you right there in that field. Maybe we could go for a walk and just talk about life and things and really get to know each other quite well. That would be real nice I think.

Another compared himself and his future children to a wolf pack:

The world will not forgive us for this, it will not forget. It seeks to destroy this beauty, our beauty. It wishes that we would vanish, that our progeny would never come to pass. It hates and loathes us. This is a heavy burden we must bear, and with it we must arm ourselves against this world. Our revolt will be joyous laughter echoing in the great hall, our revenge will be the smiling faces of our children. We shall prevail, there is no doubt. I only seek to share this great journey with you. There are untold adventures that we shall embark on, and great challenges that we shall overcome. Our pack shall be strong, taking time to hunt and feed and play. Through us, we shall exert our will upon the world and shape it in our own image. This I promise you.

This one was the simplest and most direct:

Dear Wife,

I hope you are all the things I've ever wanted. I hope you're a good Christian, conservative who despises diversity and Multiculturalism. Someone who realizes each people, deserve their own homelands. I hope you are someone who will stand by me thru thick and thin as I will with you. I want us to raise a big family that we instill the correct values and life lessons into. Not allowing them anywhere near the Marxist brain washing centers. I hope you enjoy and love life like I do. I want you and I to grow old together.

There are more, of course—love letters to the breeding white women of the world, from men who hoped I would be that woman, and who would be filled with rage if they saw my brown curls and big nose, if they found out I was part of the "Jew infestation" plaguing their world.

But here it was, laid out: the way fantasies about breeding, about birthrates, about racial continuity, were embodied, for these men, in the wombs of white women. Their laudatory words of romance were—just as their forebears' had been—inextricable from their desire for racial segregation and violent ethnic cleansing. They wanted an inferior partner, a submissive woman to love—and one who would keep their children from the Marxists and the "darkies." In the end, their visions of love were inextricable from their hatred of the modern women that they hoped to avoid on WhiteDate.

Misogyny was a natural outcome of indoctrination into white supremacy, which sees women purely as vessels for breeding. But I had suspected for a long time that misogyny could be a gateway into racism as well. Over years of being a woman online, marinating in gendered abuse being directed my way, I'd learned a lot about just how radical online antifeminism could be. Lonely, frustrated men, convening online, had decided, by the score, to slough off the conventional wisdoms of a society that had reluctantly accepted some of feminism's tenets, and indulge themselves in outright hatred of women.

The term *red pill*, adopted by racists, was originally a term that derived from the men's rights movement—a viciously misogynistic movement centered around a mishmash of pickup artistry; longing for idealized, *Leave It to Beaver*-style gender norms; and coordinated attacks on feminists. In the context of this world—the "manosphere"—the *red pill* meant learning the "truth" about society:

that feminism was a devious scheme to render men's lives difficult and women's lives a manicured garden path of hapless mates easily parted from their money. The distance from the antifeminist "red pill" to the racist "red pill" was not so far: Each, in its own way, represented conspiratorial worldviews, in which the rights of women or minorities were a zero-sum game, promoted by sinister actors to deprive men and whites of their due.

The overlap was illustrated most cleanly by one of Ashlynn's suitors—one who rejected her outright.

"I only talk to one person at a time, so my time is valuable. I'm not like the other men on here, I know my worth and my agency speaks for itself," wrote "Brendan," who said he was twenty-seven. ("Yes, I'm military, but don't lump me in with the rest of them," he wrote in his profile, indicating just how widespread the presence of members of the armed forces was on the platform.)

When I explained that Ashlynn was definitely interested in something serious, but was messaging more than one man at a time, Brendan told her that he was no longer interested in any sort of conversation.

"I only talk to one person at a time and believe that hypergamy predisposes relationships to failure," he said.

Hypergamy was a term I'd previously encountered only on message boards organized around misogyny. As he explained it, *hypergamy* meant: "The instinctual desire of humans of the female sex to discard a current mate when the opportunity arises to latch onto a subsequent mate of higher status due to the hindbrain impetus to find a male with the best ability to provide for her OWN offspring (already spawned or yet-to-be spawned) regardless of investments and commitments made to a current mate."

The pseudoscience, and the imputation that women are

evolutionarily programmed to shallowness, smacked of online anti-feminist movements, the kind that lonely men all across the internet were joining en masse.

Later, when I began infiltrating white-supremacist chats more extensively, I did so under both male and female identities. My male guise was greeted with the same rough, puerile humor, skepticism, and edgy camaraderie that typified the chats more broadly. When I created a feminine profile—an anonymous stock photo of a French braid, a femme name—the responses were much more varied: some overtly hostile, sexually harassing my avatar; others overly solicitous. Overall, there was a sense that a woman in these spaces was a rarity. And the hostility made it clear why: This was a culture born from the sticky, tarry, concentrated misogyny of the internet, the hatred of women expanded into all the hatreds white supremacy claims as its own.

To confirm that thesis, I wanted to look more closely at misogynist communities online. It would help me to explore the ways in which antifeminist radicalization could lead to white-supremacist ideology—just as white-supremacist ideology demanded antifeminism.

It's hard to disentangle white supremacy and misogyny. This might initially seem counterintuitive—after all, many classic white-supremacist images involve "protecting" and "cherishing" white women. *Birth of a Nation*, the 1915 silent film that serves as something of an ur-text for the neo-Confederate, white-supremacist mind-set, hinges on noble Klansmen protecting the virtue of white women from the sexual threat of black men. *The Clansman*—the 1905 "Historical Romance of the Ku Klux Klan" that served as the film's inspiration—warned that the consequences of "lawlessness and disorder" would be "a black hand on a white woman's throat." Countless lynchings, including the infamous murder of Emmett Till, were inspired by putative sexual threats to white women.

In the white-supremacist imagination, the chaste white woman is the guardian of all virtue. Her chastity is constantly under threat from the sexual advances of black men; she must be protected, and infantilized, during her passage from the guardianship of her white father to that of her white husband.

Laws prohibiting interracial marriage date back to 1661 in the United States; but as Kenneth James Lay points out in his monograph "Sexual Racism," such laws functionally prohibited the commingling of black men and white women, while serving to "permit and even encourage the sexual abuse of black women by white men." Rape of slave women by their white masters and overseers was ubiquitous throughout the centuries of slavery in America, dating back long before the country's founding.[1] Sociologists Ruth Thompson-Miller and Leslie H. Picca surveyed ninety-two African-Americans who had lived through the Jim Crow South in childhood and early adulthood, concluding that the wanton rape of black women by white men continued long after slavery was abolished. Rape served not only as a means of economic and social domination—employed as a punitive measure—but also "to fulfill White men's sexual gratification, particularly to engage in sex acts that would have been inappropriate to engage in with a White woman." Black women, throughout the Jim Crow era, were subject to assaults by white men who acted with impunity, and, at the same time, cast as sexually available and wanton. By contrast, white women were expected to maintain the purity, piety, submissiveness, and domesticity that typified feminine ideals of the era.

Texts from the early twentieth century romanticized the laudatory qualities of white women, utilizing such admiration to underline the need for a racial caste system. The author William Hepworth Dixon wrote of the white women of Charleston, in his 1876 book *White Conquest*: "And then, what women pace these walks, peep from these lattices, adorn these balustrades! Surely the mothers of these women must have been the ladies painted by Lely and Vandyke! Yet what a fiery energy in the men and women! It is a saying in Charleston 'that no Negro or Mulatto dares to look straight into a gentleman's face.' How many Negresses and Mulattoes would face one of these White damsels?"

In 1890, in the Southern Historical Society Papers, praise of white Southern women encompassed a romantic vision of plantation mistresses—and of the Southern woman's ongoing, postbellum commitment to domesticity. "She has been taught to believe that the influences that are the result of a happy home-life are more powerful and more important elements of politics than the casting of a ballot," wrote the Richmond-based author Joel Chandler Harris. "Her devotion and self-sacrifice in the past have consecrated her to the future."

By the age of eugenics, in the first decades of the twentieth century, this praise became less winsome, and more suffused with pseudo-science. "Women, however, of fair skin have always been the objects of keen envy by those of the sex whose skins are black, yellow or red," wrote Madison Grant in his phrenology-laden 1936 tract, *The Passing of the Great Race; Or, the Racial Basis of European History*.

A 1920 book, *The Rising Tide of Color Against White World-Supremacy*, by Harvard PhD and white-supremacist ideologue T. Lothrop Stoddard, goes even further in iterating the vital role of breeding—of unadulterated progeny—in maintaining racial purity.

Decrying the "debased coinage" caused by interbreeding, he adds that "Two things are necessary for the continued existence of a race: it must remain itself, and it must breed its best."

The "debased coinage" theory of racial purity—in which interracial mixing was an unendurable threat and both a judicial and moral crime—was manifest in the strictly policed boundaries of race. Throughout the nineteenth century and continuing through the Jim Crow era, laws and social boundaries served to punish the progeny of interracial unions. Such policing was not limited to the South; in 1897, to enforce segregation between the races, Nebraska enacted an anti-miscegenation law that prohibited marriage between whites and "persons possessing one-fourth or more Negro blood." In 1913, that law was revised to ban marriages between white persons and those having "one-eighth or more negro, Japanese or Chinese blood."[2] So-called "one-drop rules," which—as one Arkansas bill put it—defined *Negro* as anyone "who has . . . any negro blood whatever,"[3] were designed to maintain whiteness undiluted by miscegenation. The same Arkansas law made interracial cohabitation a felony.

The notion that white women were guardians of blood purity meant that sexual straying—in other words, the exercise of bodily autonomy—served as an existential threat to that purity. The sole role for women, within the romantic ideology of white supremacy, is to be chaste, except when serving as a vessel for white reproduction. There are, of course, in the present and the past, white women who have done far more than this in the service of upholding white supremacy—those who have served as its constant guardians and most loyal enforcers.

The century since *The Birth of a Nation* was released brought with it a few lurching, hard-fought strides toward progress for white women—from a measure of tenuous reproductive freedom to increasing integration into the workplace. The feminist movement, in all its overlapping and contentious waves, mainstreamed the notion that women ought to be equal partners—possessing the right, the need, and the ability to leave the archaic role of hearth-guardian behind. The women who live in the age of the internet live in a world that feminism has shaped irrevocably, imbuing us with notions of our own autonomy, worth, and relevance as independent actors. This represents a fundamental tension with white-supremacist ideas of women as passive guardians of Aryan blood. Add in the vitriolic, self-perpetuating misogyny of male-dominated spaces on the internet, and you have a recipe for a poisonous and ongoing culture war.

The animosity that white supremacists display toward feminists—and, by extension, women shaped by a culture suffused with the tenets of feminism—is continual, and often the locus of some of the ugliest rhetoric in the movement writ large. For diehard white supremacists, feminism—with its birth control, its careerist women, and its ethos of sexual choice for women—represents an existential threat to the future of the white race. As the white-supremacist murderer Brenton Tarrant expressed in his manifesto prior to shooting over fifty Muslims at prayer in Christchurch, New Zealand: "It's the birthrates."

The Turner Diaries, the 1978 novel by neo-Nazi William Luther Pierce that served as a direct inspiration for Timothy McVeigh and other white-supremacist terrorists, lays out this antipathy to feminism succinctly: "'Women's lib' was a form of mass psychosis," Pierce wrote. "Women affected by it denied their femininity and insisted that they were 'people,' not 'women.' This aberration was promoted and encouraged by the System as a means of dividing our race against itself."

Some of this hostility expresses itself in violent rhetoric toward women, particularly outspoken women online. Black feminists were among the first to sound the warning bells against coordinated racist harassment online. Organized around the hashtag #Your-SlipIsShowing, Shafiqah Hudson, I'Nasah Crockett, Mikki Kendall, Jamilah Lemieux, and others documented and exposed efforts by racists galvanized on the anonymous message board 4chan to pose—clumsily—as black men and women, in order to discredit black feminist discourse. As Hudson told *Slate* journalist Rachelle Hampton: "Nobody wants to be right about how much real peril we're all in, even if you saw it coming."

In other cases, racist spaces, such as the neo-Nazi site Daily Stormer and the "Western chauvinist" gang the Proud Boys—pointedly exclude women entirely.

The antipathy of white-supremacist spaces toward women, and the frequency with which that antipathy spills over into harassment campaigns, is well-documented. One striking case involved Taylor Dumpson, the first black student-body president of American University, being targeted from the first day of her tenure for racist harassment—including an anonymous culprit hanging bananas from nooses and writing racist messages on bananas around the college's campus. Daily Stormer posted about the story, including Dumpson's picture. The young woman received an overwhelming wave of racist and misogynist online harassment. She sued an Oregon native and enthusiastic troll named Evan McCarty, who was ordered by a court to apologize to Dumpson, renounce white supremacy, and refrain from online trolling.

One of the most extreme examples of online white-supremacist misogyny I'd ever witnessed occurred in November 2019, and it happened to two of my friends—women I spoke to regularly online. The white supremacist Paul Nehlen, a former congressional candidate endorsed by Donald Trump, creator of a racist Telegram channel with thousands of subscribers, and owner of a water-filtration business, conducted a harassment campaign so extreme and grotesque it still boggles my mind that no one was legally culpable for it.[4]

It was the height of deer hunting season, and Nehlen set out into the woods with his phone. He began filming two does, calling them yentas—common far-right slang for Jewish women. He wrote to his thousands of followers that he was getting closer to the deer, and posted pictures of the does in his rifle sights. Then he named them after my friends, one an antifascist, one a researcher of the far right—neither of whom are Jewish. He wrote that he could smell the "filthy yentas." And then he shot the does. Over the next two days, he photographed the deer partially skinned and hanging from a makeshift noose in a photo meant to mimic a lynching. "Now we're getting somewhere," he wrote. All the while, he posted pictures of one of the women continuously, alternating with photos of the flayed carcasses. He made homemade deer sausage, referring to the deer as "the horned Jew." Subsequently, he spelled out my friend's name in the homemade deer sausage, posting photos of the tableau to his channel. I reported the channel to Telegram; the threats were reported to the FBI. Despite the grotesque nature of the threats, and their obvious feeling of rehearsing a kill, Nehlen faced no legal consequences and continues to post violent rhetoric to Telegram on a daily basis.

While this particular example is extreme, lesser versions of misogynist harassment play out every day online. Women of color are subject to extraordinary harassment, but white women, too, receive disproportionate harassment online, compared to their male counterparts. This is particularly true of those who are outspoken about feminism, or who enter fields—such as video-game design and science—that misogynists view as "masculine" endeavors. In April 2019, newspapers and blogs exploded with the first documented image of a black hole: an eye-of-Sauronish red ring, like a sinister doughnut, carefully constructed by scientists. Among those scientists was a twenty-nine-year-old postdoctoral fellow named Katie Bouman, who, working at MIT, was a prominent member of the team that created the groundbreaking image. After MIT tweeted out an exuberant photo of her seeing the image for the first time on her laptop, social media users and the press alike quickly lauded her role in the achievement, comparing her to pioneering female scientists like NASA programmer Margaret Hamilton.[5] But the backlash was just as swift, and dripping with the rankest misogyny. A conspiracy theory arose—that Bouman had been given credit for the achievements of a larger group. Fake Instagram accounts in Bouman's name and YouTube videos by the score claimed that one of Bouman's colleagues, Andrew Chael, had done the lion's share of the work, only to be overshadowed by Bouman due to the rapacity of a feminism-drunk media. Chael himself emerged to rebuke the attack, noting that the software "would never have worked without her contributions" and decrying the "awful and sexist attacks" against her. On the anonymous 4chan, users speculated that Bouman was a Jew—bracketing her name with the triple parentheses that serve as a coded signifier of Jewishness in white supremacist spaces. Her fame, they said, was due to "the jewmedia."

"A woman being made a project manager on something like this almost always means that she was a complete waste of space but they couldn't kick her off the team because vagina," wrote one user. Another added: "The bulk of the much harder work was done by a large team of forgotten white men."

To find out how misogyny feeds into white supremacy, I had to make an even more radical departure from Talia Lavin, Jewish bitch journalist with an IWW membership card, than I had when I invented Ashlynn. I had to become a man who hated women more than anything.

CHAPTER 5

ADVENTURES WITH INCELS

Tommy O'Hara was born in 1998, the same year "My Heart Will Go On" hit the top of the pop charts, a gem from the soundtrack to that year's top-grossing film, *Titanic*. And like the crooning, keening voice of Celine Dion in that song, Tommy was filled with yearning.

He'd never been kissed. Never touched a single boob. Never been held tenderly after a rousing bout of coitus. Never, in fact, had coitus in the first place.

Tommy had a tense relationship with his mother, whom he regarded with open scorn, and a distant one with his father, a corporate middle manager. He was shy and introverted, speaking in a flat affect that tended to unsettle the more naturally outgoing young people he met. Even in the bustling social atmosphere of a college dorm, he was retreating further into himself, and into the world of the internet. He thought obsessively about the plump thighs of women he saw in the halls, the taut, shaved labia and cartoonishly round breasts of porn stars, and the big, limpid eyes of the girls in Japanese anime, their curves bursting from underneath schoolgirl outfits.

It wasn't that he hadn't been around real-life girls. He had, but he just never knew quite what to say to them. He'd been absorbed in his own pursuits (video games) and hobbies (video games) and rich, fulfilling inner life (video games and YouTube). He saw girls in his college classes—he was finishing junior year, studying history— but couldn't seem to strike up a conversation. He had come to regard them as alien beings, all hips, breasts, and unknowable minds. Between him and them there was a chasm of empty, air- less space, which had come to feel to him like a rift that couldn't be bridged. The chasm had been created, as Tommy saw it, by the inscrutable, inexplicable, and probably irrational behavior exhibited by the women around him. He had studied well enough to get into college, with a particularly keen focus on math and history in high school; he was on his way to what he hoped would be a comfortably middle-class life. But his lips had never touched another human being's; they felt parched with loneliness. One day, after a fellow Overwatch player jokingly called him an "incel," he started to look into precisely what that meant. The term—a portmanteau of "involuntarily celibate," aka someone deprived of sex by its cruel female keepers—was both an insult and an accurate description of his life.

What followed was a deep dive into Reddit and YouTube—videos by creators like Dr Shaym and "alfsvoid" and message boards like r/TheIncelPill and r/Foreveralone. Soon enough, his puzzlement at women soured into contempt. Tommy was angry now. Life had seemed to promise him a degree of intimacy with women; not for him the easy, tender romances of John Green novels, teen rom-coms, or even the cardboard-thin romantic subplots of the sword-and-sorcery fiction he preferred.

The ideology was self-reinforcing; contempt bred anger, which congealed into loathing. As much as he desired the women around him—and their airbrushed, hyperappealing mirror images in hentai and porn—he loathed them just as much, or more. Tommy began to obsess about his facial features a lot (weak chin, weak nose, eyes too close together) and his height (five-foot-seven on a good day) and his cystic acne, and blamed these physical qualities for his lack of romantic success. Women were shallow, vapid beings, always looking to trade up for a more physically attractive or wealthy mate. That was something Tommy knew he could never be. So, at all of twenty-one, he felt sealed in a sexless sarcophagus, doomed to never know a female hand on his hand, or on his cock, or what it felt like to be locked in a passionate embrace. All that he desired was around him—women in the dorms, in classes, donning short skirts as soon as the chill retreated from the air; he was sure they were fellating his handsomer classmates as passionately as the women in porn did, gagging to the root, then presenting themselves like bonobos in heat. But not to him. Never to him.

Tommy was an incel.

Only "Tommy O'Hara" had never really existed.

Tommy O'Hara was me.

—

The internet is rife with misogyny, even shaped by it. A majority of women who are active online face harassment, particularly on social media. A 2018 investigation by Amnesty International found that 62 percent of women given a survey in 2017 had faced harassment on Twitter, ranging from gendered and racial slurs to threats of rape and violence. This frequently leads to self-censorship on both a large and a small scale, a careful choosing of words, or a choice not to speak at all on the platforms that shape news cycles, political opinions, and interpersonal relationships. I have, as described above, experienced this in my own life, on a daily and even hourly basis; misogynistic slurs, anti-Semitic slurs, and criticism of my appearance blur together into a background hum of hatred, the atonal, dissonant counterpoint to my ability to speak to an audience.

Misogyny is also, in some respects, the background noise of American culture. Contemporary America is a country passing draconian abortion bans left and right—in which a state legislator passing such a stricture said that the abortion procedure "should be painful" in order to induce women to "allow God to take over." It's a country in which a Supreme Court nominee credibly accused of sexual assault passed his hearing easily, to the roaring triumph of conservative media. And it's a country in which a president whose most infamous catchphrase crudely described a pattern of sexual assault—"grab 'em by the pussy"—was duly elected, and is years into his tenure. At Trump's rallies, they still chant "Lock Her Up," although it may have morphed, by now, from Hillary Clinton to a generalized, ur-female opponent, Clinton a metonym for any uppity, presumptuous woman, or perhaps any woman desirous of autonomy.

In 2014, the year before Donald Trump began his campaign for president, misogyny effloresced on the internet, exploding into the public consciousness through a movement known as GamerGate. That same year, a self-proclaimed incel and mass murderer named Elliot Rodger shot his way through Isla Vista, California, leaving a trail of bodies and a manifesto about sexual deprivation in his wake. Rodger would be the inspiration for numerous murders of women, and countless alienated young men marinating in misogynist hatred would look to him as a saint. At the same time, GamerGate provided a launching pad for the mass mobilization of young men pursuing reactionary politics—and a testing ground for harassment techniques that continue to warp discourse on the internet half a decade later.

As Becca Lewis, a researcher probing the far right at Stanford University, told me of the contemporary far-right sphere: "Pretty much everything is GamerGate."

That "movement"—a loosely organized collective of internet trolls, some anonymous, others emergent ideologues—began as retribution after Eron Gjoni, a then-twenty-four-year-old man, posted a ten-thousand-word diatribe about the alleged infidelities of his ex-girlfriend, a twenty-seven-year-old indie video-game developer named Zoë Quinn. Among his allegations were that she had slept with a video-game journalist, Kotaku's Nathan Grayson, in exchange for favorable coverage. The screed spread wildly among self-identified gamers. Its immediate repercussion was the vicious harassment of Quinn—who received a cavalcade of death threats; had her accounts hacked; and had her personal information, including her address, posted online, causing her to leave her home in fear for her safety.[1] The movement soon metastasized, taking the false allegation that Quinn had traded sex for favorable coverage to entail an industry-wide crisis in "ethics in games journalism."

Despite its occasional male targets, GamerGate never lost its misogynist rancor. Prominent women in the world of video games and video-game criticism, like the feminist vlogger Anita Sarkeesian, faced snowballing death threats. Trolls learned to gamify their tactics, overwhelming selected targets with abuse or contacting en masse the ad sponsors of journalistic outlets that had the temerity to criticize them. As Becca Lewis, with coauthor Alice Marwick, put it in a 2017 report on GamerGate's broader consequences for disinformation online, the movement was predicated on "retrograde populism": "Gamergate participants asserted that feminism—and progressive causes in general—are trying to stifle free speech, one of their most cherished values. They are reacting to what they see as the domination of the world by global multiculturalism and the rise of popular feminism. This is a retrograde populist ideology which reacts violently to suggestions of white male privilege."[2]

What had initially begun as a harassment campaign against a single female game developer grew into an all-out digital war against the presence of anyone who threatened a certain view of "gamer" identity—the idea that video games should exclusively cater to young, white, male, and socially alienated audiences. Anyone female, or a member of a racial minority—or even simply critical of the tits-and-gore ethos of mainstream games—was a fair target for attack. GamerGaters were digital natives, utilizing all the tools at their disposal and innovating more, orbiting around a nucleus of reactionary politics. As one commenter on the gaming message board Escapist Forums put it, the movement was an expression of "anger at feminists and SJWs [Social Justice Warriors, a derogatory term for leftists] trying to dictate what's in games and screeching when things don't meet a 'diversity' quota"—and its end goal was a "crazy as all get out revolution."

It's unsurprising that these scorched-earth tactics extended to racialized abuse of critics, and purposeful disinformation generated to blur the white, male nature of the movement.

Shireen Mitchell, a black female activist, recalls the racist abuse that accompanied her outspoken stance against the harassment of women online at the time. "It was one of the most public racist and sexist displays," she told me. Having received abuse and threats after planning to participate in a South by Southwest panel on online harassment, Mitchell was accompanied by a security detail while speaking at another event about online harassment.

"The basis was that only white male gamers are actually good at games," she said of GamerGate. "So everyone else needs to go through some 'ethics' screening. That women sleep around and minorities are only given jobs because of their skin not because they are qualified. So that became the ruse. The narratives are used as cover."

Several figures initially rose to massive fame online during GamerGate—including Milo Yiannopoulos, who was then the technology editor of the far-right website Breitbart, and Mike Cernovich, a small-time "dating coach" and trained lawyer who emerged as a spokesperson for the movement. Both went on to participate in the alt-right's rise to prominence in 2015 and during the 2016 presidential election, riding a wave of racism to online celebrity.

GamerGate was in many ways an inflection point for the social-media age: It showed trolls that they could use tactics old and new to abuse targets en masse in pursuit of reactionary, antifeminist politics. As racist ideology became more mainstream in the era of Donald Trump, many of the men involved in GamerGate became part of campaigns that utilized the same tactics to push racism, anti-immigrant sentiment, and white-nationalist rhetoric. A campaign that began as revenge against an alledgedly cheating girlfriend morphed into a retrograde wave that encompassed racial minorities, women, and progressive ideology more generally. The young men energized by reactionary politics, radicalized by participation in harassment campaigns, and ready and able to engage in nimble, hard-to-foil propaganda operations were ripe for recruitment by America's organized racist movements.

The feminist journalist Robyn Pennacchia, who covered the GamerGate movement as it unfolded, explained that GamerGate arose, in part, from an extant internet culture among young men that employed shock as entertainment, and was constantly upping the ante. Immersion in a milieu that pushed racist rhetoric, misogyny, and grotesque jokes about bestiality and pedophilia for shock value furthered their social alienation, pushing them away from the jobs and girlfriends they felt entitled to as young white men.

"Though Gamergate was certainly the beginning of something, it was also a last gasp. In their minds, women were taking every damn thing away from them. If women were coming for their video games, they were at least going to go out fighting," she told me. "Soon, people who are actually serious about racism come in and start pushing them to take it seriously as well. They give them new reasons for why their lives suck, and they eat it up. They're already not THAT put off by racism, because of the whole 'doing racism for shock value' thing, so organized racism becomes the next step."

While GamerGate was driving feminists out of their houses—and driving video-game fans into the arms of reactionary politics—the murders committed by Elliot Rodger were radicalizing a different, smaller sector of the internet, in that same fateful year, 2014. Together with the manifesto he left behind, Rodger's rampage would transform a small sector of internet users who'd come together to bemoan their sexual deprivation into a community that would come to be defined by rage, misogyny, and the potential for violence.

The incel community—which stands for "involuntarily celibate"—is a red-hot crucible for the hatred of women, and Elliot Rodger, a man who killed women out of sheer rage with a patina of sexual frustration, would become their patron saint.

———

ADVENTURES WITH INCELS

On May 23, 2014, Rodger, twenty-two years old, killed seven people, including himself. Shortly before beginning his rampage, he had posted lengthy videos to YouTube and emailed thirty-four people a 137-page manifesto that decried his own virginity and vilified a world that had denied him what he saw as his birthright. Rodger's manifesto was titled "My Twisted World," and consisted of equal parts autobiography of his short life and seething, misogynistic screed. In his final video, titled "Elliot Rodger's Retribution," Rodger, a handsome young man with an eerily flat affect, speaks in clichés to express his loathing for the world in general and women in particular.

"You girls have never been attracted to me. I don't know why you girls aren't attracted to me, but I will punish you all for it," he says, staring directly at the camera. "I'm the perfect guy and yet you throw yourselves at all these obnoxious men instead of me, the supreme gentleman. I will punish all of you for it."

He ends with an eerily rehearsed laugh, one ripped straight from a B-movie. Later that day, Rodger murdered six people and ended his own life with a bullet to the head.

The murders—and Rodger's self-identification as an unwilling virgin, coupled with the rage he expressed, over and over again, at women—electrified a small but growing corner of the internet. On a forum innocuously named love-shy.com, on 4chan, and on Reddit communities like r/ForeverAlone, young men saw Rodger's violence as a natural extension of their own anger. In the following years, that anger would grow into a holistic, self-contained ideology, one that encompassed gender relations, social theories, pseudoscience—and a great deal of rage. They called themselves "incels"—a portmanteau for "involuntarily celibate."

Incels are a group of people, nearly all male, who self-identify as sexually deprived, and commune on the internet to bemoan their lack of sexual intimacy. Just as often, they revile the women who, in their view, unjustly imprison them in that sexless state. "Chad" and "Stacy" are incel code words for the sexually successful, socially well-adjusted men and women who oppressed them so foully.

In the incel community, to enact violent retribution against an unjust, sex-depriving world is called "going ER." And it's the subject of constant fantasies. While Rodger is the most prominent example of incel-specific mass murder, he is far from alone in transforming his frustration at women into violence. On April 23, 2018, a twenty-five-year-old Canadian man named Alek Minassian deliberately drove a white Ryder van into a crowd in Toronto, killing eight women and two men. Before he did so, he logged on to Facebook. "Private (Recruit) Minassian Infantry 00010, wishing to speak to Sgt 4chan please. C23249161," he posted. "The Incel Rebellion has already begun! We will overthrow all the Chads and Stacys! All hail the Supreme Gentleman Elliot Rodger!"

The previous year, Christopher Cleary, a twenty-seven-year-old Coloradan with a conviction for domestic violence and stalking, had posted a long rant to Facebook about his virginity, involuntary celibacy, and plans to kill "as many girls as I see." He traveled to Provo, Utah, and was arrested by police who feared he was planning to target the anti-Trump Women's March protest, a nationwide event that took place on January 21, 2017. On May 24, 2018, Cleary was sentenced to serve up to five years in prison. Also in 2018, Scott P. Beierle shot two women to death and injured five others in a yoga studio in Tallahassee, Florida. In videos posted before his attack, he urged fellow incels to fight back, and expressed sympathy and admiration for Elliot Rodger.

A quick search on YouTube reveals multiple tributes to Rodger, with his image displayed to maudlin soundtracks and descriptions like "The world was hard on you, you lived a life of injustice and pain." The blogger David Futrelle, who carefully tracks the world of online misogyny on his blog, We Hunted the Mammoth, noted in *New York* magazine that the fervid admiration of Rodger among online misogynists amounts to a kind of worship, a "cult of Saint Elliot," complete with a widely circulated image of Rodger's face photoshopped into an icon of a saint, a halo surrounding his passive, smirking face.

After Minassian's rampage, I began to explore the world of incels online, thinking to write an article about it. I wasn't the only journalist with that idea; Vox issued one of its characteristic "explainers" about incels; the BBC asked, "What is an incel?" While doing some further poking around, I came across a Reddit post on the board r/badeconomics titled "Sexual Market Value in the Planned Economy of Inceldom." There, I encountered a screenshot that offered far more detail than Minassian's isolated act of terrorism. It read, in part:

> The Incels are not the problem, but rather they are a symptom that something is very wrong in our society—and unless their legitimate grievances are addressed this could very soon spiral out of control . . .
>
> There are several ways I propose we do this:
>
> 1) Women are no longer allowed to wear makeup, i.e falsely advertise "their" beauty and hence stop them from banging guys above their league.
>
> 2) Women are ONLY allowed to date men with equal sexual market value to them. State-mandated tests should be made and everyone get a sexual-market value card, ranging from the 1/10 to 10/10, like an ID card.

3) Every time a woman sleeps with a new man she lose one (1) rank on her sexual-market value card, until she reach the lowest rank (1/10) [*sic*].

4) There's no way to rise through the ranks, other than through exercise.

5) Women with more than 9 sexual partners and single moms should be forced by the state to date and have sex with incels that can't get any women despite the above changes.

This would deal with the problem, not the symptom, and is the way we deal with everything from counter-piracy to counter-terrorism. The Incel threat is real and should be treated the same way.

A vision of state-mandated sex slavery, state punishment of female sexuality, and "sexual market value" as a real, scientifically determinable number was fascinating, horrifying, and so tantalizingly grotesque that I naturally posted it to Twitter, back in the halcyon days of 2018. "These are human beings but they live on a different planet I think," I wrote. The tweet got a fair number of views, and ten thousand "likes"—and that's when the incels found me, long before I'd penetrated their ranks, or even contemplated doing so.

Over the next few days, my time line was flooded with images of roast-beef sandwiches. They were open-faced sandwiches, for the most part, overflowing with loose, dripping meat, pink folds of beef sagging tableward. "Shut the fuck up roastie," wrote anonymous Twitter users with anime images as their avatars. "Found the roastie." "Roastie genocide soon, inshallah."

What's a "roastie," you ask? It's incel terminology, included in their official "incel wiki," a dictionary of memes, terms, and slurs, hosted on the message board Incels.co. "*Roastie* is a word for insufferable women that makes fun of something women can't change without extremely invasive surgery: their labia. Implying distended labia looks like roast beef," the wiki entry reads. The comparison is bolstered by a highly dubious and unscientific belief: that the more men women have sex with, the more stretched-out and, well, roast-beef-like their labia become. (No word is given on women who frequently have sex with a single partner, such as a husband or boyfriend.) In the incel wiki, the entry for "roastie" is accompanied by a graph that claims to depict "How Labial Elasticity Correlates to Number of Sexual Partners," illustrated with a spatter of pink dots rising to the top of the y-axis (Labial Elasticity) as sexual partners surpass thirty-five-plus. The graph is attributed to three scientists—S. Mintz, J. Russels, and P. Nilan. There was no journal name listed—just the vague credit "Cambridge University, vol 14, no. 2, 2009."

I searched for the article, on Google, Google Scholar, Jstor, PubMed, and Academia.edu, massive storehouses of academic data; in each case, I found nothing. A Google Image search for the graph itself came up with only critics mocking incels on Twitter.

P. Nilan and S. Mintz came up on Google Scholar as Pam Nilan and Steven Mintz, respectively. Nilan has written extensively about adolescents in contemporary Indonesia; Mintz is a professor of American history at the University of Texas at Austin, with a particular focus on historical views of childhood. Of J. Russels there was no sign whatsoever. A search revealed no incidence whatsoever of a "labial elasticity index"; the term *labial elasticity* seemed to refer to lungs' ability to expand, and featured most prominently in a number of articles about birdsong. Just to be certain, I asked Dr. Jennifer Gunter, a prominent obstetrician-gynecologist and author of *The Vagina Bible*. "There is no such thing as a labial elasticity index," she wrote me. "This leads me to conclude none of these men have seen labia or even a penis entering a vagina."

Despite the inaccuracy of such roast-beef-labia claims, when I published a column about incels back in 2018, a reader sent an Arby's gift card to me, courtesy of the *Village Voice*. I asked my editor to take it and give it to the first homeless person he saw; I didn't have much appetite for that particular sandwich meat just then.

There's some distance, of course, between the massacres committed by Rodger and Minassian and the act of sending images of roast beef en masse to a female writer on Twitter. But some of the memes were genuinely disturbing: One image was doctored to look like a screenshot from a first-person shooter game in which the player was Elliot Rodger, entering a room filled with young women holding Solo cups. The user who posted it accompanied it with a poem: SMOKE YOUR WEED / DRINK YOUR CUM / YOUR TIME IS COMING / ROASTIE SCUM.

The incel community was as close as I could get to an online community organized purely around misogyny—to grotesque and willful misunderstandings of women, from their social roles to their very anatomy. The ideology of inceldom falls under the loose category of "male supremacy"—a subspecies of hate organized around the thesis that women are inherently inferior. In order to further examine the hypothesis that misogyny is a "gateway hatred" that can lead to white-supremacist thought, I wanted to see if racist hate had made inroads here, among the lonely, angry men of inceldom.

R/incels—the main Reddit message board for the community, with some 40,000 members—had been banned by the site in November 2017 for inciting violence against women. R/braincels, the alternative that had sprung up, was "quarantined" by the site when I began research for this book, though it has been banned as of May 2020.

Before clicking through to a quarantined message board on Reddit, users are confronted with a message informing them that the board "is dedicated to shocking or highly offensive content." The message board couldn't be searched for specific words and terms due to the quarantine, but a light skim through the pages of content on offer showed that the "shocking or offensive" label was accurate. (And I am not easily shocked.)

There's something particularly disturbing about incel communities and their rhetoric, at least for me. Perhaps it's because there's a core of relatability in the worldview they describe: Who among us has not felt unworthy of love, obsessed about their appearance, or longed for intimacy and companionship that seemed impossible to attain? These very feelings had prompted considerable angst for much of my teenage years, even into my early twenties. The driving force of inceldom is loneliness, borne of social isolation and erotic frustration—near-universal feelings, particularly in an era of internet-driven social alienation. But in the world of incels, these natural human urges have been twisted into a holistic, ugly worldview predicated on two pillars—misogyny and self-hatred. Their loathing of women, which is inextricable from desire and longing, is visceral; so is their loathing of themselves, and their despair. The resulting universe of rhetoric is so devoid of empathy for others that what empathy one feels for the denizens of incel-world erodes, word by word, post by post.

Incels have their own vocabulary, enshrined, in loving detail, in their wiki; it's an obscure mix of slurs, pseudoscientific terms, and their own peculiar quirks and obsessions. To "rope" is to commit suicide; a "cope" is a delusional belief that allows the coper not to despair; "JB" is "jailbait"; "mogging" is undermining people by surpassing them (thus one can be "heightmogged," "looksmogged," etc.—meaning outclassed by someone taller or better-looking than you). There are also the aforementioned, ubiquitous terms *roastie*, *Stacy*, and *Chad*, along with *femoid* or *foid*—a cyborg-like, dehumanizing term for women. There is an obsession with "mewing"— a technique developed by British orthodontist Dr. Mike Mew and spread via YouTube, which dictates that pressing one's tongue against the roof of one's mouth can result in a stronger and more attractive jawline. (Jawlines, face shape, and even skull shape are a persistent obsession in the incel community, the subjects of careful analysis both in the selfies incels post and in photos and videos of celebrity "Chads" they analyze with the precision of a savant phrenologist.) The journalist Alice Hines documented for *New York* magazine the story of a plastic surgeon who had become something of a celebrity in the incel world for his willingness to aid young men in creating more masculine faces, often using custom implants, to craft angular cheekbones, shovel-like jawlines, and aquiline noses. They wanted to be big men enough to shave their bones to do it. They were working toward an idealized masculinity warped by misogyny so complete it isolated them from reality. A millimeter of bone, for them, was the way to punch a particular button in the inhuman, alien female psyche that would break down sexual resistance. There was no pattern of behavior to address; just the shape of a jaw to change, not the words it produced. This is an expensive and occasionally dangerous form of what incels call "looksmaxxing"—the attempt to improve one's appearance enough to "ascend" from inceldom into a sexually active life.

The blizzard of unfamiliar vocabulary incels use helps to create a sense of insularity, as all jargon does. The users of these terms were speaking a mutually comprehensible language that rendered life a grim gauntlet of sexual selection, and would be unintelligible, for the most part, to an outsider.

But once I learned enough incel terminology to read through the posts, I was struck most by the current that underlies all incel discourse: a potent mix of despair and rage.

Over and over again, users made reference to suicide. "Made the mistake of joining Tinder . . . Pass me the goddamn rope," wrote one user on r/Braincels. Another: "Braincels is my only cope in life. Without it, I will inevitably rope." An entire category of posts—usually about attractive men or ugly women finding sex and companionship—was dubbed "Suifuel" (suicide fuel). When one user posted that he was readying himself for suicide—had bought a gun and wasn't planning to go into work tomorrow, writing that he was "ready to die, ready for whatever comes next"—other users on the message board actively encouraged him. "Godspeed. Watch the sunrise and listen to your favorite bands," replied one user. "See you in incelhalla [incel Valhalla] lad," wrote another. "Enjoy the otherside friend."

In between the despairing posts, there was the misogyny. Pulsing, vivid misogyny, so vitriolic it seemed to burn my eyes through the screen. There were countless memes valorizing another man who had committed suicide, but not before expressing his ultimate hatred of women by murdering them: Elliot Rodger. One user photoshopped him onto the Iron Throne, the titular seat of *Game of Thrones*, suggesting that this could have been an "alternative ending" for the TV show. Another user used a Snapchat filter to gender-swap Rodger's face, suggesting that his life would have been easier if he had been born a woman. There were countless posts decrying ugly women, promiscuous women ("I don't want my child to come out of a place where hundreds of dicks have entered"; "My mother is such a fucking whore"; "Daily reminder: your crush lives only to deep throat chad's cock"), and overweight women. Users posted reports of crimes and murders committed by women as if they proved the thesis that women are evil—a common tactic on racist blogs and message boards, which are rife with reports of crimes by minorities. "Women are such careless, heartless whores," wrote one user. "Take away the lies and women are literally filthy hagravens who happens to have a pussy so everything works out in their favor," came a reply. (Hagravens are a monster in the video game *Skyrim*, a mix between a crone and a bird who attacks travelers with spells and claws.)

Beyond the "red pill" of antifeminism, incels embrace their own, deeply nihilistic philosophy, which they have labeled the "blackpill." It's a mix of carefully cherry-picked scientific theories, misogynistic social conclusions, and, often, a fatalism so deep an existentialist would faint. In the world of the blackpill, looks are not subjective; women are "hypergamous"—tending to trade upward in favor of more sexually attractive and prosperous mates—and looks are not evenly distributed among men. "It is often suggested that the blackpill means that 'it's over' for incels with a certain physical and social status—that is, that they have next to no chance of 'ascending' or attaining sexual and overall fulfillment," the incel wiki entry concludes. "It's over" is somewhere between a mantra and a meme, a repeated refrain that's an incitement to rage and hopelessness.

As a roastie—or, more generously, a "foid"—I knew I couldn't get in, or even close. I wanted to join Incels.co, an incels-only independent message board, which is not constrained by the rules of any large social-media site. The site is run by an anonymous figure who goes by the name "SergeantIncel." In an interview with *Vox* journalist Zack Beauchamp, "Sarge" expressed amusement at the anti-Semitism, racism, and misogyny plaguing Incels.co, insisting that much of it was trolling, not genuine hatred.

Nonetheless, in its Rules section, the site states that females are "banned on sight, no exceptions."

So Tommy O'Hara was born.

———

Like any area of American life, racism permeates the world of inceldom, too.

Consciousness of race is embedded in incel culture, which tends to fall prey to the same pseudoscience that online racist communities do. It's a generally agreed-upon maxim that white men have the most natural advantages in the game of sexual selection. The racial worldview expressed in the incel-sphere is one in which whiteness is an innate advantage in schematics of sexual attractiveness; whiteness remains at the top of the pyramid, in a way imbued with the pseudoscience of sloppy, bastardized evolutionary psychology.

Incel communities differ from white-supremacist spaces in that they contain significant nonwhite membership; a poll conducted by Incels.co of its community members indicated that the community was 60 percent white, 40 percent nonwhite. However, I observed significant white-supremacist activity on incel message boards; a pool of resentful, radicalized, and hatred-driven young men proved irresistible, even if not all of them were white. Racist sentiment, including pseudoscientific rhetoric that predicates sexual attractiveness on arbitrary racial hierarchies, ran alongside the rankest of misogyny. Together, they commingled into a vile worldview that striates humanity into ethnically distinct furrows of sexualized despair and rage. Different races of incels are labeled through distinctive terminology—from "ricecel" for an East Asian incel to "currycel" for a South Asian one. The figure of the white, sexually successful "Chad" has analogues in other skin colors and cultures. Like all ideologies warped by hate, inceldom bears only a cursory relationship to reality. Its logic is crude and corroded by irrational misogyny. In attempting to set forth a coarse and hate-driven total theory of sociosexual interaction, inceldom recreates in parallel the white-supremacist nature of Western societies.

Incels.co has the feeling of a barroom boast-off. The vibe is giddy but competitive—users intoxicated by the freedom of a space where they are free to express prejudice with as much violence as they wish. There's a sense of one-upmanship that pervades the place, a desire to heighten the level of extremity of speech, graphic images rendered, racism expressed. It's also a forum for the encouragement of despair. As in every incel space, the dual forces of despair and rage fight for space, but on this particular board, the atmosphere is heightened. One post was created by a user whose avatar was the face of Scott Beierle, the man who had shot two women and himself to death at a Tallahassee yoga studio. It was titled "The Fate That Awaits Us All [NSFW]"; its content was a photo of a decayed body, partially mummified, beside a table covered in thick dust. Its smooth, partially preserved face stared blankly upward, mouth agape. The accompanying text: "Dying alone and undiscovered for years." The responses ranged from the blackly comic—"The way the rent is around here, I'd probably be discovered by 6pm on the 1st"—to the flippantly nihilistic: "not if you kill yourself in public." Another suggested he might "go ER"—an incel term for committing a massacre, as Elliot Rodger did. Others posted grimmer and grimmer photographs of bodies: a swollen, drowned corpse, gray-skinned and bloated; a choked face with its tongue hanging out, its eyeballs protruding, in fuzzy, moldy-looking chiaroscuro.

That's just a sample; there are thousands of such posts. On May 25, 2018, I looked at a sample of posts on Inceldom Discussion, the forum's most popular channel. Posts ranged from the desire for suicide, to tips for appropriate anime movies to masturbate to, to apocalyptic fantasies ("Is creating AI for destroying the whole of humanity really immoral?"). In public view, the conversation was extreme, and saturated with racism. There was a long and heated discussion over whether Italians could be considered truly white, which included dark insinuations from a user called "Eugenicist" about whether the Italian mafia had merely been a front for nefarious Jewish activity. Non-white incels rarely pushed back against this sort of hate-peddling; the idea of a racial hierarchy was embedded in their ideology. In a poll conducted on Incels.co in March 2020, asking users, "Do you wish you were white?" an overwhelming majority of nonwhite respondents voted yes—31 to 7. There was some public grousing about the number of white supremacists attempting to recruit, however; some incels argued that white supremacy was just another "cope"—just another self-deluding attempt to cover over the grim truth of the blackpill.

If this was what they said in public—so filled with hate and misery—what on earth were they saying in private, where the watchful eyes of reporters, researchers, and a curious public couldn't reach?

In order to enter the backroom at Incels.co—to post, reply, or join the chat room perpetually throbbing on the site—you have to register, and, in the process, offer your reasons for being an incel.

My initial answer, as Tommy, was somewhat perfunctory: I wrote that I was a virgin at twenty-one, a "truecel" (authentically involuntarily celibate), and wanted to join the community. My membership bid was rejected; the reason provided was a prompt to "go into more detail about your situation."

So I switched usernames, from "blackpillbaby" to "Tommythe-manlet"—*manlet* being an incel term for a short man, whose height provides an obstacle to sexual success. This time, I wrote:

My name is Tom. This is my second attempt to get onto the board because I really do want to be part of this community.

I am 21, never been kissed even once. I see foids on the street and I long to touch them and be touched but I think because of my ugly face I will never be loved. I feel despair and rage. I am so angry at seeing foids date men who never care about them when I know I would cherish them and make them feel special but they do not ever look at me. I have cystic acne and weak wrists, I am only 5'7", and no matter how hard I try I can never have a successful conversation with a foid.

I am angry at the feminist bitches who treat men like we are disposable. I do feel disposable but it's unfair the way foids treat me and guys like me who just want to love and be loved. I want to hold tits with my hands at least once before I die. I think about suicide a lot but have decided the best revenge on foids is to find my own friends and community. that's why I want to join—I am a truecel and I want to talk to others like me. I feel very alone and very angry and I want to talk to others. I am fucking sick of Chads who tell me to "just lighten up" and automatically I will be swimming in pussy. I am a short manlet with acne and an ugly face and that's not something I can control.

I see foids walking down the street in short shorts and tit shirts and I feel both rage and desire in ways that feel so hard to control. It will only get worse as summer arrives. I want to be part of this community.

Thanks,

Tom

It worked. I was in.

I clicked on the main forum. On one thread, users had selected a graduation photo of an interracial couple—the man black, the woman Asian—taken from Reddit and were discussing how unattractive their children would be, using racial slurs and suggesting chemical castration for ugly women.

Steeling myself, I clicked over to the chat room.

A user calling himself "Adolf_Hitler" was advocating rebuilding concentration camps. He was laying out a plan for creating an ultra-right party, picking up where the more nebulous cultural movement of the alt-right had failed. He was lauding Einsatzgruppen leader Helmut Oberlander for his jawline, and Joseph Goebbels's service to the Third Reich, despite his inferior forehead shape.

No one was arguing, just egging him on.

Over on the chatting app Discord, where I joined a private incel chat room after jumping through a few more hoops (laying out Tom's story again, linking to his profile on Incels.co, begging), the discourse was chaotic. There were about three hundred members, about sixty online on a Saturday afternoon in May 2019.

The principal difference between the Discord chat and the message board was the frenetic, recursive pace of its memes—which mainly involved using images of a particular overweight Reddit user who had once posted selfies to a forum on male grooming, only to become the unwitting mascot of the incels and called "Hamlossus." There were also the usual cherry-picked news stories that portrayed women as sluts and criminals. There was a lot of porn.

In the #nsfw (not safe for work) channel, there were porn clips, for the most part fairly vanilla blow jobs and nudes. But there were also a lot of anime breasts—pliant and willing and belonging to kiddie-faced, big-eyed girls. One user posted an image of a man having sex with a Fleshlight (an artificial vagina) sewn onto an anime body pillow. "I need to do this," he wrote.

Back on the main site, Incels.co, I discovered that multiple users had taken to praising the desirability of women in anime over their flesh-and-blood counterparts—calling them "2D girlfriends." One post polled users as to whether they would rather choose "sex with ugly 20+ 3d femoid" or "fap [masturbate] to cute 2d lolis [lolitas, or characters drawn to resemble young girls]." Twenty-seven users had voted in favor of having sex with a real human woman, ending the celibacy they had gathered to bemoan. Nineteen—41 percent—voted in favor of masturbating to anime. Despite these bleak personal choices, I noted elsewhere on the site that several users attributed their lack of sexual success to "Jewish conspiracy." (It's always, always convenient to blame the Jews.)

Tommy O'Hara had done his job—he'd peered into the heart of incel discourse. And here was the equation laid out: Radicalized misogyny had led users straight into the arms of white supremacy, with its anti-Semitism, its specious and violently expressed concern for the survival of whiteness, its willingness to engage in pseudo-science and racial abuse. Seeking to express their hate for women, the users of Incels.co had been drawn to other hatreds. Having rejected social norms surrounding the personhood of women, they were willing to degrade other personhoods, in service of their identification as a uniquely marginalized and imperiled group. And the hate was violent; casual posts about mass murder and suicide abounded. Just as white supremacy leads to misogyny, the causal relationship could be reversed. No hate is an island. Here, these angry young men were telling each other what they considered to be truths—the truth about the evils of women, the truth about the Jews, the truth about the ultimate desirability of whiteness. There was no one to stop them, and the steam was building, until the next murder occurred. Reading the posts, I wondered who among those who idolized incel shooters would be the next. I wondered how many women would die, and if, in the age of ubiquitous gun violence, I would even hear the news.

CHAPTER 6

THAT GOOD OLD-TIME RELIGION

My daily research for this book involved a lot of lurking in and surveilling fascist and neo-Nazi chats on Telegram. I mostly kept all the channels on mute so I could dip in when I wanted to, but occasionally forgot to do so immediately when I joined a new one, leading to some nervous fumbling when messages from "Holocaust II" or "Expose the Nose" cropped up on my phone with no warning. Suddenly, in one day, across a bevy of racist channels, word of an explosive new event started spreading. It was going down in November 2020, somewhere in Kentucky.

The event was informally dubbed Christgang vs Pagang. It was a fund-raiser for Augustus Sol Invictus (Latin for "majestic unconquered sun"), born Austin Gillespie. Invictus is a white-supremacist lawyer and a practitioner of Thelema, a black-magic religion based on the teachings of Aleister Crowley; he had been a headline speaker at the deadly 2017 Charlottesville Unite the Right rally. He has publicly denied the Holocaust and agitated for a second Civil War. With these dubious qualifications, Invictus is running for president of the United States in 2020, on a platform that includes planks like "Better dead than red," "Eat the bankers," and "End White Genocide." ("We will halt the flood of immigrants, cease all so-called diversity programs, and terminate the trend of Whites becoming unwelcome minorities in their own countries," he wrote on his official campaign website.)

Invictus's first brush with electoralism—a quixotic bid to replace Marco Rubio as senator for Florida in 2015 as a candidate for the Libertarian Party—was derailed, in part, by allegations that he had sacrificed a goat and drunk its blood. ("I have performed animal sacrifices as part of my religion," he told *Politico*.)[1] So who was so enthused about the campaign of a goat-blood-drinking satanist neo-Nazi in a bid for the Oval Office? A bevy of white-nationalist Christians and pagans, ready to come together . . . but only to a point. They wanted to settle their religious differences with their fists, for a profit.

The Christgang vs Pagang event was set to be an MMA and fistfighting bout between practicing Christians and Pagans within the white-nationalist movement, with a pay-in designed to raise funds for Invictus's campaign. Christians versus pagans, punching each other in the face to raise money for a satanist. The fund-raiser seemed quite necessary: Federal Election Commission data for Invictus's 2020 presidential campaign—as a Republican, naturally—showed just over $4,000 in contributions.[2] All sixty-one campaign donors were anonymous, with the exception of a nutritionist named Emily Phillips in Lisbon, Iowa, and Invictus himself.

I wanted to know the fund-raiser's precise date and location, so I activated a long-dormant sock-puppet account and messaged a man named Colton Williams, a white supremacist and leader of the Christian extremist organization the Legion of St. Ambrose. It's an antigay, militantly misogynist, and racist group. Williams is a former member and close associate of the Traditionalist Workers' Party, a neo-Nazi and racist group founded in 2015. The TWP fell apart in spectacular fashion in 2018 after its leader caught the group's chief spokesman having sex with his wife—an event archly dubbed by antifascists "The Night of the Wrong Wives," in reference to the infamous intra–Nazi Party purge known as the Night of the Long Knives. Williams, who had been a TWP member, took some of its principles—in particular, an overtly religious push against "anti-Christian degeneracy"—into forming his new crew.

The Legion of St. Ambrose specified that they had "around 90 members" when I contacted them, under my real name, through a publicly available email. "Given the rapid growth of our fraternity, it is hard to tell what our total numbers are, at this time." The group advertises itself as an explicitly Christian and deeply theological endeavor.

"We believe that the Americas were founded and forged by European Christians, from the French Catholics and Russian Orthodox in the furthest north of Canada to the Spanish and Portuguese Catholics in the furthest south of South America," a spokesperson wrote to me. "We believe that all cultures and heritages should be celebrated and preserved, including the Christian European culture and heritage that transformed these lands in the name of Christ." In this context, I was practicing dual roles—that of the respectable journalist and the infiltrator. In fact, given my notoriety within the white-supremacist community, even to get such an anodyne quote from a spokesperson I had to press, cajole, and threaten, eventually telling the spokesperson that I was going to write about the Legion with or without their cooperation. They had no idea I was already inside their chat rooms, in disguise.

Their rhetoric sounded fairly harmless at first. But a closer look dispels the notion that the Legion is a celebratory, heritage-focused religious group. In a section on their website titled "Traditional Values," the group enumerates a rejection of "homosexuality, trans-genderism and pedophilia," aspiring for a return to "traditional" sexuality—one dominated by a stifling ideal of submissive women and dominant white Christian men. I scrolled through their mission statement, which ranged from a desire to "return to a patriarchal society," to a ban on kosher and halal slaughter, and to the outlawing of anti-Christian rhetoric. It called for the United States to cut all ties with Israel—a far cry from the Christian Zionism of the mainstream US evangelical right.

In the chat rooms, Williams goes by @ColtonWilliams1483—a spin on the white-supremacist dog whistle "1488"; it's a combination of the white-supremacist slogan the "14 words," and "88," which, because *H* is the eighth letter of the alphabet, stands for "Heil Hitler." For Williams, though, *83* is a spin that indicates the true thrust of his public identity—*83* stands for "Heil Christ." This showcases not only the white-supremacist adoration of coded symbols—it also shows just how serious extremist Christians are about marrying their religious and racist values. Williams's motto is *In Hoc Signo Vinces*—a Latin motto first recorded in the time of the Emperor Constantine, meaning "In this sign thou shalt conquer."

Moreover, a quick dip into the Legion of St. Ambrose channel on Telegram reveals that this religious group is a means to honor and celebrate white supremacy. It's rife with racist and anti-Semitic memes. Williams posted a video of himself in a black trench coat firing a handgun at some trees, after attempting to entice racist women with pickup lines like "I have respect for any soldier in the war against global Jewry." In their chats, icons of saints are sandwiched between assertions that Jews murder Christian children to drink their blood and praise for anti-Semitic graffiti.

Talia, the Jewish journalist, couldn't get much further than simple, and misleading, statements from a public email. So I had to resort to getting deeper on different terms, and as a different person. I chose the name "Tommy" yet again—a name that I consistently used to represent white-supremacist male personas. I'm not sure why "Tommy," in particular, seemed like such a fitting nom de guerre; the name has a certain genial, unthreatening, Middle American resonance. This Tommy wasn't an incel. He had his own tale to tell—one that, as usual, I was frantically making up as I went along.

"mr williams im interested in attending the Christgang vs Pagang rumble!!" I wrote to Williams on September 27, 2019, on the Telegram channel. "lets stomp some degenerates."

Even though my alter ego "Tommy" had never spoken in any Telegram chat before, it was that easy. I'd be able to get info and access to the Christgang vs Pagang event. I was immediately invited into two chats: "Pagans vs Christians: 21st Century Rematch," a planning and shit-talking channel for the event; and the private channel for the "Christgang" side, "Augustus Fight Night: Holy League Coordination."

By posing as Tommy, a West Virginian with a pickup truck and a readiness to offer rides, I was given the date of the event and its tentative location, somewhere in Kentucky. The exact address was TBD; but once in, I'd wait until the location had been firmed up. I was also dubbed a "holy warrior for Christ" for my professed desire to stomp pagan heads. More saliently, I got a peek into just how superficial the differences between the Christians and pagans of white nationalism are.

The chat was an immersive bath in toxic masculinity. The stench of homophobic, racist, masculine posturing hit me like a slap with a rank fish. The few female members of the chat were immediately told they would be banned from fighting at the Christgang vs Pagang event ("women fighting is gay"), but would be allowed to be "war brides," offering sexual rewards for the winning side. They were also dismissively called "dishwashers"—as in "who wants to listen to a dishwasher?"

Pagans were called "peggins"—a reference to pegging, the practice of performing anal intercourse on a man with a strap-on dildo, and a prime example, in this case, of homophobic trash-talking. Christians were blamed for putting forth a "doctrine of human equality" that has led to the ascension of nonwhites and Jews.

All the participants talked about their training regimens and how good at fighting they were. Everybody called everybody else the n-word. Dual worship before the fight was proposed, to take place in "different parts of the woods." The pagans bet they would consume the mead of victory. The Christians pledged to punch out their foes for the one true Lord. And all of them were game to raise money for a candidate who wanted to strip the country of nonwhites.

Somewhere in Kentucky, the Rumble in the Bumblefuck (my appellation) was going to go down, and it was going to smell like blood, sweat, and beer. All I had to do was wait for them to tell me where, so I could inform the public at large via Twitter—and my antifascist contacts in private. Despite my (that is, Tommy's) avowal that I was ready to "stomp some pagan heads," I knew which side I was really on: The side that thought all these creeps were racist losers, but too dangerous to ignore. The side that didn't want any blood spilled at all—whether in the name of Odin, or the name of Christ.

There is a deep strain of extremist Christianity within many iterations of contemporary white supremacy. There is also an ascendant pagan or heathen subsect of the community. While the two factions have far more in common than not, it's both fascinating and horrifying to look closely at the ways white nationalism combines with religion on the extremist right.

While researching that religious expression, it was easy for me to get bogged down in who's drinking goat blood for Satan and who thinks a cone-shaped Crusader helmet is an extremely cool fashion accessory and who's climbing mountains to sacrifice to Odin in hopes of awakening the white race. Sifting through the details, and observing the nonstop, puerile nature of their speech, it can be easy to wonder precisely what the point of decoding all this hate is. Isn't it just hate? Aren't these just losers pontificating and arguing on the internet?

The thing about hate, though, is it metastasizes. The thing about channels that are filled, twenty-four hours a day, with stochastic violence—testosterone-filled megaphones shouting for blood—is that, sooner or later, someone is going to take them up on it. From Robert Bowers to Anders Breivik to Brenton Tarrant, racist networks have proven over and over again that the steady dissemination of murderous propaganda leaves a trail of blood behind it. And when that happens, being able to trace, isolate, and identify these ideologies means that racists can't hide behind slippery code words or private vocabularies. In identifying their inspirations, and their ideological and theological motivations, we give them less room to operate in the shadows. We give them less room to be the mysterious nightmare creatures they so long to be. The chat rooms would continue without my sock puppet or with it. But if I'm there, I can tell you about it. And if you learn about it, you can help me strip the shadows away, and disinfect these crusty dens of hate with a blast of much-needed sunlight. Part of dismantling and understanding white supremacy is a need to understand the myths extremists tell themselves—about their own superiority, and about the origins of whiteness. It's a story that's usually a clumsy grab bag of history, myth, and outright falsehood—and, for extremists, it stretches back a millennium, to the Middle Ages.

Every cause needs a myth, a founding story that imbues its adherents with purpose, making them feel that they are part of something bigger than themselves, something grander and necessary. American nationalism is founded on notions that our country is more principled than others, and mightier, forged in the heat of insurrection against injustice. Other nationalisms are founded on other myths: For Poland and Ukraine, it was a matter of shoring up their distinct languages and histories to attempt to break off from the Russian empire. National heroes were forged from oral tradition and previously obscure literary works, a sense of continuity from ancient days infused into the political struggle for independence. The further back the created past stretches, the greater the political impetus for the cause. In the late nineteenth and early twentieth centuries, the political visionaries of Zionism took biblical verses and Jewish angst at persecution and wove them together into a case for moving thousands to the hot, occupied, and malarial lands of Palestine. Their determination to create a sense of continuity with the ancient yearnings of the biblical past was so strong that they elected to choose Hebrew—a language long dead, lacking a vocabulary for a world more modern than ancient Babylon—and re-formed it as a new, living tongue.

In this sense, transnational white supremacy—the notion that all whites across the world share a common cause—is no different. It requires reaching back past the invention of race in the eighteenth and nineteenth centuries and reframing prior religious movements, wars, and achievements as those of "whiteness" writ large. It requires creating a shared heritage out of disparate cultural artifacts, retrofitting the failures and brutalities of the Crusades and the piratical, ancient culture of the Vikings as parts of the relatively novel concept of whiteness. All told, the construction of a mythos of whiteness requires weaving a new mantle from the threads of ancient and contemporary desires—and claiming, anachronistically, that the battle was for whiteness all along. For Christian white supremacists, it's a viewpoint that pits white against black, and adorns that struggle with a blood-red Templar cross. For pagans, it's a matter of blood, mead, the ravens of Odin, and the Valhalla that awaits white warriors felled in the pursuit of swarthy foes.

———

The Crusades, in particular, crop up again and again in white-supremacist rhetoric and action. A dramatic example occurred in 2016, when three white men named Curtis Allen, Gavin Wright, and Patrick Stein—middle-aged men who had long been part of the armed militia movement in the form of the Kansas Security Force militia—created an even more radical new group. They called it the "Crusaders," and plotted to carry out a devastating act of terror against a Somali Muslim community in Garden City, Kansas. The men were arrested in October 2016. They had planned to bomb an apartment complex with many Somali residents on November 9, the day after the US presidential election. Their plan involved four cars loaded with explosives. The complex contained a small, makeshift mosque; it was where some 250 Muslim refugees lived and prayed.

A former member of the Kansas Security Force, Brody Benson, testified at Allen and Stein's trial. According to Benson, they were given to calling Muslims "cockroaches," and complaining of governmental conspiracies bringing Muslims into Kansas "by the planeload." The former militiaman added that he had heard Stein say that, in the event of a major natural disaster or break in the rule of law, every Muslim man, woman, and child in Kansas should be killed—what amounted, Benson said, to an "extermination."[3] In a conversation recorded by an FBI informant, one of the defendants, Curtis Allen, said he wanted to do "something that almost shuts the state down."[4]

Their motivation wasn't simply hatred. It was an overwhelming fear of Muslims that drove these men to the brink of mass murder, one that has percolated through white-supremacist thought. As the federal government put it in a motion in the case, each defendant expressed that "current U.S. policies concerning Muslims presented an imminent, existential threat to the homeland." In one conversation recorded by the FBI's informant, Dan Day, Stein said: "That's why we're doing this shit. To save this country, to save the future of my kids, my grandkids, your kids and grandkids. That's what this is all about." Allen added: "We're losing the whole country."[5] The visceral fear of "losing one's country"—of being outbred, outnumbered, of becoming a minority—was what drove these "Crusaders" to plot what they deemed to be a holy act. In murdering women and children, they were stemming the invasion they perceived, a brown tide washing whiteness away.

It all squared with David Lane's infamous, influential "White Genocide Manifesto." Stein's recorded comment could have been a paraphrase of the white-supremacist slogan the "14 Words": "We must secure the existence of our people and a future for white children." In the uncompromising, visceral ideology of white supremacy, birth is a zero-sum game, a competition between the races. And murder can be an equalizer. Immigration took on a similarly apocalyptic cast. While some might see humanitarian policy in the resettlement of refugees, Stein, Wright, and Allen could see only invasion, loss, and a loathing borne of terror.

At one point, Stein, Wright, and Allen explicitly mocked pro-immigration ideology. The FBI recorded the following exchange:

STEIN: Oh, these are refugees from a war-torn country.
WRIGHT: Yeah, so sad.
STEIN: . . . they don't have anything, their families are tore apart.
   They don't have a country no more.
ALLEN: Bullshit.
STEIN: We gotta take 'em in!
ALLEN: They don't have a country no more? They just fucking
   walked off and left it!

The "Crusaders" produced a handwritten manifesto, its jumpy script skittering down a legal notepad. The brief screed alternated between ire against the federal government, the United Nations, a decline in manufacturing jobs, and the erosion of constitutional freedoms. "We have to take a stand," they wrote. "Take a stand before it's too late to. It might already be."[6]

In their case, "taking a stand" involved stockpiling ammunition and guns, attempting to manufacture explosives, and setting a date to blow up the apartment complex on Mary Street. They conducted surveillance of the building, and discussed strategies to pack bombs with shrapnel to inflict the maximum amount of pain. According to the chief prosecutor in the case, Tony Mattivi, the men planned to "blow up a bomb, flatten the building, and murder every single man, woman, and child inside."[7]

The FBI obtained a recording of the three men planning to promulgate their manifesto after the bombing.

"This is our call to action. All these people in these militias are like all over. They'll be like, 'Goddamn, it's starting,'" Allen said.

"Fucking Crusades," Stein replied.[8]

Thankfully, the Crusaders' plot was interrupted, and all three men were convicted in 2018, sentenced to decades in prison.[9] But the most deadly act of white-supremacist terrorism in decades took place just two months later—and it was also targeted directly at Muslims.

———

Christchurch, New Zealand, is about as far as it's possible to be from Kansas. Half a globe separates them, but on March 15, 2019, white-supremacist ideology pushed them into a terrible kind of kinship. In one of the most extreme examples of white-supremacist violence in modern history, the Australian far-right extremist Brenton Tarrant drew the danger of white-supremacist ideology in letters of blood.

The details of the story are grotesque, an atrocity custom-designed for the internet age. Tarrant livestreamed his murders on Facebook; posted a link to the video on 8chan, along with a manifesto; and drove to the mosque to a meme-influenced soundtrack, "Remove Kebab," a 2006 Serbian anti-Muslim song that went viral. In the massacre's aftermath, 1.5 million copies of the video were uploaded to Facebook, as the social media giant raced to take it down wherever it recurred. Tarrant's manifesto, titled "The Great Replacement," is woven through with references to the Crusades and medieval Christian struggle. On the gun he used, he painted the words *Tours 732*—a reference to the Battle of Tours in 732, in which a Frankish king conquered Spanish Muslim invaders. Just above it, on the gun's barrel, he wrote: *Refugees Welcome to Hell.*

Tarrant's manifesto is an odd document, a mix of cheeky references to white-supremacist memes and deadly serious dissemination of the ideology's foundational myths. Its very title, "The Great Replacement," is a reference to a secular vision of a clash of civilizations, a purported demographic crisis in which the white Christians of the West are being outbred, outnumbered, and swallowed up by darker races. Tarrant, and his fellow ideologues, seek to connect this theory to a mythical history of whiteness, one in which noble warriors have fended off swarthy hordes for millennia.

In this manifesto, Tarrant referred to his own act—gunning down dozens of innocents at prayer—as a "grand crusade," and included the text of Pope Urban II's appeal to would-be Crusaders in a section titled "To Christians." It was a call to holy war, soaked in the blood of his victims.

In a section titled "To Turks," Tarrant revived the medieval notion of a conflict between Christians and "Turks" as the central, civilizational conflict envisioned by contemporary white supremacists. "If you attempt to live in European lands, anywhere west of the Bosphorus. We will kill you and drive you roaches from our lands," he wrote. "We are coming for Constantinople and we will destroy every mosque and minaret in the city."

Beyond the Crusades themselves, Tarrant's manifesto is a remarkable example of a violent appeal to whiteness that draws on texts and authors from across centuries. He quotes Rudyard Kipling, Dylan Thomas, and the mid-twentieth-century British anti-Semitic fascist Oswald Mosley. This appeal to solidarity is grounded in an all-white view of history, patched together across centuries. It's also an explicitly Christian document, one that invites its readers to embrace a revanchist, medieval vision of holy war. Using the framework of religious duty, Tarrant puts forth a notion of "racial responsibility"—that is, the responsibility of whites to murder anyone perceived to be acting against white racial interests, from Angela Merkel to "your local drug dealer." In the context of this religion-soaked document, it is clear that, to Tarrant and his ideological fellow travelers, racial duty and religious duty are impossible to separate. Tarrant's text reminded me of the ultra-Christian posturing in the Telegram chats I read daily. Calls to racial violence in the name of Christ were something I'd become almost inured to by now. But this one had come true, to deadly consequences.

Six weeks later, another killer inspired by Tarrant's example utilized the Christian faith as a justification for murder.

In another house of prayer, back in the United States, on April 27, 2019, gunfire rang out. This time, the alleged perpetrator was John Earnest, a nineteen-year-old nursing student and devout church-goer. He allegedly walked into a modest synagogue in a suburb of San Diego during Sabbath morning services and opened fire with a semiautomatic rifle, killing one woman and wounding three other people.

In an open letter he posted on 8chan prior to the attack, Earnest laid out a vision of virulent anti-Semitism, laced with expressions of Christian faith. The document quotes Matthew, John, Thessalonians, and Revelation to bolster his view of a world in which "international Jewry" has sealed "the doom of my race." Earnest also admitted that he'd "scorched a mosque in Escondido"—an arson attempt in a mosque had been reported in that city a week earlier—but it was Jews who were the focal point of his ire, in a tirade that encompassed grievances both ancient and modern.

Earnest opened with the proud statement that he was a man of European ancestry, of Irish and Nordic stock. The anti-Semitism exhibited by Earnest echoes some popular white-supremacist and neo-Nazi fixations. He accused Jews of pushing mass immigration, sexual degeneracy, feminism, and race mixing. But Earnest cited his

Christian faith as the justification for his alleged murderous act. He referenced Jewish persecution of Christians of old and Christians of the present—some accusations pulled from the pages of the New Testament, some from the web pages of fervent, extremist-Christian conspiracy sites.

Earnest blamed Jews for the murder of Christ—a common Christian charge across the centuries, although contemporary Catholics have moved away from this charge in their formal doctrine. And he pledged his belief in a medieval myth—the blood libel—that had been the driving force behind countless pogroms. The blood libel is an enduring falsehood that accuses Jews of kidnapping and torturing Christian children for the sake of their blood, which Jews bake into matzah, the traditional unleavened bread of Passover. Needless to say, not only is there a biblical prohibition against eating blood in the first place in Jewish law, matzah is merely a rather tasteless yet crunchy mix of flour and water, not some sort of grisly, cannibalistic black pudding.

Referencing the ancient blood-libel myth of Simon of Trent accented the hybrid nature of Earnest's ideology, a toxic admixture of contemporary internet hate and medieval anti-Semitism.

On Easter Sunday, 1475, the body of a two-year-old Christian boy named Simon Unferdorben was discovered in the cellar of a Jewish home in the northern Italian city of Trent. Immediately, authorities of the Holy Roman Empire, which controlled the town at the time, arrested every Jew living in the city. Even as they awaited sentencing, a mythic narrative sprang up around the dead toddler: that he was a saintly martyr, a victim of ritual murder by the Jews, who used his blood to make their bread.

After prolonged torture, eight Jews were beheaded or burned at the stake for their alleged roles in the boy's death. Late-medieval

Christian networks broadcast the myth of Simon's death at the hands of evil Jews across languages and countries. Simon's tomb became a magnet for pilgrims from across Christendom. The bishop of Trent financed the writing of poems and hagiographies that both praised the martyred child and denounced the perfidy of Jews. Scapegoating of Jewry is an old tactic in many parts of Christianity; on the extremist fringe, only its method of transmission has changed. One does not need to finance the writing of a hagiography anymore to spread lies about the evils of one's racial enemies.

In 2019, a full 544 years after the death of Simon of Trent, Earnest used 8chan to promote his own vision of Jewish perfidy. And while the dissemination was instant, its roots were tethered to a vision of white Christian continuity that stretched from the earliest days of the Church, to the high Middle Ages of Simon of Trent, to the present. To fulfill his Christian vision, Earnest urged his peers on 8chan to "shoot up a mosque, synagogue, immigration center, traitorous politicians, wealthy Jews in gated communities, Jewish-owned company buildings, etc. and get away with it as well." Repeating several times that Tarrant had inspired him, he added, "You cannot love righteousness if you do not also hate sin. You cannot love your own race if you do not hate those who wish to destroy it." He wrote to his "brothers in Christ," urging them to be strong: "Although the Jew who is inspired by demons and Satan will attempt to corrupt your soul with the sin and perversion he spews—remember that you are secure in Christ." It was his faith that propelled him forward, and drew him to pull the trigger.

For both Tarrant and Earnest, internet slang and memes were threaded throughout manifestos that referenced ancient deeds. Sacred texts, poems, and papal decrees rubbed elbows with the casually dropped racial slurs and staccato sentences that fill anonymous message boards daily. Both documents shift wildly in register, reflecting a desire to synthesize 4chan-friendly rhetoric and high-minded statements of purpose.

In both cases, the internet had furnished these violent young men with a vision of history—snow-white, venerable, and filled with conflicts between pure white Christians and dark hordes of unbelievers—that led them to murder. But similar language is replicated daily across chat clients, message boards, and encrypted apps—the forceful commingling of sacred and profane, sarcasm and single-minded earnestness. The two manifestos reflect aspects of a created history, a founding myth for white supremacy, that undergirds prejudice with profound purpose. These two killers weren't isolated cases in that sense; Templar crosses, symbols of Crusader knights, are ubiquitous in white-supremacist spaces. Shields with the Templar symbol were carried at the deadly Unite the Right rally at Charlottesville. White supremacists that weekend chanted "Jews will not replace us," and filled the air with cries of *deus vult*—"god wills it," a Crusader battle cry.[10]

An obsession with medieval Christianity is not entirely new among white supremacists. The Ku Klux Klan made repeated gestures toward courting the heritage of chivalric whiteness, evident in the names of its chapters. In 1975, David Duke founded the Knights of the Ku Klux Klan, aiming to establish White Christian government.[11] The theme of taking on the mantle of medieval Christian warriors echoes through the extremist group today. Current Klan chapters include the White Knights of the Ku Klux Klan; the Church of the National Knights of the Ku Klux Klan, in South Bend, Indiana; Alabama's statewide Global Crusaders: Order of the Ku Klux Klan; and Mississippi's American Christian Knights of the Ku Klux Klan.

The burning cross—one of the Klan's trademark symbols, a method of intimidation and aggression—is also drawn from pre-

Enlightenment European history. In response to an English invasion of Scotland in 1547, the Scottish Regent, the earl of Arran, was said to have sent out a "fiery cross" across the land to summon soldiers to war. An 1850 collection of legends of old castles and abbeys describes the fiery cross as "two slender rods of hazel, formed into the shape of a cross, the extremities seared in the fire and extinguished when red and blazing in the blood of a goat,"[12] a description echoed in other nineteenth-century histories. An original illustration in *The Clansman*, the 1905 "Historical Romance of the Ku Klux Klan" that was the source material for the hugely popular racist film *Birth of a Nation*, shows a medieval-esque scene of two Klansmen, crosses on their white robes, holding a burning cross aloft. One exclaims: "The Fiery Cross of Old Scotland's hills!" Much of the symbolism of the Klan inclines toward a medievalism influenced heavily by popular images of the period, including fantastic ones. After all, this is an organization whose leader is called the "Grand Dragon."[13]

What all these obsessions—with medieval Christianity, with Christian symbolism, and with the Middle Ages in particular—reflect is not just a desire to devolve to a society that was more warlike, built on casual and deadly violence. It also reflects a desire to create an origin myth for whiteness—and imbue a thrown-together and internally inconsistent ideology with an intoxicating whiff of ancient virtue.

Central to the white-supremacist project is the idea of whiteness itself. That sounds obvious—trivial, even—but it matters: The very idea of whiteness is a construct, created to exclude and oppress non-white people by stratifying society along the lines of race. Trivial differences in melanin levels, in eye shape, in hair morphology, in facial structure are used to underpin an ideology about who deserves to live and who deserves to die. About who is the source of uncleanliness and disease, and who is pure. About who should reproduce, and who should be sterilized. These ideas truly came to fruition under the eugenics movement in the nineteenth and twentieth centuries; but like any group that pursues what they see as a high ideal, white supremacists are not content to settle for the notion that the thing they hold most sacred—whiteness—was invented by haphazard skull measurers with prissy-sounding names less than two centuries ago. As noted earlier, white supremacists draw from a grab bag of ideas from throughout history to create their patchwork ideology. So it should be no surprise that among those ideas, and among those texts, are ones that reach further back, beyond the nineteenth century. Consequently, many white supremacists adopt and interweave religious expression into their racist worldviews. The obsession with medieval Christianity is particularly strong when it comes to the Crusades. After all, bigotry seems nobler when retrofitted to a millennia-old tradition of holy struggle. When it comes to religiosity in the white-supremacist movement, no single image looms larger than the Crusades—conceived by contemporary white supremacists as the ultimate holy war between white knights and black foes.

For David M. Perry, a journalist and former professor of medieval history, a fixation on the Crusades among white supremacists is analogous to the ways Confederate imagery crops up in the same contexts. "The Crusades operate as a Lost Cause, a defeat filled with glorious heroes fighting dastardly villains who fell through accident, betrayal, infighting, and more," he told me. "Second, it sets up the 'clash of civilizations' narrative for extremists." Valorizing the Christian warriors of the Crusades aids in creating a vision of the world that is a dualistic struggle between Islam and Christianity, between nonwhite and white—a sacred war that cries out for the valor of those who would do violence in its name.

The idea of the Middle Ages as a utopia of shapely, nubile peasant women, lily-white nobility, and white warriors taking up arms against swarthy foes wasn't invented by the radical far right. It's an image that mass media, depicting any sort of vague Ye Olde Times, has been more than happy to abet. Works like J. R. R. Tolkien's *The Lord of the Rings* and George R. R. Martin's *A Song of Ice and Fire*, and countless other works of fantasy, have shaped the vision that white supremacists imagine themselves to have sprung from.

Much of our entertainment is full of fantasies of pallid, armored warriors scourging dark, scurrying foes; strong knights taking women at will, pure daughters of noble houses, as wives to bear their heirs. Heroes of the pure blood of Númenor shape broad American cultural understandings of what Europe was before modernity.

While the Middle Ages in Europe were not a white utopia— historians and medievalists have worked diligently to record a world that was "multiracial, multifaith, and multicultural," as Professor Dorothy Kim, who teaches medieval literature at Brandeis University, told the *Daily Beast*—cultural images of the period portray it as such. In real life, there were black people, Jews (like my ancestors in the ghettoes of medieval cities), North Africans, and other ethnic minorities in medieval Europe. But the all-white image of the Middle Ages is reflected in just who is attracted to celebrations of the period.

The prevalence of medieval symbology in white-supremacist contexts hasn't escaped the attention of academic medievalists, a number of whom have spoken out against the widespread adoption of the Middle Ages as a mythic locus for the origins of whiteness. "We are allowing the Middle Ages to be seen as a pre-racial space where whiteness can locate its ethnic heritage," wrote Dr. Sierra Lomuto, a medievalist and professor at Macalester University, in a public blog post pleading with other medievalists to be on the lookout for white supremacists embracing their bodies of work.

—

"Jesus was also a kike and deserves to be burned," wrote user "Parzival Æthelwulf," in a Telegram channel titled Radical Agenda. "Every bible should be burned."

It was July 2018.

The channel I was observing was fluid, with about two hundred members, and militantly racist. It was run by the podcasters who called themselves the "Bowl Patrol," in homage to racist mass murderer Dylann Roof's haircut. The conversation was wide-ranging, from gossip about hate groups like the National Socialist Movement to racist cartoons to endless, juvenile homoerotic humor. The user Parzival was no outlier in expressing his overt hostility to Christianity.

"Jesus was nothing but a fucking Jew," replied the user "Mr. Dr. Uncle Dad." "If he were in Auschwitz I'd give him a tattoo."

It's important to note the elaborate and deliberate choices that go into how white supremacists represent themselves: They are consumed by history, poring through it to find models and inspirations. Both parts of the user name Parzival Æthelwulf hearken back to premodern Europe. *Parzival* was a thirteenth-century romance written in Middle High German by the knight Wolfram von Eschenbach, a story of the Arthurian hero Parzival. Æthelwulf, meanwhile, was an Anglo-Saxon king whose reign lasted from 839 to 856, and who was deposed from his kingship soon after returning from a Christian pilgrimage to Rome. But the Telegram user Parzival scorned Christianity; like other contemporary white supremacists, he viewed Christianity as tied too closely to its Jewish roots. Jesus, after all, was a Jew, even if Jews had been killed for centuries in his name. Could a religion started by a Jew ever be free of the Jewish taint? This is perhaps the ultimate example of how difficult it is to transcend anti-Semitism; you can *literally be Jesus Christ* and it won't be enough for some people.

While any number of contemporary hate groups, and their sympathetic shit-posting legions, profess no religion in particular, others look to an alternative faith tradition to adorn their bigotry. Consider the archetypes, in popular culture, of the warriors who roamed premodern Europe. Legends of manly, horn-helmeted Vikings, worshipping pagan gods and raiding villages at will, are featured in nearly as many novels, films, and TV shows as their Christian counterparts. Small wonder, then, that some white supremacists have chosen to adopt what they see as an all-white religion, free from the taint of Jewish perfidy: worship of the Norse pantheon. For a militantly misogynist, violence-glorifying crew, what could be better than worshipping hammer-bearing Thor, or grimly knowledgeable, staff-wielding Odin, who hung from a tree for nine days to gain the world's most secret wisdom? After all, didn't their followers once bring rack and ruin to their foes, as they struck fear into the sights of all who saw their shield-studded longboats? Didn't Odin and Thor and Loki, and their counterparts, once demand blood sacrifice; didn't they once glory in war?

Bypassing the Jewish stain of Christianity, white supremacist neopagans claim to be the "untainted remnant" of true European blood in America. The idea of a racialized culture belonging to whiteness is a key engine of the far right. Racist groups, from the Klan to Identity Evropa, speak frequently of a "white cultural genocide," driven by immigration.[14] For some white supremacists, embracing the worship of the Norse pantheon is a way to concretize the idea of a white racial culture—a means to worship whiteness with sacrifices and prayers.

At any racist rally, you can often find both Christian and pagan symbols: The typical blood-red Templar cross of the Crusades and the runic Black Sun (*Sonnenrad*) fight alongside each other. Men adorned with Celtic tattoos and Crusader helmets form ranks and strike out at antifascists with the same glee. Although they may have their differences, white-supremacist Christians and pagans both aim to justify persecution of nonwhites and Jews by claiming to be part of something big and ancient and macho. This manliness is represented by the sword-and-torch zealotry of the Crusades or the mead-and-blood–soaked cult of the Viking.

The Norse pantheon dates back at least a millennium, but contemporary worship of Scandinavian gods—a faith known as Ásatrú—is a comparatively recent phenomenon. In the United States, the modern history of worshipping Scandinavian gods dates back to the counterculture of the late 1960s, when the Odinist Fellowship, an explicitly racist heathen religious group, was founded by Danish weaver Else Christensen.[15] Soon thereafter, in 1970, the Viking Brotherhood was founded by Texan Stephen McNallen. Both McNallen and Christensen envisioned Ásatrú in an explicitly racialized way, picturing the Norse faith as a way to reclaim the cultural inheritance of white, European-descended Americans—the scholar Damon T. Berry calls it the "biologization of spirituality."

Numerous white supremacists of the 1970s and '80s embraced the cult of Odin, known as Wotanism, as their primary religion. Among them was David Lane, a member of the infamous bank-robbing, murderous racist terror group The Order.[16] In the 1990s, Norwegian black metal musician, neo-Nazi, and dedicated promulgator of Odinism Varg Vikernes was convicted of murder and serial church arson, serving fifteen years in various Norwegian prisons. The Anti-Defamation League (ADL) has reported that Odinism is a popular faith among incarcerated white supremacists. The connection between Ásatrú—a broader name for worship of the Norse pantheon—

and white supremacy is simple: For racist heathens, Ásatrú or Odinism is, in the words of author Mattias Gardell, "a religion of the blood, eternally connected with Aryan man as his spiritual root of existence."[17] It's an expression of the myth of a whiteness that stretches back centuries, all the way back to pre-Christian Europe.

While Christianity has a long history of anti-Semitism to draw on, with its own organic myths and pogroms, the explicit anti-Semitism of racist pagan Telegram channels offers a simplistic, almost Manichaean view of white history. Heathenry reveres nature; therefore the Jew is responsible for the white man's alienation from his agricultural and hunter-gatherer past. Words like *society*, *economy*, and *industry* are often presented in the triple-parentheses "echo" symbol that is a white-supremacist code for malevolent Jewish influence. One channel in particular appeared to intimate strongly that Jews were responsible for the entirety of the Industrial Revolution and the modern world—a prima facie absurd claim that nonetheless sums up the animosity racist pagans hold toward Jews. Heathenry, in the racist conception, values masculine manhood; therefore, the Jew is responsible for feminism, gay rights, and other phenomena that challenge traditionalist gender roles. This is an idea echoed in other facets of the racist movement, but while Christian fascists have a history of anti-Semitism within their religion to draw on, heathen racists must create their own justifications for loathing Jews. Moreover, Christianity itself is deplored as a pan-ethnic religion that embraces adherents of all races, as opposed to racial heathenry, which sees itself as the "authentic" heritage of ancient whiteness— and the purest form of whites-only worship in the present day.

Within the world of racist Ásatrú, race, faith, and culture are synonymous. Modern iterations of racist heathenry, like the group Folk Right, embrace ethnonationalism, and claim that their religion is a reclamation of the "unique and diverse ethnic identities . . . for the people indigenous to Europe."[18] The Ásatrú Folk Assembly (AFA), founded by Stephen McNallen in 1996, similarly embraces the role of pre-Christian European religions in "awakening our European-descended kin everywhere."[19] According to Gardell, Mc-Nallen founded the AFA because he was disgusted by the number of black people who had begun to participate in worshipping the Norse pantheon.

Since 2016, after which McNallen left the AFA, the group has grown increasingly, stridently reactionary in its rhetoric—now officially espousing homophobia, celebrating "our beautiful white children," and promoting a return to restrictive gender roles. (McNallen himself, through the newly formed Wotan Network, is now encouraging other heathens to climb mountains and offer sacrifices to Odin in the name of European heritage.) Other organizations focus less on religion and more on hate, but retain a heathen, Viking patina. The Vinlanders Social Club, a white-supremacist skinhead group named for "Vinland"—the name used by early Norse explorers arriving in America, including Leif Erikson—was founded in 2003 and dissolved by 2010 amid the arrests of some dozen members for violence, ranging from fatally shooting a white woman in an interracial couple to domestic abuse.

More recently, the Soldiers of Odin, an anti-immigrant, anti-Muslim group that originated in Finland and arrived in the United States in 2016, has become known for conducting "street patrols" and provoking violent clashes with antiracist protesters. The all-male, white-supremacist biker gang the Wolves of Vinland has been photographed performing elaborate rituals of animal sacrifice in the woods of Virginia.[20] A member of the Wolves of Vinland was arrested in 2012 for attempted arson of a black church. And in 2015, two adherents of Ásatrú were arrested by the FBI for plotting to bomb black churches in Virginia in order to start a race war. For those who are motivated to violence by the thought of a threat to white supremacy, a purportedly indigenous, pan-European faith can be a powerful boost to the animating notion of an imperiled white heritage, worth defending with spilled blood. For the less intellectually inclined, adopting a Viking aesthetic overlays a patina of old-school machismo onto white-supremacist violence. Of particular attraction is the idea of Valhalla—the Viking vision of a heaven for warriors. In Norse myth, it is a great mead hall in the sky, home to warriors who fall in battle; those who reside there fight all day and feast all night, attended by Valkyries. In the white-supremacist idiom, Valhalla emerges as the place where those who die in battle for the white race aspire to go. In August 2019, twenty-one-year-old Philip Manshaus allegedly murdered his seventeen-year-old adopted sister, who was Chinese, and went on to storm a mosque in Baerum, a suburb of Oslo, with multiple weapons, opening fire. He was overpowered by a sixty-five-year-old man who was present in the mosque. But before engaging in this orgy of violence, he posted to Endchan, calling for a "race war" to be taken offline and made "irl" (in real life.) He ended his post with a salute to Odin: "Valhalla awaits."[21]

Once the idea of a racialized, white-supremacist form of Odinism had reached the mainstream for extremists, plenty were willing to profess a heathen faith without any kind of formal affiliation. Judging by the number of Norse-oriented heathen racist channels I joined on Telegram, it was much more about adopting a pseudo-biker, tough-guy look than an authentic or solemn connection to Odin and Thor. Peering in at the planning for the Christgang vs Pagang event in honor of a satanist, that thesis was well borne out. While white-supremacist Christians worship Christ, and white-supremacist

practitioners of Ásatrú revere Odin (and all adhere to their religions within the semi-serious, semi-ironic framework of online
shit-posting), both groups abhor nonwhites, Muslims, and Jews far
more than they loathe each other. Each hearkens back to a chalk-
white myth of European history that never existed, but propels hate
nonetheless.

American white supremacists' obsession with Europe manifests in
the somewhat schizoid attitude of extremists toward the continent
in their news outlets and rhetoric. On one end of the spectrum,
pre-Enlightenment Europe acquires a quasi-sacred status as a land
of alabaster-white Crusaders and nobles, the birthplace of the "West"
that many white supremacists declare themselves bound to defend.

One example of reflexive worship of the "West" is the Proud Boys,
a group of extremists best known for street brawls with antifascists,
an initiation ritual that involves being beaten by other Proud Boys
until the initiate names five different types of breakfast cereal, and
a prohibition against masturbation. The Proud Boys describe themselves as "Western chauvinists" while explicitly denying that they are
white supremacists.

The sacrality of premodern Europe appears in different guises, but
is a near-unanimous foundational assumption across a wide variety of white-supremacist groups. At the same time, contemporary
Europe appears in white-supremacist rhetoric as a subject of scorn,
contempt, and fear.

The view that Europe is on the verge of destruction is common
on the right of the political spectrum in the United States. Right-
wing news outlets, such as Breitbart, the Daily Wire, and the Daily
Caller, highlight isolated cases of immigrants committing violence in
Europe. The impressionable President Trump, perennially glued to
Fox News, has repeated that myth, denigrating Sweden in particular

because it "took in large numbers" of immigrants and thus has faced "problems like they never thought possible" in a 2017 speech.

The myth that certain neighborhoods in European cities have become "no-go zones" due to immigration is repeated uncritically in right-wing news outlets, such as Fox News and Breitbart; an op-ed in the *Wall Street Journal* by far-right propagandist Andy Ngo referred to an apocryphal, but terrifying, "Islamic England." He described himself as being "frozen" in fear at the sight of women in niqābs. The elegiac tone of Ngo's article, and his description of rather mundane things, like seeing a mosque or people speaking Punjabi, as a cascade of horrors and a sign of social decline, provoked a swift backlash from residents of Luton and London. At one point in the article, Ngo implied that a sign noting that alcohol was prohibited in a certain area of Whitechapel Road was a Muslim innovation. As the British writer Libby Watson pointed out, such alcohol restrictions are not the product of some sharia takeover of the British legal system— they're targeted at "areas where lads and louts gather to drink warm piss beer."[22]

Extremist news outlets offer a warped mirror of contemporaneous right-wing and mainstream news outlets, filtered through explicit ideology. Whereas outlets like Breitbart, the Daily Caller, and the *New York Post* choose their topics through a right-wing and xenophobic framing, explicitly white-supremacist news outlets like Infostormer, the White Information Network, VDare, and the Daily Stormer act as parasites, leeching onto the most sensationalistic news and making every subtext explicit. The stories they choose to highlight and re-frame in explicitly racist, white-supremacist terms, often using crude language, are reflections of their own worldview, but are drawn, for the most part, from more mainstream right-wing news outlets, and the mainstream press at large. Most of the time, and particularly in the Trump era, extremists are simply picking up on extant social preoccupations, on the general weft of social prejudice in America— and are simply willing to take it to its logical conclusions.

The preoccupations of the right-wing press, in particular, are reflected in far-right outlets, but with an extremist flourish. The mainstream right's sensationalized coverage of migrant crime in Europe becomes an obsessive preoccupation for extremist news sites, which work to create a perception of Europe as a continent under perennial violent siege by nonwhite immigrants.

Blanket coverage of isolated crimes by immigrants in different countries contributes to a mind-set in which immigration in Europe has led to a continent overrun by criminality. On August 3, 2019, a headline on the racist news site Infostormer used a sword attack by a Syrian immigrant in Germany to hit back against the purportedly too-liberal attitudes in German government and media. The same outlet utilized a disturbance at a pool in Kehl, Germany, to condemn "colorful invading migrants." The Daily Stormer breathlessly covered an alleged gang rape in Austria, using the occasion to parody left and centrist attitudes on immigration. The article was titled "AUSTRIA: FIVE VIBRANTS CONVICTED FOR GANG-ENRICHING A 13-YEAR-OLD GIRL."[23]

At the same time, contempt for the EU, and for centrist and leftist European leaders, forms a concomitant, parallel fixation; criminal activity, these articles posit, is caused by "multiculturalism." The contemporary white-supremacist view of Europe as a sacred spiritual homeland under siege is juxtaposed against a present shaped by multiculturalism, gay rights, and a perceived out-of-control willing-ness to admit immigrants from the global South.

In reality, European leaders of all political persuasions have sought to limit immigration in recent years, although to a movement that would gladly murder or expel every nonwhite resident of Europe, no restriction could be enough.

The contrast between the mythic white past and the "degenerate" present of Europe serves as a factor inspiring militancy, reinforced by rhetoric in news outlets and chat channels that continually present the bleakest possible image of a Europe whose historic whiteness is on the verge of being eradicated by black and brown depravity. It's a rhetoric of violence, rooted in a mythos that sees itself as the noble heritage of millennia of European history.

Back on Telegram, "Tommy," my pseudonymous character, was gaining purchase with Christian extremists—and taking a close look at the ways pagan extremists exchanged both barbed words and friendly banter with their Christian counterparts. In a shit-talking chat designed to hype up participants, the Christians and the pagans outlined their battle plans—offering prayers to Christ and blót to Odin before battle, respectively—before sharing their weight-training regimens and their eagerness to beat the shit out of one another. It was juvenile, but more about camaraderie than hate: They saved that for the ways they talked about black people, Jews, immigrants, and Muslims.

Long before November, the event planning for the Christgang vs Pagang fight fell apart. ("It just didn't work out," Williams told "Tommy" via Telegram chat.) Among other problems—incessant infighting being the foremost—the beneficiary of the fund-raiser, satanist presidential candidate Augustus Invictus, had bigger issues to face than his dim political prospects. He'd been arrested for kidnapping his wife at gunpoint and transporting her across state lines against her will—and was cooling his heels in jail. Misogyny, violence, and white supremacy were as tightly bonded as ever. Still, whether Christian, pagan, or satanist, it had become abundantly clear to me that white-supremacist religiosity, regardless of the faith tradition that it was derived from, was a way to deepen and ennoble extant systems of prejudice. It was a means to elevate the grim, dirty business of racist violence.

Ultimately, Christian and pagan white supremacists were both seeking a way to root their hate in something that felt ancient, unassailable. Something from God—or from the gods. But it was still just another face, another facet, another deep, poisoned root of hate to deracinate.

CHAPTER 7

TWEEN RACISTS, BAD BEANIES, AND THE GREAT CASINO CHASE

It's a hot day in August 2019, and I'm arguing online about whether I've, in fact, been "chased" from a casino.

I'd spent the day at the Minds IRL Conference, a conference for right-wing YouTubers and their fans. *IRL* is online slang for "in real life"—i.e., not online—and, as such, this was a gathering for people who spent a lot more time on the internet than anywhere else. The conference organizers had invited a few token liberals and their slogan was: "Minds IRL: Ending Racism, Violence and Authoritarianism." The big draws, according to conference attendees, were YouTubers who skirted the line between the far-right and the mainstream, or had crossed it fully into propaganda. Figures like Carl Benjamin, aka "Sargon of Akkad," a massively popular right-wing YouTuber; Blaire White, an antifeminist trans YouTuber with close to a million subscribers; right-wing gadfly Tim Pool; and fascism-adjacent dickwad Andy Ngo. These figures, internet-famous on the right, were the headliners, and their fans had flown in from all around the country. The event had initially been set to take place at a theater in New Jersey, but an antifascist initiative, known as "No Hate N.J.," had inundated the theater with calls and protests and a few threats. The event had hastily been moved to a Philadelphia casino.

Not having a blond wig handy, I decided to attend as myself, Talia Lavin—knowing that people might recognize me from my Twitter photo, and having been the subject of not a few videos from the likes of Tim Pool myself. It was an attempt to do research in person, not just online; I wanted to see what it would be like to be behind enemy lines for a day. I thought it would be a good opportunity to see the people who considered themselves devotees of right-wing YouTubers, not just viewing the slick, processed video content on creators' feeds. Naïvely, I hoped that the conference's disingenuous branding as a home for "tolerance"—despite the virulent right-wingers who made up the primary speakers—might dampen any potential for harassment. I would soon be proved wrong.

It was a long hot day pacing the dingy ash-colored carpet of the SugarHouse Casino. In the press room behind the main conference hall, I briefly interviewed Tim Pool and Andy Ngo, both of whom recognized me. Pool had created two separate videos about me, posted to his 700,000 subscribers, including one gloating about the fact that a course I was set to teach at New York University, on the far right, was canceled due to low enrollment; that video got nearly 200,000 views. Ngo, who had risen to prominence castigating the antifascist movement and writing for the Canadian racist publication *Quillette*, had written and tweeted about me numerous times to his audience of hundreds of thousands. It was an odd experience, encountering them in the flesh, and in an environment where the public profile of the event demanded some approximation of civility. I stood mere feet away from men who had sicced their digital armies on me so many times, asking them questions. The tension was as thick as the shag rug in the casino backroom; they lied to my face, but politely. "Did you know that the list of journalists sympathetic to antifa in the article you edited wound up in an Atomwaffen 'kill list' video?" I asked Ngo. "No comment," he replied, in his soft voice. I asked Tim Pool if he had any comment on appearing in an infamous photo with several notable figures in the alt-right. He said he'd once appeared in a photo with a Soviet general. When I responded that the Soviet Union had disbanded in 1991, he offered no reply.

When I emerged from the press room into the broader room where the panels were taking place, I heard a woman onstage describing a T-shirt with the slogan I HATE CHINKS, GOOKS, WOPS AND SPICS, BUT NIGGERS ARE OKAY. The audience, almost entirely white, laughed uproariously. "It was a funny shirt," she said.

I spent most of the day lurking by the door to the casino, talking to the conference attendees who smoked about their politics. I shared cigarettes with them, asked seemingly innocuous questions—"How would you describe your politics?" and "What brought you here?" and took photos, with their consent. Most didn't recognize me. Then I live-tweeted the proceedings. I spoke to lots of people. People like Anna, who, from beneath a cloud of brown frizz, proclaimed to me that "Nazis are the real leftists." I met a heavily bearded man named Jeff who wore a bandanna around his unruly curls. He claimed to be a staunch libertarian; when I posted his photo online, my Twitter followers informed me that this was Jeff Thomas, a known alt-right personality and second-in-command of the Philadelphia far-right organization PA Alt-Knights, who had attended the Unite the Right rally in Charlottesville, and was known for palling around with Holocaust deniers. He smiled at me and told me he was planning to vote this year.

I also met "Tyler," a white man with a cropped brown beard and a large bandage over one eye. He told me he was a Christian and a nationalist, and a free-speech absolutist. "In no other country could you say niggerfaggot and not get arrested for it," he said. I took his photo; he was giving a thumbs-up, and I tweeted it out.

An hour later, I went back into the casino. Word of my Twitter posts had gotten around among the attendees. Tyler, the eye-patched man in a beard, ran up to me and began pursuing me around the conference floor, calling me a "liar" and a "propagandist." As it turns out, he was angry because I'd labeled him a "Christian nationalist" in my tweet; he was, in fact, he said, a Christian and a nationalist, separately. (This was an honest mistake; transcribing hastily, I'd missed the pause in between the two words.) I spoke to the affable gentleman in a security vest at the back of the room, saying the man was harassing me.

"I'm not harassing her," said Tyler. "I'm just telling everyone she's a liar, not to talk to her."

The harried publicist who'd given me my press pass urged me to exit through the back when I was ready to leave.

But by then, it was too late. As I took my seat for a crowded panel on "Ending Political Violence," a woman came up to me, with a male companion in tow. I'd been live-tweeting the conference, a not atypical occupation for a journalist in 2019, and Jeanesca—one of the women I'd introduced myself to, told I was a journalist, taken a photo of, and posted about—was pissed. It just so happened that after I'd asked her a pretty anodyne question—"So they're talking about some contentious stuff up there, like race. What do you think about that?"—she'd told me, without further prompting, exactly what she believed. "People can fuck who they want, I'm a libertarian, but I'd never marry outside my race," she'd told me, then agreed when I asked if she believed in the separation of the races. I tweeted it out, naturally, not using her last name, to nearly a hundred thousand people. Now she was pissed, and my phone was dead. She knelt beside me, urging me softly to delete the tweet. I explained that nothing I'd recorded was inaccurate. Her male companion, sitting across the aisle and glaring, told me to delete it anyway. "I'm a mother," she said, pleadingly. "But I told you I was a journalist," I replied.

I told them once my phone had some juice—it had died after a furious volley of tweets—I'd consider what they'd told me, and pulled out my laptop to plug the charger in, sweating a little as they reluctantly retreated. Then I turned to whisper to my friend, who'd driven us there and spent most of the day playing blackjack and poker while I talked to white nationalists and libertarians who were wearing Tommy Robinson election gear.

"Let's get the fuck out of here," I murmured to him.

Jeanesca's male companion was waiting for us at the bottom of the escalator, though. When I took a sharp right, he followed me a few hundred feet, into a bank of buzzing slot machines. The beeps and boops and clattering chips resounded all around us as he glared at me.

"You're not going to delete the tweet, are you?" he asked, bridling, and drawing himself up to his full height.

"I told her I was a journalist," I repeated. "I didn't say anything inaccurate."

And then I turned to my friend, jerked my thumb toward the exit, and ran.

I dodged past him and ran into the blinding sun, out into the casino parking lot, out to the bright little car I was banking on for my salvation. I could hear Jeanesca yelling after me, grasping at my friend's arm. There was a small crowd surrounding him, yelling after me. He broke away and got to the car, slid in, and hit the gas. My heart was thudding in my ears like a skittering rodent. I felt like a wheezy, overbuxom James Bond in an ill-fitting dress.

I tweeted: "I must admit 'being chased by racists through a casino' wasn't on my life bingo card but life is a rich tapestry."

We headed to meet up with friends at an anarchist bookstore and get some cheesesteaks. I hadn't been to Philly since I was twelve and kept kosher. At Pat's, the peppers are sharp enough to cut through the fat and any lingering bitter taste in the mouth.

By the time I rolled back into New York, a debate was brewing at the Minds IRL Conference. The conference organizers and some far-right-friendly media outlets, including a digital Canadian rag called the *Post Millennial*, were responding to my post alleging that running away while being yelled at didn't count as a "chase."

I never claimed I was pursued by a mob carrying pitchforks, *Beauty and the Beast*–style, just clumsily half-sprinted to the getaway car, but nonetheless.

The *Post Millennial* wrote an article quoting Tyler, the eye-patched Christian/Nationalist, who had apparently taken the mic and called me "a pigeon-shaped lady interviewing people and lying about you on Twitter." I was being accused of creating a hoax, as if booking it after being followed and pestered and screamed at wasn't a "chase."

Eventually, the *Post Millennial* quoted an anonymous conference attendee as saying I simply "waddled away" from the conference, presumably of my own volition. The headline: ACTIVIST JOURNALIST LIES ABOUT BEING CHASED OUT OF MINDS IRL FREE SPEECH CONFERENCE. They published a photograph someone had stealthily taken of me in the back of the room, and a brief interview with the casino's beleaguered-sounding security director, who denied that anyone had been chased out of SugarHouse. They claimed they could get the security footage and release it. But they never did. Antifascists surveilling the event who witnessed my getaway called it being "chased out." I'd met them briefly while smoking outside. They were wearing colorful sweaters.

The point of this lengthy story isn't so much to relitigate the particular events of that bizarre August day, although I'd be lying if I said I wasn't still pissed about it. (I am not shaped like a pigeon. I'm more of a noble heron, or perhaps a heavily pregnant stork.) In a sense, I wasn't surprised that my body shape, credibility, and intentions had been publicly challenged—it's part and parcel of reporting on the far right, and part of the reason I'd been so hesitant to do reporting in person before. I knew what I was undertaking, and its price. It occurred to me only later that I had been physically vulnerable; I was glad I'd gotten out. As I personally witnessed, the conference organizers and panelists of Minds IRL count on their ability to release a tsunami of digital harassment on anyone who challenges them. Their counteroffensives are a mess of smears, misogyny, and misinformation, designed to intimidate anyone who takes a close look at just what ideologies are being represented by the extreme right. The Minds IRL conference was designed to bring together an entire ecosystem of people who spend their time promoting racist ideas and groups, demonizing the left, and furthering a culture war in an environment so hypercharged with partisanship that further incitement bears the real risk of violence.

The landscape of right-wing social media personalities is a colorful crowd—although mostly white—and together they form a greasy slope toward right-wing radicalization. Their videos are slickly produced, glibly argued, and create a full-fledged landscape through which viewers can sink deeper and deeper into ideological homogeneity. It's big business—YouTube monetization can be quite lucrative as YouTubers rack up more and more subscribers—and it's an algorithmically aided rabbit hole that can lead someone, over weeks or months or years, from trying to catch up on the latest news to believing that communist Jews are actively working to take over the globe. It's a digital complement to right-wing disinformation purveyors like radio personality Rush Limbaugh and the slate of miscreants at Fox News; while older viewers might be sucked in via basic cable, it takes only an internet connection to inculcate younger people into a world where salvation is white of skin, where feminists are sinister harpies, where everyone "other" is to be scorned and subjugated.

I'm not trying to sow fear, here—this isn't a local-news story about razors in candy bars, or kids eating Tide Pods, or the latest phantom danger that can send suburban moms into a tizzy. The process of far-right radicalization is real, and widespread, and it rarely starts with overt Nazism. Average Americans tend to shun swastikas, if only due to their historical associations. It takes a process of being exposed to and absorbing far-right ideas—and then more and more of them—to break down a person's inherent opposition to racism, or misogyny, or anti-Semitism. Critical to this process are people like those at the Minds IRL Conference: ideologues whose personas are groomed to seem reasonable, who introduce far-right ideas more subtly than a Sieg Heil, who you can watch in the living room without setting off alarm bells to all and sundry around you. I call these figures launderers: They are in the business of repackaging the same ideas zipping around Telegram and neo-Nazi news sites, but in a way that's palatable to the clicking masses. They make money by beckoning viewers onto a journey that ends somewhere sticky, dark, and difficult to extricate oneself from—an ooze-pit redolent with the stench of hate.

Without the launderers, far-right rhetoric—genocidal, puerile, extreme, and unruly—would be a far harder sell. The movement would be starved of fresh meat, limited to those rare individuals naturally drawn to overt racism, anti-Semitism, and outright detestation of women. The launderers inculcate their fans in a worldview that casts the modern world in an irredeemable and fearsome light, one full of sinister conspiracies engendered by the left. It draws on primal fears, on ego, on tribalism—on any number of human foibles—and ushers viewers inexorably rightward.

In a groundbreaking article for the *New York Times*, journalist Kevin Roose, who has studied YouTube radicalization extensively, revealed one individual's pathway through the video site to the far right.[1] Caleb Cain—a twenty-six-year-old college dropout who spent five years as part of the alt-right before renouncing it publicly, and buying a gun to counter the death threats he received—sent Roose the entirety of his YouTube history, which consisted of more than twelve thousand videos. Cain alleged that he was radicalized by a "decentralized cult" of far-right YouTube creators who, Roose writes, "convinced him that Western civilization was under threat from Muslim immigrants and cultural Marxists, that innate I.Q. differences explained racial disparities, and that feminism was a dangerous ideology."

Underlying this push toward radicalization was not just YouTube's algorithm, which has a documented propensity for recommending extreme content to increase engagement and watch time. There's a consistent pattern of cross-promotion, collaboration, and high production value that builds audiences for far-right content and draws viewers deeper into the rabbit hole.

Roose documented a single forty-eight-hour binge-watch by Cain that started with right-wing commentators who specialize in anti-feminist content; escalated to overt conspiracy theory videos; and concluded with racist propaganda, including videos that called black men "coons." It was a journey that began with alienation, and led him to feel that he had been inculcated into a special club of the elect, trafficking in forbidden knowledge. By 2016, Cain was watching and promoting content that focused on the "white-genocide" conspiracy theory; he alienated friends with his turn toward the far right. YouTube denied to Roose that its algorithm promotes extreme content, but a study by the online investigative journalistic outfit Bellingcat found that the most frequently cited means to radicalization referenced in far-right chats was YouTube videos.[2] From slickly shot rants on the subversive feminism of J. J. Abrams's *Star Wars* reboot to overt embrace of anti-Semitism, the path to radicalization is paved by glossy content with hundreds of thousands of views.

In 2018, researcher Becca Lewis of the think tank Data & Society laid out the metrics of the laundering scheme with remarkable clarity in a report titled "Alternative Influence: Broadcasting the Reactionary Right on YouTube," which mapped out dimensions of the rightward rabbit hole far-right videos draw viewers down into.

The report describes what Lewis calls the "polished well-lit microcelebrities" of reactionary YouTube. Lewis tracked dozens of channels, members of what she dubbed the "Alternative Influence Network," a set of ideologically reactionary YouTubers. The study found that these reactionary personalities built an audience by deliberately cultivating an air of authenticity and allegedly "countercultural" appeal. Declaring that right-wing ideology is the new punk, these "political influencers" draw on the tactics of social-media marketing to sell their viewers on ideologies that range from mainstream conservatism to radical white nationalism.

I'd met, or seen from a distance, several members of the Alternative Influence Network at the Minds IRL casino conference—figures like "Sargon of Akkad," whose YouTube moniker is that of an ancient Akkadian king and who is best known for videos like "Feminist Tyranny," "Political Correctness Is Killing Comedy," and "The Farm Murders in South Africa"—the last a nod to a popular white-supremacist conspiracy theory that postulates that the white population of South Africa is facing an imminent, existential threat of violent extinction by black South Africans. "Sargon"—real name Carl Benjamin—has just shy of one million subscribers, and his videos regularly garner hundreds of thousands of views. In 2018, Benjamin ran an unsuccessful campaign for European Parliament in his home country of Britain, under the umbrella of the far-right UK Independence Party. During his run, he suggested to followers that he would rape Labour MP Jess Phillips if he found her more attractive, but, as it was, "Nobody's got that much beer." Within the context of the far right online, however, Benjamin is a relative moderate—and a gateway to those with even more extreme views. One of Benjamin's most-watched videos is a four-hour-long, livestreamed debate with white nationalist Richard Spencer, in which the latter took full advantage of Benjamin's platform to articulate his hateful ideology at great length.

"Radicalization is not caused purely by the YouTube recommendation algorithm, as many media narratives have suggested. It is a social and media process where influential broadcasters build trust with their audiences and introduce them to more extremist content over time," Becca Lewis told me in an interview.

There are multiple techniques members of the Alternative Influence Network utilize to draw their viewership toward more and more extreme right-wing ideas. These include hosting guests from the fringes of the right, ostensibly for a "debate"—and, in the process, exposing their viewers to the far right's top ideologues. Engaging in a debate implies that the opposite side has legitimacy; debating with

Richard Spencer implies that his ethnonationalism is a substantive position worth sharing with your audience. It's a pernicious influence masked in "reasonableness."

The Minds IRL conference, which brought together dozens of mostly far-right YouTube creators on its speakers' bill, was a striking example of a gathering of the most hard-core fans of such content. The conference, rather disingenuously, claimed to be about sparking "open dialogue," and had invited a few token left-wing speakers; but of the dozens of fans I spoke to, none identified as progressive.

A few hours before my unceremonious exit, I spoke with one fan— an older gentleman named Alan, wearing a cowboy hat and a shirt that said, TRUTH IS THE NEW HATE SPEECH—who said he was impressed by the diversity of opinion at the conference. I asked whether he'd met anyone who identified as progressive—he said no—and then whether he'd met anyone he fundamentally disagreed with.

"Yes," he said. "I met an ethnonationalist. But I'm a civic nationalist."

There was, it must be said, no hint of irony in his large, dark eyes.

———

One of the biggest YouTube influencers on the far right—until recently—was a high school freshman whose public persona was a tomboyish look and approximately 90 pounds of pure bile. Due to her young age I will only use her YouTube alias, "Soph."

A resident of wealthy Marin County, Soph attained infamy, and nearly a million YouTube subscribers, for the seeming disconnect between her tiny frame and foulmouthed anti–social-justice rants.

According to the internet-ephemera archive Know Your Meme, Soph first rose to internet fame at the age of eleven, primarily as a foulmouthed video-game streamer. She rapidly gained a following in the tens of thousands under the pseudonym "Lt. Corbis," streaming herself playing games like *Counter-Strike* and *Call of Duty* while cursing like a tiny sailor. On Reddit, Soph soon developed an avid community of fans. They tracked and celebrated her rising subscriber counts—she is still in high school—made memes and fan art that featured her, and sometimes skirted uncomfortably close to the line of sexualizing an eleven-year-old. (One example featured a meme of a man in prison looking at a picture of Soph. "Her ID didn't say 18, but her memes did," read the caption. The word *memes* was written over a crossed-out *breasts*.)

Gaming has a male-dominated, profoundly reactionary culture, one hot for war with feminism, in particular, and progressive political causes, in general. While video games have a far broader cultural appeal than far-right ideology, self-identified gamers make a fertile recruiting ground for right-wing ideologues: The culture of gaming is self-consciously directed at male audiences, female characters are designed to be sexually appealing and not much else, and the "gamer" identity is a jealously guarded one, adopted primarily by white males. From nearly the beginning of Soph's middle-school streaming career, immersed in gaming culture, she proved herself susceptible—or naturally inclined, or both—to embrace and disseminate reactionary positions.

On February 15, 2015, under her alias Lt. Corbis, Soph made a video titled "BUZZFEED VS MEN," attacking BuzzFeed Canada editor Scaachi Koul. Koul had tweeted that she was seeking long-form content from essayists and journalists, adding that "BuzzFeed Canada would particularly like to hear from you if you are not white and not male." Conservative media had picked up and run with the story, claiming that BuzzFeed in toto as a company was rife with discrimination against white men. (Sample headline, from right-leaning media industry blog Mediaite: BUZZFEED CANADA IS LOOKING FOR WRITERS, WHITE MALES NEED NOT APPLY.) It was a typical conservative-media faux scandal: a milquetoast series of tweets from an editor seeking diversity in submissions spun up into the phantom of antiwhite discrimination. Anything—an errant wind, a dumb tweet, a conspiracy theory invented from whole cloth—can drum up the forces of white grievance, a seemingly limitless resource. And that grievance is a bottomless well content creators can draw on, laundering more violent sentiments.

In the case of Koul, reactionary elements in the web-savvy gaming world picked up the story, which was featured heavily on Reddit. On YouTube, videos accosting Koul with titles like "BuzzFeed Canada vs White Men" acquired hundreds of thousands of views. Koul herself, an archetypal target of right-wing internet bullying—a young woman of color in journalism—endured a significant degree of harassment over these anodyne remarks.

So far, so typical—these tempests in teapots, in which online reactionaries seek to turn fleeting incidents into a holistic worldview in which white men face disproportionate, enduring, and unendurable discrimination, occur daily. What made Soph's video stand apart was the commentator: a tiny, fragile-looking girl with long brown hair, dressed in a dark-blue sweater, in a middle-class-looking bedroom with a game controller in her hand. Gunning down video-game enemies with a massive weapon, Soph accosted BuzzFeed as a "company full of idiots," "racist against white people," and called Koul a "feminazi extremist." She condemned feminism as a whole, saying it was hijacked by extremism, and compared Koul to "shitty" and "retarded" teachers.

The nascent overtly political bent of her channel didn't prevent her from receiving positive attention from the YouTuber community—or fawning coverage in the press. An article in the tech-focused publication the *Daily Dot* hailed Soph uncritically: "LtCorbis is the smartest, funniest new video game streamer on YouTube, snapping off sharp, witty commentary about streaming-channel culture and the internet over gameplay footage from Call of Duty and Counter-Strike," wrote journalist Jay Hathaway. The article included links to multiple Lt. Corbis videos, and the headline crowed: THIS SWEARY, SAVVY, 11-YEAR-OLD GAMER GIRL IS THE FUTURE OF YOUTUBE.

Soph's first video is relatively tame: It's a description of a run-in with a teacher she'd hated in fifth grade, the prior year, told as running narrative over a video of her playing *Counter-Strike: Global Offensive*. Her hair is long and tidy, her face fragile and small.

By 2019, however, the *Daily Dot*—and observers of the far-right internet—were expressing cautionary notes about Soph. In the same publication that had hailed her as "the future of YouTube," journalist Samira Sadeque cited the rapidity and alarming nature of Soph's political journey, titling her article, "This 14-Year-Old's 'Edgy' YouTube Channel Parrots the Far Right." Which, by then, was just about the mildest thing you could say about Soph and her channel. It was something of an astounding transformation, and in and of itself a master class in internet radicalization.

In the interim, Soph had grown a few inches; stopped brushing her hair; and started expressing more and more extreme forms of racist and misogynistic vitriol. She wasn't streaming video games anymore, either. She started making videos filled with the kind of nihilism that only a teenager could muster—and directing every inch of it at racial, gender, and sexual minorities. Her videos often credited a producer named "VapoRub Boy," whose presence online had been scrubbed by the time I began reporting on Soph. Online chatter speculated that he was her brother, that he was slightly older, but I couldn't ascertain precisely who was helping her produce ever-slicker and more virulent content. Her videos featured quotes like "Kill yourself, faggot" and

"Doctors are really fucking Jews who want to take your shekels." She also gained hundreds of thousands of followers, reaching nearly a million before her channel was banned from YouTube.

Her most provocative—and most viewed—video was titled "Be Not Afraid," and came out in late 2018. It featured her wearing a chador while giving a fluent and rage-filled rant about freedom of speech, among other topics. She said she'd become a devout Muslim, was being raped by her forty-year-old husband, and enjoyed "stoning the shit out of the gays." The video was at least partly a response to a controversy in which posts on the chat app Discord she'd made under the name "lutenant faggot" had surfaced, instructing her inter-locutors to "kill muslims." "I WISH THERE WOULD BE A HITLER FOR MUSLIMS," she wrote. "GAS THEM ALL." In the video, she made a sarcasm-laced apology to the "peaceful followers of Allah," and condemned the "muzzle" placed by social-media companies on the head of "anyone whose speech eludes the narrative."

By this point, Soph's notoriety had begun to spread to the circles of people who tracked far-right content online; she was notable for her extreme youth and viciousness in combination, and caused no small amount of consternation among journalists debating how—or whether—to cover the phenomenon. To find out more about her, I wrote to Soph's publicly available email with a few questions, phrased generically, in the hopes of beginning a conversation. My queries were innocuous—"What made you start vlogging?"—and her answer hit me like a jet of pure vitriol:

> ive been contacted by many vulturePredators like U before, and i cannot believe your audacity. at least da otha ones TRIED to hide their pozlvl* [a far-right term for being AIDS-positive] but i guess u just dont care. that means U suck at

your job, since youre a crypto (u think ppl dont notice that u flow betwen "im a Jew" and "im White", they do. not sure why u do that, feel free to clarify:O). ur like the king in the kings new outfit story and im Seeing ur bare buttnaked pimple-ridden eczema ass RN bc youre too fucking dumb to figure out how to hide it. nowonder you got fired from the new Yorker dude; youre too obvious, they pay4subtlety. U gotta do ur job like internet viagra delivery stuff: untraceable, unnoticeable. now that Ive noticed beforehand, u Wont have the chance to tell evryone abt how U talked to a NAZI!!!! undercover. guess Youre just stupid and one day, those dadbux will run out and u will windup drinking curbwater to keep hydrated and get zika. i personally want you to know that the only reason U exist is bc some evil rich Fugk has decided to curse the world by funding your excuse for cultural analysis with his infinite money.

thank u for the invite ms. Bugpig Areola but i will have to decline as im currently Trying to focus on my Pro b-ball career:) hope that book sells a lot (it wont), also hope u can pay ur college debt some day (you never will). Suffer for Eternity, i hope you like the taste of truck tires and defeat.

    I didn't respond. She also posted a screenshot of it to her Twitter page, and her followers swarmed me, accusing me of Jewish pedophilia.

    The email was laced with far-right language—the term *pozlvl* is a common far-right meme alluding to the idea that degenerate sexual promiscuity means that everyone on the left is "positive" for the AIDS virus. In addition, her fixation on my "crypto" Jewishness—and the notion that I was trying to sneakily pass for white—read like something ripped straight out of a Stormfront post. It was an astonishing glimpse into the mind of a very young teenager who had thoroughly swallowed the entirety of an internet-savvy, far-right ideology, and was busy disseminating it to an eager audience of hundreds of thousands.

I decided to speak to Soph's parents, if I could: I was curious about how a young teen could be so openly hate-filled, with such a vast public profile, and what the family environment that produced such a young person was like. With the aid of a people-search database, I was able to find Soph's father, an executive at a Bay Area biotech company. I reached out to him via email and text message, telling him I wanted to discuss his daughter's videos and ask what role he played in them—whether he helped her produce them and what he thought of her recent content. I asked him what he thought of the white-supremacist videos she posted to her channel.

"Not sure you have actually listened to her videos," he responded.

I gave him a few choice quotes, coupled with time stamps, of Soph using antigay and anti-Jewish slurs.

"Sorry, I have to hop off," he responded. "Thank you."

Soph's mother did not respond to any form of inquiry.

But in May 2019, a few weeks after I'd spoken to Soph's father, her content was pulled into the journalistic mainstream. A BuzzFeed news article, titled "YouTube's Newest Far-Right, Foul-Mouthed, Red-Pilling Star Is a 14-Year-Old Girl," detailed Soph's videos at length, linking directly to her channel and blaming YouTube directly for the proliferation of hate-filled content like hers. The author, Joseph Bernstein, also focused on Soph's extraordinary propensity to respond to any limitations on her content with threats of violence. In response to concerns over pedophilic commentary on Soph's content, YouTube had removed the comments sections on her videos.

In response, Soph uploaded a twelve-minute rant directly threatening the life of Susan Wojcicki, YouTube's CEO.

"Susan, I've known your address since last summer," she said, staring directly into the camera. "I've got a Luger and a mitochondrial disease. I don't care if I live. Why should I care if you live, or your children? I just called an Uber. You've got about seven minutes to draft up a will. . . . I'm coming for you, and it ain't gonna be pretty."

After Bernstein's exposé, Soph became something of a cause célèbre on the right; she made appearances on countless channels, and was featured in articles like an RT commentary that cast Soph as the innocent victim of liberal overreach. BUZZFEED & THE OUTRAGE MOB HOUND FOUL-MOUTHED 14YO OFF YOUTUBE read the headline, and the article condemned the "horde of Twitter liberals" who objected to Soph's content.

At any rate, the title was inaccurate: It took three more months for Soph to be banned from YouTube, which finally happened in August 2019. It appeared that not even a direct threat on the life of its CEO could make the company, which profited handsomely from her nearly one million subscribers, move any quicker than that, despite ample attention to the extreme nature of her content in the press.

But at that point, Soph was in far too deep to leave the far-right community. As of the time of this writing, she is continuing to make content—her videos slicker, better packaged, and better produced. Along with the dregs of the far-right internet, like Milo Yiannopoulos, Soph's content is now hosted on Censored.tv, a far-right site created and spearheaded by forty-nine-year-old Gavin McInnes.

McInnes could be—and certainly has been—the subject of his own lengthy spiel, but suffice it to say that he was a cofounder of Vice Media in its edgy days, the early oughts, and has spun that initial success into a long, embarrassing, and occasionally violent second career of spouting racism and encouraging violence. He's also the founder of his very own far-right street-fighting gang, the Proud Boys, who have been involved in countless melees and physical assaults against their political opponents all around the country. Soph's content now appears alongside the tag "This site also contains adult content, coarse language, and potentially offensive satire. We don't think there's any nudity but who knows?"—and her videos have grown increasingly radical, asserting a definite link between homosexuality and pedophilia, and winking and grinning at anti-Semitism.

Soph isn't in prison for her content, although her videos are now locked behind a paywall subscription, requiring ten bucks a month and the desire and knowledge to check out a site chock-full of rancid far-right videos. What's unclear is how, if ever, she'll crawl out of the rabbit hole she's been in since age eleven—and how many others she's radicalized along the way.

Journalists' protestations often enough do not suffice to rout hate from spaces like YouTube, Twitter, and Facebook, and the simple act of pointing out hate speech earns journalists harassment, death threats, and intimidation campaigns, as I can attest to personally. To cite one small example, in September 2018, I took to Twitter to point out the consistently white-nationalist messages broadcast by the YouTube channel Red Ice TV—then an influential outlet with hundreds of thousands of subscribers—and reported the channel repeatedly to YouTube. In response to my public comments, which garnered thousands of "likes" and retweets, one of the channel's authors, Lana Lokteff, found an old bikini picture of me and posted it to her following, adding mocking commentary and encouraging her followers to do the same. On a subsequent video on the channel, Red Ice commentators called me a "whale" and speculated that I had changed my name from "Levin" to sound less Jewish. Which . . . would not have been a particularly successful endeavor, given my constant references to my own Jewishness. At any rate, Red Ice remained on YouTube for over a year after my initial appeal to the public, until October 2019.

The fact that social-media companies have failed so badly to address the issue of white-supremacist violence exploding on their platforms is compounded by the fact that the issue was extremely easy to anticipate. White-supremacist online activity is older than Facebook, Twitter, and even Google. In fact, white supremacists were some of the earliest adopters of the internet nearly forty years ago, back when it was brand-new—long before it became a staple of commerce and socializing. The Texas Ku Klux Klan had a website by 1984; by 1985, using dial-up modems and Apple IIe computers, the Aryan Nations were posting lists of the addresses of their Jewish enemies online. They were quick to recognize that the internet's communication had the potential to radicalize dormant populations, to link white supremacists around the world, and to retain some level of anonymity while inciting violence and coordinating violent attacks.[3]

Because once they're radicalized, white supremacists continue to use the internet. It's how they connect. And not just across the United States, but around the world. Above all, the internet allows white supremacy to become an internationally linked movement. It's been evidenced in some of the worst atrocities to come out of the movement in recent years—Brenton Tarrant, for example, openly stated in his manifesto that he was partially inspired by a hope to spark civil conflict in the United States. Tarrant also donated a significant amount of money to Martin Sellner, leader of the Generation Identity white-supremacist movement in Europe. Sellner, in turn, has an American wife, Brittany Sellner, née Pettibone, who has gained a sizable following on YouTube for her white-supremacist content. It's a world map with pins in every country where a white-reactionary population exists in any numbers.

As I encountered all of this—in person and online—it left me with a feeling of despair, and anger, at the tech companies that had knowingly allowed this sort of hate to bloom, for profitability, for engagement. I'd tasted a bit of it in my own life, as a frequent subject of these channels' users' ire, for having the temerity to oppose hate in public. I'd been called a cunt, had my hygiene discussed as a source of nausea, had my body minutely analyzed; I'd been impersonated, repeatedly, on 4chan, by someone I didn't know who kept posing as me to rile up the internet's most harassment-happy neo-Nazis. These neo-Nazis had begun somewhere—somewhere mainstream, somewhere familiar. They had been through a process of ideological inculcation, of grooming, and now they were doing what neo-Nazis do best: making it harder for everybody else to get by.

Every day on Telegram, white supremacists in Eastern Europe, Western Europe, Australia, and the United States commingle, sympathize with one another, and spread propaganda. Not just propaganda, either: An international network of white supremacists facilitates the cross-border spread of money, tactical coordination, and even personnel. In numerous cases, white supremacists from the United States have trained with the Azov Battalion, a Ukrainian far-right militia that forms part of that country's national guard.

The ongoing conflict in Ukraine's east has drawn foreign fighters from around the world to fight with both pro-Russian and pro-Ukrainian forces. American white supremacists tend to have been drawn to the latter, finding common cause with an explicitly neo-Nazi strain of Ukrainian militarism. The Azov Battalion is often called a "state within a state" in Ukraine, boasting of their influence over civilians and politicians. A 2018 FBI criminal complaint alleges that the group is "believed to have participated in training and radicalizing United States–based white supremacy organizations."[4] Four members of the white-supremacist Rise Above Movement were found to have trained with Azov, and the leader of RAM took part in a highly touted boxing prizefight against an Azov member in Kyiv in 2018. In September 2019, two former US Army soldiers, Alex Zweifelhofer and Craig Lang, were arrested for their alleged involvement in the murder and robbing of a Florida couple, allegedly to finance a trip to fight in Venezuela. Both had trained with the far-right Ukrainian militia Right Sector. A third soldier, Jarrett William Smith, was apprehended by the FBI earlier that month for "distributing information related to explosives, destructive devices, and weapons of mass destruction" after making terroristic threats against a US news network and personally threatening the life of an anti-Nazi podcaster. Smith had sought to travel to Ukraine, he said, to train with the Azov Battalion. Azov has reached out to its counterparts in Western European nations as well, and looms large in the imaginations of white supremacists around the world, who see it as a pure expression of whiteness, militarism, and manliness—three of their highest values.

While an expensive plane ticket to train in Eastern Europe might still be beyond the reach of most white supremacists, the distribution of propaganda is free, and an assortment of home-brewed memes, videos, and an ad hoc library of fascist classics circulate regularly around Telegram and far-right message boards.

One of the things that surprised me, as I researched the different types of far-right propaganda spreading through the hate-swelled infosphere of neo-Nazism, was the popularity of audiobooks. There were dozens, read aloud by users of hate-friendly platforms like Bitchute and Telegram. These included books of Nazi-era racial science; books of black magic and occult esoterica; survivalist books; neo-Nazi tomes; survivalist tracts like "Lessons from the History of Guerrilla Warfare"; and one book by Corneliu Codreanu, an inter-war Romanian fascist, a romantic roman à clef to his legion of paramilitary followers.

Pirated e-books and audiobooks were passed from channel to channel, viewed by hundreds at once, just as fascist literature had once been photocopied, *samizdat*-style, and transmitted from hand to hand at white-nationalist conferences and gun shows. But these books were being passed to hundreds of people at once, without any lag time, and without having to leave the comfort of one's home. It requires far less motivation and specialized knowledge to click on a link than to buy an obscure book of fascist ideology from the 1930s. The internet provides the pipeline into far-right ideology; then, once a user is radicalized, it offers community, solace, and the opportunity to deepen and flesh out one's commitment to violent ideologies.

While far-right internet users maintain insular communities in which to socialize and further radicalize one another, another crucial element of their online behavior is the desire to engage with out-siders. The far right's attempts to create an "alt-tech" structure—independent crowdfunding platforms, social-media sites, and forums free of even the few constraints of mainstream websites—have largely failed, thanks to a combination of user apathy and vigilance on the part of antifascists and journalists, who appeal to internet service providers, advertisers, and platforms to attack disseminators of hate. One example was Hatreon, a would-be alternative to the popular crowdfunding site Patreon. The site is currently a stub, notifying users that "This site's services were suspended by VISA in November of 2017." Other sites—like Gab, the social network used by Pittsburgh shooter Robert Bowers—attempted to create a far-right-only social-media environment, but have largely petered out into obscurity due to lack of interest by users. Far-right social networks tend to wither when fascists don't have feminists, people of color, Jews, and anyone else they disagree with to pick on.

But thanks to the laxity of major social-media companies, the far right doesn't need to create alternatives to the social media you and I already use. And their presence on these platforms is both more diffuse and more pernicious—more difficult to quash. On Twitter and other mainstream social-media sites, fascists engage in purposeful, continuous, and aggressive harassment of their ideological foes. This serves both to salve the rapacious id, and provide free advertising: those drawn to the scrapping, who might want to inflict pain of their own, are only a click away from neo-Nazi and white supremacist cliques on mainstream social media sites.

Even so, anonymous message boards like 4chan thrive in large part due to the complete anonymity they offer, as well as the ability of users to engage in coordinating harassment campaigns on a massive scale.

Far-right news sites—like InfoStormer, The Renegade Tribune, Western Voices World News, the Daily Stormer, and legions more—have prospered in an era of fragmented consciousness, in which news consumers are drawn to hyperpartisan outlets that offer them the world, refracted through the specific prism of their hatreds. They focus on stories of black, migrant, and Jewish crime, particularly—and obsessively—on those instances when such crime has white victims and occurs in Europe or the United States.

They also offer a kind of running far-right commentary on the political issues of a given day, parroting—often in full-paragraph block quotes—the top news stories disseminated by mainstream media, with white-supremacist patter interleaved throughout. They are depositories of grievance and manufacturers of rage; they also often provide the social-media handles and contact information for specific (black, Jewish, immigrant, journalist, academic) figures of opprobrium, laying the necessary groundwork for readers to engage in mass harassment. That harassment takes place in another world: the internet you and I use, and which the far right uses, too, for strategic purposes.

A handful of technology companies are responsible for the transformation of white supremacy into a white-internationalist movement, and for the coordination of fascists with one another across the country and the world. These companies—Google, Facebook, Twitter, Telegram—are unelected, wildly profitable, and largely unaccountable to the communities that stand to be wounded by this ideology.

Public pressure, aided by the steady work of journalists, has unearthed some of the most scabrous public examples of white-nationalist rhetoric on social networks, and companies usually, eventually, accede to pressure campaigns waged against specific purveyors of poisonous content. But an increasingly strained and undermanned press corps in the United States hardly suffices to patrol the nigh-endless digital deeps of the contemporary internet landscape.

In a speech to the Anti-Defamation League in November 2019, comedian Sacha Baron Cohen pointed out the inherent risks of the so-called "Silicon Six"—"Zuckerberg at Facebook; Sundar Pichai at Google; at Google's parent company Alphabet, Larry Page and Sergey

Brin; Brin's ex-sister-in-law, Susan Wojcicki at YouTube; and Jack Dorsey at Twitter"—being totally responsible for, and unconstrained in, making such momentous decisions as whether Holocaust denial and antiblack hate speech have a role in public discourse. Silicon Valley has long operated on a libertarian, reckless, "move fast and break things" ethos that is far more conservative about reining in hate speech than allowing it to reverberate in the public consciousness unchecked. Consider the sheer dollars generated from people like Sargon of Akkad and Soph. And the human price of such unchecked hate, which was immeasurable.

The results of this laissez-faire attitude from Silicon Valley are self-evident in the exponential growth of white-nationalist movements around the world, fueled by reactionary impulses that gather in strength until they have turned into the full and vitriolic force of hate. Without regulation constraining such caustic and dangerous speech, without meaningful social checks on consuming such content, and without protections for the general public from the soldiers of hate, it is safe to assume that these movements will continue to grow, fueled by slickly produced propaganda disseminated in the guise of "just asking questions" about a multiracial democratic order. Wrapped up in a glossy layer of reasoned inquiry, hate is cunningly smuggled through the bright screen.

Through the same internet on which you can order groceries, check out pictures of your friend's cat, or chat up a prospective lover, neo-Nazis and budding neo-Nazis find one another and engage in a dance of mutual radicalization. That grim tango moves, for the most part, in only one direction: toward more and more egregious hate rhetoric; toward brutal harassment of selected targets; and eventually, for the unstable, the desperate, the lonely, those truly mired in hate, toward real-world violence, which rips through communities with senseless, concussive force. The result is that synagogues have posted armed guards more than ever before. The result is that Asian-Americans are at greater risk for hate crimes in the wake of misinformation about the novel coronavirus sweeping the world—and the tide of rhetoric about the "China Virus" and the "Kung-Flu," beginning in the Oval Office and sweeping through an endless sea of YouTube channels. The results are all around us. The idea of relying on corporate generosity to combat hate is naïve at best; hate generates a profit. It is on us to demand more, and better—and to fight back.

CHAPTER 8

GETTING TO THE BOOM:
ON ACCELERATIONISM AND VIOLENCE

On Yom Kippur 2019, the holiest day of the Jewish year, a young German man set out to end the lives of as many Jews as he could. Yom Kippur is a solemn day of fasting and prayer, a day on which congregants implore God to extend their lives another year; it's unclear whether Stephan Balliet knew about the aspect of the holiday's liturgy that is a recital of all the ways God can kill his supplicants, but Balliet's goal was to ensure that deaths were many, and terrible.

The city was Halle, Germany, an ancient city on the banks of the river Saale, neighbor to Leipzig and a cultural center of the state of Saxony-Anhalt, some hundred miles from Berlin. According to the *New Yorker*, about 93 percent of Halle's modest Jewish population had perished during World War II; the community was renewed by a wave of migration from the former Soviet Union after its collapse.[1]

The synagogue was secured, as most synagogues in Europe are, but modestly: locked wooden doors, a community member in a jacket that said SECURITY. There were about fifty attendees at Yom Kippur services, and when the sound of gunfire erupted outside, they crowded around the security camera's feed to see what was happening.

Twenty-seven-year-old Balliet, a German native, was uploading live video in real time to the video-game streaming site Twitch through a smartphone mounted on a helmet. Balliet prefaced his brief rampage with an anti-Semitic rant that echoed familiar themes. Angling his high-cheekboned face and wide green eyes toward the camera, Balliet said, "I think the Holocaust never happened. Feminism is the cause of the decline of the West which acts as a scapegoat for mass immigration. And the root of all these problems is the Jew."

Although he had trained in the German army, he did not have ready access to guns, thanks to the country's strict gun-control laws. Instead, he had built weapons of his own, using open-source guides he'd found online; he'd constructed homemade explosives in the same fashion. They were made clumsily enough not to be able to penetrate the wooden door of the synagogue, which held together, protecting the congregants inside. On the video, a curly-haired woman casually walking down the street passes by Balliet after his failed attempt to storm the synagogue. She says something to him in German and he shoots her and she falls down dead. He quickly adjourned to a nearby kebab shop, where he hoped to find Muslim targets, and he killed a man. Then he surrendered to authorities and it was over; his confession was immediate and extensive. But he'd left a manifesto of sorts, as fame-hungry killers tend to do. He said he would like to kill "as many anti-whites as possible, jews preferred [sic]." There was a page of "Achievements," similar to video games that offer goals to attain as you progress through levels. They had cutesy titles like "Why not both?"—which meant "Kill a Muslim and a Jew." "Chosen to die" was "kill a Jew"; "Gender Equality" was "kill a Jewess"; "Think of the Children!" was "kill a kikelett." But at the core of the document was an ode to guns.

GETTING TO THE BOOM: ON ACCELERATIONISM AND VIOLENCE

There were loving photographs of each piece of handcrafted weaponry, soldered together from pipes, pieces of wood, and assorted bits of metal. Balliet had crafted his own bullets, too, with a crude mix of potassium chlorate and sugar. He had made five guns and his own hand grenades, and carried a gothic longsword. "The whole deal," he wrote, "is to show the viability of improvised guns."

He did not succeed in that particular goal. The doors held, the hand grenades failed, the congregation was unharmed. Random passersby died instead of Jews, and Balliet attained none of his grisly "achievements." But his abortive rampage illustrated the deep fascination with weaponry that runs throughout the far-right internet, where bomb-making instructions and open-source weapons guides and survival manuals are passed around routinely.

White supremacy is where the cult of racism, the cult of anti-Semitism, and the cult of the gun fuse together, creating an environment filled with people preparing themselves for a civilizational collapse they view as inevitable. And, increasingly, as less radicalized, more staid and political sectors of the far-right flail, fail, and fall away, a radioactive core of accelerationists remain. This is the story of the far-right since 2016: a winnowing away of most of the factions that yearned for respectability and mainstream acceptance, until those who remain are poised at the brink of explosion.

———

It's nearly 3 a.m. in Ukraine, but my interlocutor hasn't gone to sleep yet. His name is David, he lives in Kyiv, and he's sending me videos about how to make a gun out of pipes. He's trying to flirt with me. He's Ukrainian, but he wants an American wife. He wants to make a whites-only United States, and he believes I may be his ticket to do that. I'm back in character as Ashlynn, only this time I've infiltrated the Vorherrschaft Division (Supremacy Division), a chat group composed of Americans and Europeans fixated on disseminating images of terror and discussing the need for a race war now. I'm using the screen name "AryanQueen" to say hello to the most violent racists online. Vorherrschaft is one of several knockoffs of the widely feared white-supremacist terror group Atomwaffen Division that have sprung up in recent months. *Atomwaffen* means "atomic weapon" in German. The knockoff groups have Germanic names, organize primarily on Telegram, and traffic in the language of terror. (Another example is the Rapekreig Division.)

I've decided to use a female identity in hopes of coaxing more information out of participants, and David is ready to oblige. His screen name is "Der Stürmer", named after the favorite tabloid of the Nazi Party, and he admires Hitler openly—though his truest hero is Christchurch mosque mass shooter Brenton Tarrant. Like Tarrant himself, David has a preoccupation with all things American. He'd like to visit me in Iowa, and to establish his bona fides, he tells me he was once part of a group called "Cherniy Korpus"—Black Corps—a guerrilla military group that served as a forerunner to the Ukrainian far-right militia now known as the Azov Battalion. He tells me that he left in order to spread national socialist ideas throughout Ukraine, that he's working an office job to afford ammo. He wants a white wife with traditional ideals. He shows me some photos of his militia garb and the gun he used on the front lines in the grinding Ukraine-Russia war in Donbass. I quickly find out that he is one of the administrators of a Ukrainian-language channel I've been monitoring for just under a year. Explicitly designed to evoke stochastic terror, it's called "Brenton Tarrant's Lads."

GETTING TO THE BOOM: ON ACCELERATIONISM AND VIOLENCE

He shows me photos of a Ukrainian translation he's made of Tarrant's manifesto, "The Great Replacement," and tells me he's printed and distributed hundreds of copies. The open-source intelligence website Bellingcat, which closely tracks the far right in Eastern Europe, had published a few months before an investigation of the translated booklet, documenting numerous selfies of men in Ukraine and Russia holding copies of the pamphlet—some reading it by the sea; a group of men holding it up while giving Hitler salutes; and an extremist antigay group that attacked marchers in Kyiv's Pride Parade in 2019 encouraging its members to buy copies. The fish that had landed in my net unwittingly was surprisingly big: He was single-handedly aiding in the radicalization of potentially thousands of men, disseminating a document that had already inspired copycat terror attacks. And he was proud of it.

Every day while the "Brenton Tarrant's Lads" channel glorified terror against Jews, black people, and Muslims, its owner was trying to seduce me. David—he assures me he's "not a kike," despite the name—wants to visit me the next time he comes to the United States. I tell him Ashlynn has learned Russian because she wanted to go to Donbass to meet guys—the most hard-core guys around, the American white supremacists who go to Ukraine to fight. We start speaking in Russian and sometimes Ukrainian. (Unbelievably, he falls for this.) I record voice messages in Russian, with my voice pitched to a sexy-baby timbre and a heavy American accent. He calls me "My Ash." He tells me he loves me.

It's a heady, precipitous flirtation with fear—what happens if he finds out it's me somehow, under the fake pictures, the fake phone number, the fake name? It's also a chance to find out more about the ways in which white supremacy has spread its tentacles around the world. I tell him I'm a waitress. He asks if I serve "n—s" at my job. I say Iowa is mostly white (true). I send him a photograph of "my" face—the same woman I used to create the Ashlynn persona. (Once again I make sure the images are cropped, screenshotted, and impossible to trace back via image search on Google or Yandex.) I send another photo, and he sends me a clip from the front lines in Donbass, of someone he says is "one of his lads" shooting an automatic rifle between rows of sandbags. Above the man's head, a swastika flag is proudly waving. I can tell he wants to impress me.

He says he's only twenty-two.

My blood is cold, cold, cold as I coax out more and more details— what his parents do, where he lives. Ashlynn is fleshed out enough at this point that I can continue to supply analogues of my own. I've memorized the dates of Iowa's hunting season, I can conjure up sorrow when I talk about Ashlynn's dead mother, admiration for her Aryan Nations father. I tell him not to trust anyone, but I want him to trust me, this terrorist. I want to thwart him, and I feel no remorse. I have a few ideas about how to do it, too.

In the end, the operation takes five months. There are moments that veer precipitously into the comical. In order to get him to reveal his face, I ask him to "prove he's not a Jew," and he offers to send me a photo of his foreskin. I decline and ask to see his nose instead.

Here's a snippet of conversation from just after he's revealed his face to me, in a picture in which his mouth is obscured by his phone. I'm fishing for a complete face photo, so I can send it on to antifascists and journalists.

Ashlynn
youre so cute:)

GETTING TO THE BOOM: ON ACCELERATIONISM AND VIOLENCE

Der Stürmer
Thx
Did u really like me?

19:36 – **Ashlynn**
tak!!! ale de tviy scar [Ukrainian translation: Yes!! But where is your scar]

19:36 – **Der Stürmer**
I'm so nervous right now
19:37
On my mouth
19:37
I will show u tomorrow

Ashlynn
i guess i will just have to imagine your mouth . . .

19:37 – **Der Stürmer**
Just picked this photo
19:38
Cause of no mouth
19:38
But it's a very small scar

19:38 – **Ashlynn**
i will dream of kissing your pretty scar

19:38 – **Der Stürmer**
After knife

19:38
I fought with my classmate in high school
19:39
And he cut me next to my mouth

19:39 – **Ashlynn**
chomu? [why?]

19:40 – **Der Stürmer**
Cause I said to him that Luhansk it's not a country
19:40
It's city that belongs to Ukraine
19:40
He was refugee from Luhansk

19:40 – **Ashlynn**
are you worried i will think you are not cute
19:41
because of the scar

19:41 – **Der Stürmer**
Nope
19:41
It's a small one
19:41
Just reminds me of him

19:41 – **Ashlynn**
bc what matters to me is the heart ❤ loving whites, hating jews

GETTING TO THE BOOM: ON ACCELERATIONISM AND VIOLENCE

19:42 – Der Stürmer
This filthy bastards from Luhansk, Donetsk, jews, kebabs
19:42
Too many people that we need to destroy

19:42 – Ashlynn
we'll do it together baby

19:43 – Der Stürmer
I love you.

It's a fucked-up act. But it works. He spontaneously sends me a picture of his car, its license plate plainly visible. I discover that you can get an awful lot of information by Googling someone's license plate. He tells me his real first and last names—David Kolomiiets. I say I'm "Ashleigh Grant."

"Like the M1 Garand," he responds, referring to a World War II vintage semiautomatic rifle.

I make a fake Twitter account for Ashlynn, so I can get his Twitter handle by asking him to follow me. I tweet halfheartedly about kikes and such—bare bones, but enough to be believable. I get him to prove to me through screenshots that he's actually one of the moderators of the Brenton Tarrant's Lads channel—perhaps the largest Ukrainian-language extremist channel, and awash in stochastic terror. He sends me a video he's enjoying watching. It's of 911 calls with callers who disappeared before they could complete the call. Their voices, thick with distress, are amusing to him. I tell him I think that's hot.

What concerns me the most about David, far away on the other side of the world, is that he keeps sending me videos and images of guns. He says he has an M4. He sends me a screenshot of his *Counter-Strike* game: He's named his AK-47 in the game "DIE MUSLIMS!!!" He says he was inspired to join the white-nationalist movement by Brenton Tarrant. He says he wants to kiss me someday. And that he wants to buy an AR-15 when he comes to America. I send him heart-eyed emojis and bide my time.

Eventually, after shopping the story to a few different journalists, I start up a conversation with Michael Colborne, who had authored the investigative piece at Bellingcat about the Ukrainian translation of Tarrant's manifesto, a project David had spearheaded. I tell Colborne I've got all the information on one of the Tarrant channel's co-runners: his name, his face, his license plate, his email, the city he lives in. "Jesus Christ are you serious? How . . ." Colborne messages me on Signal.

"It's complicated, but the short answer is antifascist catfishing," I reply.

After two journalists who cover Eastern Europe have completely ignored the story, I'm struck by the avidity of Michael Colborne's response. That's when Colborne tells me that David has created, and disseminated, a violent video death threat against him and his coworkers.

Colborne sends it to me. It's an extraordinarily disturbing video. It opens in the woods, with links to the Brenton Tarrant's Lads channel displayed on-screen. The music is jaunty. It's formatted like a meme. We cut from the woods to a video clip called "Who's That Pokémon?"—a frequently used segment in the Pokémon anime series to introduce new cute fuzzy monsters. Only instead of a Pokémon, the video then displays Colborne's face—"It's Michael Colborne, beaten Bellingcat faggot," a computerized voice says. Then the video cuts back to the woods, where a paper target of Colborne's face has been glued to a bottle. An unseen hand fires a gun and the bottle explodes, Colborne's face blown to pieces. The process is repeated with more journalists, mainly Colborne's colleagues at Bellingcat. David has sent it to multiple extremist channels, accompanied by the message, "This video is a kind of instructive response on how to deal with our enemies." It's not subtle. It's an invitation to murder.

A few weeks after we first touch base, Colborne tells me he's going to publish the piece soon, and I should probably extract myself from the conversation with David. We'd been talking more sporadically; knowing the jig was about to be up, I was less invested, though he was still telling me he loved me regularly. I send him a message.

"hi David," I write on March 18, 2020, just after midnight. "i have to tell you something."

"Hi," he replies.

"i'm an antifascist and you're about to be exposed," I tell him, filled with a mixture of loathing and fear and glee.

"Makes no sense," he replies. "For what we texted from Nov then?"

"So I could get as much information from you as possible you genocidal asshole," I say.

"I'm scared," he says.

"good," I say, and block him.

So the story comes out. The next morning, Colborne publishes the piece, titled "Revealed: The Ukranian Man Who Runs a Neo-Nazi Telegram Channel."

Colborne wrote, "For all the chatter on neo-Nazi Telegram channels about the need to preserve anonymity and security from all manner of 'feds' and 'journalists/spies,' [David Kolomiiets] was willing to throw caution to the wind because—well, to put it plainly, because he seemed to think he might get laid."

Bellingcat took what I gave them and offered more: David's Facebook page. His page on Vkontakte, the biggest social-media site on the Russian-speaking internet. After the story dropped, David balked. He dropped out of public view entirely—but not before pretending to be his own mother on Twitter and email, begging Bellingcat to unpublish the story, and offering monetary bribes to the journalists to take his name out of circulation. He also deleted all his social-media pages. He seemed genuinely afraid, and embarrassed— and his peers reacted with contempt toward him. Brenton Tarrant's Lads announced his expulsion from the chat room and sent out an increasingly unhinged series of warnings about information security, the need to avoid "e-girls," and the need to not be stupid.

I had outed a violent Nazi—perhaps one with the potential to become a mass shooter—and sown dissension and fear in the ranks of extremists. How could they rebuild the white race, and preserve a future for the white children they claimed to want, if any woman could be a trap? The less they trusted each other, the less cohesive their movement would be. The less cohesive their movement was, the less damage they could wreak. And, what's more, although they didn't know it yet, I had made their worst nightmares come true: Behind the beautiful Aryan they desired was a fat, cunning Jew, biding her time. The man who had so confidently told me that kikes need to be destroyed was cowering, pretending to be his own mother, and had been completely disowned by his peers. It was sweet. And a bit perverse. And it felt completely worth it. It was even sweeter when, a few months later, I got word that Ukrainian security services had arrested a Russian citizen and neo-Nazi who served as an adminis- trator in the Tarrant's Lads channel. It wasn't David. His name was Aleksander Skachkov, and he had SS tattoos on his arm. I wondered if David had played a role in his apprehension, known, as he was, to all and sundry.

Before I shut down my "AryanQueen" account, it started getting flooded with death threats. "Just tell me your name," one man says to me in Russian. "Your house. Your address. I'll show up. I have a gun."

———

The eleventh chapter of American Nazi Party founder George Lincoln Rockwell's 1967 book, *White Power*, is titled "Nightmare." It begins with a protracted fantasy sequence, told in the second person, in which the country has devolved into a series of race riots barely kept in check by local and federal authorities. Then, the protagonist, a white man, is faced with a hellish scenario. First, the power goes out in his home, then the water; the phone is cut off, and he turns on the transistor radio, only to hear the radio host being murdered on air. A black mob begins to riot in the city center, then sets his neighborhood ablaze. He has only a few guns with which to combat the mob, which has set about looting, raping, and burning with abandon. He watches his neighbors die, watches white women being raped and murdered, hopelessly outmanned and outgunned, though he kills a few of the "black terrorists" wreaking havoc. He herds a crowd of survivors into a basement, then watches as his formerly liberal female neighbor stabs a dying black man. "Mrs. Moody is no more 'liberal.' Now she's a member of the great White Race—a fighter! But it's too late!"

At last the Army arrives, and the protagonist thinks he has at last been rescued—only to witness the tanks, driven by black men, being turned on the infantry and mowing them down en masse, as "the great majority of the blacks in the armed forces and the National Guard have joined the black rebellion." An announcement is blasted from sound trucks to the survivors: "This is the new Socialist Democratic People's Government of the United States . . . Resistance is useless." The UN ambassador, "Alfred Goldberg," has assented to the new order, and Chinese troops have invaded the country to secure its new socialist state. "You are alone," writes Rockwell, "against a world gone mad."

In order to stave off the impending menace of black socialist revolt, Rockwell urges his readers to recapture "the fighting ferocity of our forefathers."

"The average White American has forgotten his heritage of violence," he writes. "I know I had, until I launched the American Nazi Party."

Rockwell was murdered in 1967, the same year *White Power* was published—not by a ravening black mob, but by his own, white, twenty-nine-year-old protégé, neo-Nazi John Patler. But the "heritage of violence" he touts in *White Power* is his legacy. The racist paranoia he stoked, with its culmination in an apocalyptic war of the races, has redounded through the generations, inspiring thousands of white supremacists to fantasize about—and prepare for—a "race war." Many of them seek to hasten it, believing, as Rockwell did, that in a war between the races, white liberals will at last cease to be race traitors. But barring the actuality of a black socialist revolt, because Rockwell's fantasy is one borne of pure paranoia detached from reality, a growing number of white nationalists seek to drive American society into chaos through their own actions—in a dedicated campaign of terror.

Rockwell's vision of tapping into a heritage of violence, and being perpetually prepared for apocalyptic warfare, forms a core part of the practices that a number of white-supremacist groups carry out. One of the most common forms of contemporary neo-Nazi propaganda is training videos, featuring masked men shooting guns, often in the woods. Rhetoric within neo-Nazi Telegram chats often feature fitness advice geared toward tactical preparedness for violence. And, through the violent neo-Nazi group Atomwaffen, which is linked to five murders in the United States, the work of another protégé of Rockwell has gained increasing influence.

The book *Siege*, by James Mason, a sixty-seven-year-old neo-Nazi and former member of the American Nazi Party, has acquired a totemic significance among accelerationist neo-Nazis. Mason is aware of his own standing within the movement, and particularly of his significance for Atomwaffen; in 2019, he appeared in a propaganda video for the group, wearing an Atomwaffen patch and surrounded by young men in Atomwaffen's signature skull masks. *Read Siege* or *Take the Siege pill* are common phrases among the most violent fringe of the far right. To be "Siegepilled" is to operate under the idea that a violent revolution is necessary to force America to become a whites-only country. Mason's core notion is the idea that the "System"—the current American government and societal fabric—must be implacably resisted; that intrawhite solidarity will be created under conditions of sufficient duress; and that neo-Nazis must consider themselves revolutionaries working toward the broad goal of tearing down what exists in order to build a new, whiter order.

Siege is a piecemeal, cobbled-together text. It was published by Mason between 1980 and 1986 as a series of newsletters for the National Socialist Liberation Front, then collected and published as a book by neo-Nazi black metal musician Michael Jenkins Moynihan in 1992. It's a rambling, poorly written collection of rants, with intermittent, random capitalizations and enough ellipses to be reminiscent of measles on the page. In a typical essay from 1980, Mason exhorts his readers to eschew passivity in the face of the Jew-run "System" that is oppressing whites. He writes:

The diabolic nature of the Big Brother System in power today may be largely responsible for breeding a race of docile "consumers" who roll over like a spaniel when kicked and otherwise outraged, but for us that is no reason, no excuse, for revolutionary inaction. It CAN be done!

. . . The object is not to kill Blacks . . . it is to FAN THE FLAMES! If we can't get the Whites off their asses to retake control of their destiny then we can at least put them in a position where they will have to fight for their miserable lives! And with a general conflagration going on that will involve police and armed forces, we can, if we are slick about it, assume the guiding position amidst the disorder and coordinate it into what it must become: a revolution to smash the System!

In an essay published in 1981, he writes:

In short it would seem to me that any intelligence at all would lead comrades to know to stop hitting the Enemy where he laughs and start hitting him where he SCREAMS!

Strike hard and strike deep to build the climate for revolution where even the most craven of White cowards will be COMPELLED to join in or else die!

Despite his early membership in the American Nazi Party and ascension in its ranks, Mason fell into relative obscurity and financial hardship between the days of publishing *Siege* and his adoption decades later, as spiritual father and mentor, by the young, internet-savvy neo-Nazis of the Atomwaffen Division. In the interim, he wrote a book titled *How I Paid Off My House: Six Steps to Living Debt-Free*, and served several stints in prison in the 1990s for child pornography and menacing of a minor. While his ideas may have found a new audience and new potency among young internet neo-Nazis in 2019, Mason himself, living in Denver, relies on government-sponsored Section 8 housing and food charity in order to survive, local news reporter Jeremy Jojola of Denver's 9 News discovered.[2]

While Mason initially refused an interview with Jojola for "tactical reasons," the intrepid reporter confronted the neo-Nazi in a super-market parking lot. When Jojola pressed Mason about the ways in which his rhetoric inspires violence, Mason at first disavowed the idea, saying, "I say don't do it."

Pushed further, however, he added: "If you must do it, it seems to me to be only common sense that you'd want to do it right, because it's the end of your life. You may die out there in the street via SWAT team, or you may spend the rest of your life in the joint. Make it count for god's sake."[3]

There are many who have taken that message to heart, and who have stockpiled weapons, made plans, and carried out acts of grisly violence in their attempt to "do it right." Perhaps most chillingly, white supremacists embraced the social chaos created by the economic collapse and fear caused by the novel coronavirus in 2020, reveling among themselves about its implications as a precursor to their beloved "Boogaloo."

On March 24, 2020, thirty-six-year-old Timothy Wilson was shot dead in a conflict with the FBI in Kansas City, Missouri. He had been under investigation as a domestic terrorist for months, and had been planning to bomb a building in the Kansas City area to gain attention for his white-supremacist views. Amid the terror surrounding the novel coronavirus, the FBI said, he decided to take advantage of "the increased impact given the media attention on the health sector" and planned to set off a car bomb at a hospital.

One particularly grim and representative incident of acceler-ationism occurred in August 2019, when a twenty-one-year-old named Patrick Crusius allegedly gunned down twenty-two people in cold blood in a Walmart in El Paso, Texas. The largely Hispanic border town was a purposeful target; Crusius drove 650 miles from his family's home in a suburb of Dallas to carry out the attack. In a manifesto posted to 8chan shortly before the attack was carried out, Crusius decried a purported "Hispanic invasion" of Texas. Like the gunman in the Chabad of Poway synagogue, and my Ukrainian interlocutor David, he claimed Christchurch, New Zealand, gunman Brenton Tarrant as his primary influence, but the ideas he touts are drawn straight from decades of national-socialist rhetoric.

After the August 3 shooting, federal authorities—under pressure from a frightened and angry public and under the direction of FBI director Christopher Wray, who had recently told Congress he considered white nationalism a terror threat—began to crack down on white nationalists who were already on their radar.

In late October 2019, twenty-four-year-old Kaleb Cole had a cache of military-style weapons seized by the Seattle police. Authorities found that Cole posssessed Atomwaffen propaganda calling for "Race War Now"—and on his phone, they found a photo of him and other Atomwaffen members, wearing skull masks, posing before the gates of Auschwitz. Cole had been identified as an Atomwaffen member in February 2018, in an exposé on the hate group by the investigative reporting powerhouse ProPublica. As a result of assiduous journal-ism, he was intercepted before he could carry out violent plans—but other white supremacists slipped through the cracks before they could be stopped.

According to a report from the *Guardian*, federal intervention prevented no fewer than seven white-nationalist mass shootings between August 3 and August 22, 2019.[4] Authorities arrested young men in Nevada; Connecticut; Florida; Ohio; Tennessee; and California. Each had spoken about plans to carry out violence against minorities, Jews, or women. A twenty-three-year-old arrested in Las Vegas, Conor Climo, was affiliated with the Atomwaffen Division, and had planned to firebomb a synagogue and an Anti-Defamation League office. Guns and bomb-making materials were found in his home.[5]

This surge of activity against white nationalism by federal authorities in 2019 was uncharacteristic, to say the least. For decades, observers have noted that in the frenzied heat of the war on terror, the FBI and other investigative organizations shifted their focus to surveilling, infiltrating, and criminalizing Muslim communities in the United States—at the expense of keeping watch over violent white supremacists. As a result, catastrophic massacres like white supremacist Dylann Roof's 2015 shooting of nine black parishioners in a Charleston church took authorities completely by surprise. In 2017, the violent Unite the Right rally in Charlottesville was not subject to federal intervention. Despite the fact that, as the Anti-Defamation League's Center on Extremism has documented, 71 percent of murders related to extremism in the United States between 2008 and 2017 were committed by members of far-right or white-supremacist movements, federal authorities have maintained a sustained myopia toward white terror. As one New York Times report put it, authorities have approached white supremacy with "willful indifference"—and that indifference has cost hundreds of lives.[6]

Add to that the documented propensity of law enforcement to be sympathetic to white-nationalist groups—and the frequency with which police officers and soldiers have surfaced as hate-group members—and there is a clear conflict of interest that renders federal authorities not just ill-equipped but also uniquely unsuited for the job of dismantling violent white-supremacist groups.

Which leaves the question of who can protect us from this threat if the police cannot. Are we damned, as Rockwell wrote, to be "alone against a world gone mad"? Or can we rely on something else entirely—each other?

CHAPTER 9

ANTIFA CIVIL WAR

In late 2017, certain segments of the right-wing internet were gearing up for a cataclysmic, blood-soaked civil war in America. The culprits who would destabilize the country, leading to a hitherto unimaginable level of gore and horror, were the black-clad, oft-villainized, and nebulous force known as "antifa."

Antifa is short for "antifascists" (or "antifascism"), a leaderless, loosely organized movement whose primary purpose is to block, outmaneuver, and dismantle far-right and fascist organizing. It takes a number of distinct forms—from identifying and publicizing the real names of far-right activists; to infiltrating far-right groups and attempting sabotage from within; to counterprotesting at fascist rallies. It's the latter activity that garners by far the most attention: In particular, those counterprotesters who adopt a tactic known as "black bloc," donning a uniform of anonymizing black and wearing face masks, are easy to sensationalize. Black bloc members can be unabashedly bellicose. Numerous far-right events around the country have devolved into thrown punches between far-right groups and black-clad activists, flanked by hordes of geared-up riot cops.

Antifascist street mobilization is by definition responsive—reactive to already-planned far-right events. The black bloc subset of antifascists operate under two primary principles: that bigotry and Nazism should have a social cost, which can include a black eye or two ("Punch a Nazi" is a popular slogan); and that by putting their bodies on the front lines, they are engaging in harm reduction, preventing fascist groups from roving around cities inflicting harm on visible minorities and queer individuals. Unsurprisingly, this process gets messy sometimes, and, like all spilled blood, draws in the hungriest sharks in the area—in this case, the news media.

All things in nature strain toward symmetry, but none more so than mainstream news outlets. While antifascists in the United States have never committed murder, images of black-clad leftists tussling in street brawls with far-right groups are the perfect fodder for reflexive both-sidesism in centrist media, and are known to cause veritable epidemics of hand-wringing among self-proclaimed sensible pundits. Any number of op-eds emerged in the wake of the deadly Unite the Right rally in August 2017 in Charlottesville, decrying the notion of "punching a Nazi" as a prelude to an inevitable Jacobin-like epidemic of beheadings, a breakdown in civil discourse, and a rent in the social fabric of the United States.

Far more operatically, however, right-wing press and politicians have adopted antifa as a bête noire, and an all-purpose foil to reports of far-right extremist violence. This was most famously evident in Donald Trump's post–Unite the Right remarks, in which he placed "blame on both sides" for the murder of protestor Heather Heyer by white supremacist James Alex Fields. In a press conference following nationwide controversy after the president declared there were "very fine people" in a white-supremacist march, Trump added denigration of the "alt-left" that came "charging at the alt-right": There were, he said, "troublemakers and you see them come with the black outfits and with the helmets and with the baseball bats—a lot of bad people." In June 2020, during a national uprising over police brutality, Trump reiterated that "ANTIFA" was responsible for civil unrest—going so far as to accuse a seventy-five-year-old protester pushed violently to the ground by police in Buffalo, New York, of being an "ANTIFA provocateur." Trump himself is famously a creature of the right-wing media, consuming and promoting content from Fox News and other right-wing outlets constantly. In turn, right-wing media outlets work diligently to amplify the threat of antifascists, in service of inculcating a mind-set among their viewers of existential besiegement. There are countless examples of right-wing media going all-in on anti-antifascist hysteria. But none is more instructive—and more groundless—than the Antifa Civil War that never came to pass in November 2017.

It all started with a series of protests planned for November 4, 2017, by a small group, founded in the 1970s, known as the Revolutionary Communist Party—"Revcom" for short. The group's septuagenarian, domineering chairman, Bob Avakian, had founded Revcom in 1975 as a splinter movement from better-known '60s-era activist groups like the Students for a Democratic Society.[1] In literature from the party, its leader is often referred to as "Chairman Avakian," like an avuncular, square-jawed, white Mao. Over the next half-century, the group participated in a variety of protests—and, in fact, a member of the group burning an American flag in 1984 was the impetus for a US Supreme Court case that enshrined flag-burning as protected speech under the First Amendment.[2] But by 2014, one sociologist had denounced the group, a scant collection of roving Maoists, as "parasitic," tending to glom on to extant protest movements, rather than significantly advancing causes.[3] The November 4th protests seemed like more of the same—an attempt by a hoary and oft-dismissed group to capitalize on preexisting, seething resentment of the new Trump administration.

The protests were promulgated on a website called RefuseFascism .org, and their lofty ambition was to emulate, or even to surpass, the massive Women's Marches that followed Donald Trump's inauguration that January. While the protests were always planned to be nonviolent, their goals were sweeping: to create a series of "ever-expanding" protests in which "many thousands of people will fill the streets of cities and towns, beginning a struggle that must continue day after day and night after night, eventually involving millions of people." The protests were initially announced in a press release on August 6, 2017, urging supporters to "take to the streets." Revcom's stated goal was to emulate the ouster of South Korean president Park Geun-hye, who was impeached in March 2017 following mass nonviolent demonstrations now known as the "Candlelight Struggle." (At its height, Refuse Fascism had about 75,000 followers on Facebook—hardly comparable to the Korean protests, which routinely drew hundreds of thousands of citizens to the streets of Seoul.)

A corps of genuine, self-proclaimed communists, planning to take to the streets, was catnip to the right-wing–conspiracy-industrial complex, an intoxicating lure. The fact that the proposed protests were decidedly nonviolent was quickly eclipsed by a more lucrative force: fear. Fear is the driver of the right-wing conspiracy machine, a primal force without which it would wither and die, along with all the brain-booster pills and bomb-shelter accoutrements shilled to a credulous audience suspended in perpetual terror. In the case of the Antifa Civil War that wasn't, right-wing paranoia bloomed, quickly, into something efflorescent and absurd.

It's difficult to pin down exactly who posted the first article scaremongering about Refuse Fascism, but by mid-August, reports were circulating on right-wing sites that utilized images of black-clad anarchists to promote a terrifying nightmare of coming chaos. The earliest example I found came on August 18, 2017. A site called YourNewsWire (slogan: "News. Truth. Unfiltered.") transmogrified the small and relatively unknown Revcom group into the broad, ill-defined, and terrifying movement known as "ANTIFA." (Despite its name, Refuse Fascism is not an antifascist group, nor does it describe itself as such.) A mere five days after the deadly events in Charlottesville—which had thrust antifascism into a national spotlight that quickly turned critical—far-right fear-mongerers sensed a chance to capitalize on the sentiment. The headline at YourNewsWire blared: ANTIFA PLAN NATIONWIDE RIOTS ON NOV. 4TH TO FORCIBLY REMOVE TRUMP.[4] The article began with two pithy sentences meant to pump their readers with adrenaline:

> According to two ANTIFA-based websites, plans are being made to end the "Trump/Pence regime" via acts of violence and terrorism across the United States. Don't be caught flatfooted. Call your congressman, senator, sheriff, mayor's office and ask them: "What are you going to do to ensure these domestic terrorists don't get away with killing more Americans?"

The article quoted directly from Refusefascism.org and Revcom.us, although the most violent word those sites used was *demand*. There was, admittedly, a very irritating use of two colons in a single sentence, although this is not technically violent. The press release stated, "We will not stop until our single demand is met: This Nightmare Must End: the Trump/Pence Regime Must Go!"

The brief article on YourNewsWire.com was written by Sean Adl-Tabatabai, a British-Iranian entrepreneur living in Los Angeles. A former employee of David Icke, the British conspiracy theorist most famous for his elaborate descriptions of lizard-like aliens who secretly run the planet, Adl-Tabatabai is an infamous figure among those who track disinformation online. Along with his husband, Sinclair Treadway, Adl-Tabatabai has garnered a massive audience running YourNewsWire—a slurry of outright fabrication, aggregation, and conspiracy that journalism watchdog Poynter branded "one of the most infamous misinformers on the internet." A *Times of London* exposé also revealed that among the site's myriad other flaws, Adl-Tabatabai had his mother write many of its news stories.[5] BuzzFeed reported that YourNewsWire had produced nine of the top fifty most-shared hoaxes on Facebook in 2017.[6] The site was rebranded as NewsPunch in 2019, after Facebook's fact-checking program, run in partnership with third-party fact-checking sites, began systematically rating YourNewsWire links "false," limiting their reach on the social network. From this seamy funnel of low-quality, inflammatory content, news of the impending "civil war" poured forth—and was quickly picked up, in superheated fashion, by numerous other right-wing outlets.

Chief among those was Alex Jones's InfoWars. In 2017, Jones still presided over a media empire made up of radio shows, video broadcasts, and articles; according to the web traffic-ranking tool Alexa, Infowars.com was averaging millions of hits daily that summer. On August 22, 2017, a brief article by InfoWars correspondent Paul Joseph Watson raised the stakes still further. "CIVIL WAR": ALT-LEFT PLANS ANTI-TRUMP RIOTS IN MAJOR CITIES ON NOVEMBER 4, blared the article's headline.

After quoting the same press release as YourNewsWire, Watson dug deep into a long post made the day before by a Revcom spokesperson, Andy Zee. In that August 6 post on Revcom.us, Zee hyped the November 4 protests and added a long-winded four-thousand-word rant denouncing Trump's misogyny, anti-immigrant stances, and flouting of democratic norms. In a paragraph about Mike Pence's "theocratic Christian fundamentalism," Zee made a reference to a seventy-two-page pamphlet written by the party's leader, Bob Avakian, in 2005, which he recommended to readers. The pamphlet was titled *The Coming Civil War*, a collection of talks by Avakian on everything from abortion rights to North Korea to Bill Cosby's respectability politics, with a whole lot of old-school communist rhetoric. (Sample chapter title: "The Revolutionary Potential of the Masses and the Responsibility of the Vanguard.") On this dubious basis—a glancing mention of a pamphlet published twelve years earlier—Paul Joseph Watson of InfoWars inserted *Civil War* into the headline, and thereby introduced the idea that the bloodiest conflict in US history was about to be reprised. Even Watson, however, evinced some skepticism at first about the viability of Revcom's plan to flood the streets of major cities with protesters. "Whether the demonstrations turn into riots or another damp squib of hammer & sickle flag-waving idiots chanting moronic, mindless slogans before going home having achieved absolutely nothing remains to be seen," he wrote.

At the time, InfoWars's influence over the conspiratorially minded right-wing sphere was nonpareil. "Around 2017, pre-deplatforming, InfoWars was best understood as acting as an amplifier," Anna Merlan, author of the 2019 book *Republic of Lies*, which focuses on American conspiracy theorists, told me.

Driven into the superheated heart of conservative paranoia by Watson, the "Antifa Civil War" myth began to effloresce in earnest. On

YouTube, videos like "ANTIFA CALLS FOR OPEN CIVIL WAR IN U.S. NOV 4TH," and "ANTIFA Planning a Civil War against Trump Nov 4th!!!!" began to crop up, garnering thousands of views each. "Antifa, Civil War Agenda, Plans for Nationwide Anarchy November 4" drew 28,000 views by claiming to predict the nature of antifascist violence by means of "Vedic astrology." As conspiracy theories tend to do, the notions put forth quickly devolved into anti-Semitism; ranting talking heads posited that George Soros, the liberal Jewish billionaire, and/or the Rothschild banking family were bankrolling the operation in which black-clad hordes would take over America's cities and towns.

InfoWars, sensing a receptive audience, continued to feed the speculation, piling up articles, segments, and radio content about the purported violent anarchy its viewers seemed to both crave and fear. At one point, Alex Jones spoke with a granddaughter of a Weather Underground member, reaching back generations to find a suitable example of far-left violence. By October 2017, Jones was claiming, on air, to an audience of millions, that "members of Antifa are illegally crossing the Syrian border to receive military training from Kurdish militias as part of a dark triad between Antifa, anarcho-communist Kurds, and Kurdish members of ISIS." (Needless to say, there was no evidence to support this claim.)

Then—as is the case whenever conspiracies build up too much steam—things got even weirder. A popular anonymous Twitter user who goes by the pseudonym "Krang T. Nelson"—a play on the name of a villain from the Teenage Mutant Ninja Turtles franchise—caught wind of the increasingly popular conspiracy theory wafting from the fetid fever swamps of the right-wing internet. On October 27, "Nelson," a surreal humorist, tweeted:

"can't wait for November 4th when millions of antifa super-soldiers will behead all white parents and small business owners in the town square"

There wasn't even a period at the end of the sentence, but this humble tweet was enough to ignite the parched underbrush of conservative paranoia. In an instant, what had been relegated to the fringe of wild-eyed YouTubers and InfoWars rants migrated into the conservative mainstream—a boundary that, in the Trump era, has become increasingly porous anyhow. The popular—if crackpot-friendly—right-wing website Gateway Pundit took Krang T. Nelson's tweet completely seriously, publishing an article on October 30 that blared the satirical tweet from the headline: ANTIFA LEADER: NOVEMBER 4TH . . . MILLIONS OF ANTIFA SUPERSOLDIERS WILL BEHEAD ALL WHITE PARENTS.[7]

Decrying the "anti-white racism" embodied by the tweet, the article's author, Lucian Wintrich, went on to describe antifa as both a collection of "white, pale-skinned, stick-thin men, and obese pimple-ridden women" and an existential communist threat to America.

I spoke to the anonymous writer behind the "Krang T. Nelson" account, who told me that his satirical tweet prompted some truly bizarre responses. "There was one guy in like Arkansas I think who put tape all over his guns that said 'antifa supersoldier hunter' and 'KT Nelson Eraser' and shit like that," he wrote via Twitter DM. "He was this potbellied old dude and he had some kind of 9mm handgun with a double drum mag that he had just shoved like, perfectly down the middle of his ass crack so it looked like he had a little tail."

With the threat of mass beheadings looming, some conservative publications began to advocate for armed self-defense. "Unless something changes, we can look forward, at the very least, to mobs in the streets, assaults by black-clad masked goons, shops destroyed, cars overturned and set ablaze," wrote a commentator at the journal *American Thinker* that week. "Fear God, dread naught, and keep your powder dry."

The media furor also drove an investigation by federal authorities, revealed by the *Daily Beast* through documents obtained under the Freedom of Information Act. Spurred on by reports of the "antifa civil war," the Department of Homeland Security began dredging up information about the Refuse Fascism protests—as well as cataloguing information on other left-wing groups planning protests in the same period. At least some at DHS took the ravings of far-right YouTubers seriously, it seemed—further underscoring the closeness between the far right and law enforcement.

"There are currently a large number of Youtube videos related to an unconfirmed nationwide plan by ANTIFA to cause disruptions on November 4, 2017," one email from a DHS senior special agent, obtained by the *Daily Beast*, read; the email was sent to DHS intelligence centers in Maryland and Virginia. "Some videos claim there is a plan to overthrow the government and/or harm law enforcement officers."

On the eve of the civil war, Fox News, the behemoth empire that both creates and disseminates the right-wing news cycle, felt impelled to weigh in—and up the stakes. ANTIFA APOCALYPSE? ANARCHIST GROUP'S PLAN TO OVERTHROW TRUMP 'REGIME' STARTS SATURDAY, read a headline on FoxNews.com, published on November 3, 2017.

Uncritically warning of "violent masked anarchists," the article noted "violent images" in Refuse Fascism's materials, such as a rope pulling down a Trump statue. In September, the FBI had warned of the potential of "domestic terrorist violence" perpetrated by antifa, citing as an example a violent clash between the Golden State Skinheads, a white-supremacist group, and antifascists in Sacramento. Fox ate up the claim, and regurgitated it with a flourish, dredging up the specter of the end of humanity.

When November 4 finally rolled around, of course, the United States did not collapse in an onslaught of anarchist violence. *Newsweek* reported that around three hundred people showed up in Times Square for the New York iteration of the Refuse Fascism protest; about five Trump supporters showed up to counter them. The photojournalist Ford Fischer captured the DC protest, which drew a grand total of three people. None were armed, masked, or particularly threatening, and all were seemingly over the age of fifty. Not a single small business owner or white paterfamilias was beheaded. The sun rose, set, and resumed its journey across the horizon without a hitch.

Nonetheless, conservative furor about antifa—and the perennial suggestion that brutal far-left violence is brewing just under the surface of the United States—hasn't abated. It may have chilled out for a while after the civil war that never came to pass, but "antifa" as a communist menace to the very fabric of God, guns, liberty, and the United States of America serves an obvious rhetorical purpose. It promotes both unity among conservatives and a sense of being under threat. Fear is great for selling survivalist kits and colloidal silver that turns you blue (which is integral to Alex Jones's business model) and keeping baby boomers glued to their television sets (which is Fox News's game). It also serves a psychological need: As evidence of far-right violence accrues, right-wing media needs a foil, a foe to minimize its own responsibility in the peddling of violent, xenophobic politics. Antifascists, who are most famously depicted with black masks and signs that would upset a grandmother in Des Moines (or Long Island), serve as the perfect scapegoat. And this portrayal has bled over from the right-wing sphere into centrist media like CNN and MSNBC. Debate over leftist tactics, after all, fits very smoothly into the bellowing, gladiatorial panels that make up most news shows. Such prevaricating also allows mainstream media, which is perennially critiqued as overly liberal, to punch leftward, maintaining a veneer of objectivity. Press-shy antifascists are unlikely to object, and in their masks and black garb, they seem the perfect (obscured) face of highly rebukeable extremism. The fact that no deaths in the history of the United States have been attributed to antifascist activism is almost beside the point. They look scary.

Moreover, the mask-clad figures of antifa activists form a kind of imagined storm trooper in the repeated narrative of brewing civil war. Gun culture on the American right is premised on the idea of having the right to resist "tyranny"—but what, precisely, that tyranny will look like is often left vague. At the heart of conservative culture is an innate respect for soldiers and law enforcement.

After the 2013 protests against the killing of unarmed black teen Trayvon Martin gave birth to the Black Lives Matter movement, the protests broadened in scope and intensity the following year after police officer Darren Wilson shot unarmed teenager Michael Brown in Ferguson, Missouri. Conservative backlash rose up in the form of a competing pro–law-enforcement movement that called itself "Blue Lives Matter." A jingoistic embrace of the US military and concomitant consideration of soldiers themselves as sacrosanct and immune from criticism form an assumptive backbone of conservative propaganda. Yet, at the same time, many members of the mainstream right wing staunchly defend their rights to amass arsenals of deadly weapons in case "the government" writ large decides to oppress its citizens. It's a paradoxical but passionately maintained set of positions. One way to square the circle is by inventing an enemy somehow aligned with nebulous but nefarious "deep state" interests, abstracted from the cops and soldiers that commonly feature in heroic images on the right. The masked faces of black-bloc antifascists make them a perfect proxy for the faceless, commie, gun-grasping automatons of the paranoid conservative mind. The potency of these images in popular conservative culture was made strikingly manifest in a B-movie starring *Hercules* actor Kevin Sorbo. The movie, titled *The Reliant*, is a full-fledged InfoWars fantasy, starring masked black-bloc hordes coming after the God-fearing, gun-hoarding protagonists of the film. Against a landscape of burning American flags and bat-wielding leftists unfolds a fantasy of revanchist American masculinity. At one point, an enraged Sorbo points his gun up at the sky and shoots into the heavens, screaming. "THE 2ND AMENDMENT UNDER ATTACK," a trailer for the movie blares in an all-caps intertitle, between shots of black-clad antifa stand-ins hurling Molotov cocktails. "WHEN GUNS ARE OUTLAWED, ONLY OUTLAWS WILL HAVE GUNS."

But beyond the headlines, the eye-catching B-roll, and the rumors of a perennially brewing civil war, who are antifascists, and what are their goals? For one thing, I consider myself an antifascist. Now that you've delved far enough into this book, I'm trusting that you won't put it down in a huff. I consider myself an antifascist because I've met antifascists, and I've met fascists, and I know which I prefer.

The first thing to understand about antifascism is that it is not a centralized movement. There's no group of people—black-clad or otherwise—who get together for antifa conferences, or workshops, or symposia. In fact, chances are you couldn't get 100 antifascists under the same roof without sparking 150 arguments—such are the legendary internecine squabbles of the sectarian left. The movement, rather, is a collection of individuals scattered throughout the country who are loosely pursuing the same goal: preventing fascist, far-right organizing through a variety of tactics. Any description of antifascist ideology isn't unitary or singular, and neither is an honest discussion of antifascist tactics.

Antifascism is fundamentally about community protection, although antifascist actions can sometimes reflect the proposition that the best defense is a good offense. Ultimately, though, antifascism is a responsive ideology—a way to counter the rise of fascist movements. It is an ethos—and a set of tactics—that are more complex and deeply rooted than media portrayals would have you believe. Antifascism is a way of looking at the complex relationship between extremists, their opponents, and the state that doesn't necessarily mesh with a comfortable liberal worldview. But more than anything, it's a way to keep ourselves—and our more vulnerable friends and neighbors—safe in a world where hate wants to swallow us whole.

CHAPTER 10

WE KEEP US SAFE

In August 2019, I took a long, quiet train ride down to Charlottesville, Virginia. Two years had passed since the events of August 12, 2017, the fascist rally that had transfixed the nation. In the small, verdant college town, the Unite the Right rally and its deadly fallout are referred to as "A12," in a collective act of resistance to using the name of the city as a euphemism for an orgy of hatred. But in the rest of the country, the events of that day are more commonly referred to as just "Charlottesville." I wanted to speak to some of the people who had been there—fighting—at the very moment that the American fascist movement had come violently to the country's attention, who had put their bodies on the line to protect their home.

It's a remarkably beautiful town, and the train ride down from New York is meandering and green. The Virginia fields opened up around me through the Amtrak windows, all in emerald, the sun so Southern-strong the glass could have singed my palm. I came in early; I wanted to get to know the town a little. There was an ice-cream shop that could have been lifted unchanged from the 1940s, more Confederate monuments than a Northerner like me was used to, and the air swam with heat haze. And, true to the town's role as the location of the University of Virginia, a magisterial and very old university, there were indie bookshops every half-mile or so where MFA students did their readings and locals browsed poetry books. There was an excellent vegetarian pho restaurant. Upscale dining, a lovely theater, public playgrounds with luxurious sprinklers that chased away the worst of the midday heat: That was why a loose-knit confederacy of racist groups had chosen this town as their battleground. In the grand tradition of George Lincoln Rockwell's trips to Boston and New York, it was a chance to flex their muscles against the backdrop of a diverse and mostly liberal populace, garnering opposition—and headlines—along the way. But bringing together hundreds of sociopaths united only by their loathing was always a risky endeavor. And neither the town, nor the racist movements that besieged it, would emerge unscathed.

Honorary Heather Heyer Way, the section of Charlottesville's Fourth Street named for the thirty-two-year-old woman who was murdered on August 12, 2017, was ghostly quiet in the oppressive late-afternoon heat. The city had blocked off the street to traffic with a couple of trucks. A few solemn observers trickled through; no one spoke above a murmur. There were bouquets of purple flowers leaning on the lampposts, and boxes of chalk for passersby to leave memorial messages. All along the red-brick walls there were testimonials to Heather, exhortations to peace in multiple languages, symbols of anarchy and antifascism. There were so many hearts, big and small, in every pastel color available, some scuffed by passing feet or stirred by a little wind into bright dust. Just under a month before, Heyer's killer, twenty-two-year-old James Alex Fields, had been sentenced to life plus 419 years on twenty-nine federal hate crime charges. Fields had driven from Maumee, Ohio, to join the hate group rally. On

August 12, Fields had been spotted carrying a shield emblazoned with the emblem of Vanguard America, a white-nationalist group whose slogan is the Nazi phrase "blood and soil." He had plowed his Dodge Challenger into a crowd of counterprotesters, killing Heyer and injuring dozens of others, including some who had to undergo major surgery.

Two years on, the small city was making its way through a normal Monday, but there was a spare hitch of tension to people's movements, an extra layer of silence or perhaps a hiss of warning in the hot air. The year before, in 2018, Jason Kessler, the organizer of the first, fatal Unite the Right rally, had attempted to arrange a sequel in Charlottesville. But a combination of infighting and mass social censure directed at the individuals who had marched, and been identified, at the first Unite the Right rally had defanged the event. There had been a few arrests of those who committed crimes during the first rally, including that of James Alex Fields; and a calculated antifascist operation to sow discord among Kessler's organizers led to infighting and public disavowals of the event. In the end, Unite the Right 2 was a pale shadow of the prior year's mayhem—just a few bellicose racists carrying signs in Washington, DC. What would happen this year? There were no plans for a Unite the Right 3 at all, as far as anyone I spoke to knew. But Unite the Right had been a profound anomaly in the first place; the nature of white-nationalist violence tends to be sudden, striking symbolic or vulnerable targets with deadly force, not part of an enormous gathering scrutinized by national media. That same August day two years later, the whole town, with hot light spilling on pedestrian walkways, café tables spilling out onto the curbs, seemed ripe for healing, or for revenge.

That evening, there was an interfaith memorial service held at First

Baptist Church in Charlottesville, a historically black church on West Main Street. The theme was "Navigating Troubled Waters," and a mixed-race audience filled the pews and mezzanine. The leaders were members of the Charlottesville Clergy Collective—a group of rabbis, reverends, and Buddhist and Baha'i clergy. There were rousing songs of faith, testimonials from survivors, and speeches that mixed self-castigation on the part of white clergy with a renewed commitment to antiracism. Sitting in the audience packed with Charlottesville activists, clergy members, and antiracist community members, I felt profoundly moved—and afraid. I felt my eyes flick repeatedly up to the mezzanine and back; that deeply American fear of mass shooting, of sudden bullets that would end some lives and shatter others, had lodged itself in me. This time, this place, this audience—I wondered where the gunman would stand, how best he could access so ripe a target. In the mezzanine, I figured, where he could shoot penned parishioners in the pews below. What would he shout? Hymns rose around me, but I itched in my seat, a nagging terror at the corners of my consciousness. Police protection from the Charlottesville Police Department had been promised to the First Baptist Church, but on entering the event, I had seen no cops at all, just friendly ushers with clip-art flyers listing the evening's program.

The left-wing activist community in Charlottesville was familiar with police failing to protect them. Part of the horror of the images of August 12, 2017, was the ranks of uniformed riot cops, from both the city and the Virginia State Police, staying secure behind barricades—while the city devolved into chaos.

An independent review of the events of the summer of 2017, commissioned by the City of Charlottesville and written by Timothy Heaphy of the law firm Hunton & Williams, serves in part as a damning indictment of police inaction in the face of armed protest by hate groups. In the report's executive summary, Heaphy describes police planning as "inadequate and disconnected"; the police department as "inadequately equipped"; and officers' decisions not to intervene in physical confrontations between protesters and counterprotesters a failure to "protect public safety."

"The result," Heaphy writes, "was a period of lawlessness and tension that threatened the safety of the entire community." One header for a section of the 207-page report states it baldly: "Law Enforcement Failed to Intervene in Violent Disorders and Did Not Respond to Requests for Assistance."

A single wooden sawhorse, and no police at all, had "protected" the crowded intersection where Heather Heyer died. Two years on, there were no squad cars outside the church, no burly men in blue to guard the rabbi giving his sermon or the church choir filling the room with joy in bass and alto and soprano. There were no sirens; just us, the gathered for the dead, singing.

When I went out for a nervous cigarette, I saw the community's answer to dereliction on the part of the police department. It came in the form of a tiny blond woman named Molly Conger.

I'd become acquainted with Molly over Twitter, where she tweets under the handle @socialistdogmom. It's fitting: She's a former co-chair of the Charlottesville Democratic Socialists of America, and has two small dachshunds, named Buck and Otto. She's also attended and documented many American far-right trials over the past three years, and faced down cops and far-right groups alike at protests in Philly, Boston, and Charlottesville, as well as Stone Mountain, Georgia; Newnan, Georgia; and Shelbyville, Tennessee. She's been pepper-sprayed, beaten, and ridden down with a bike by cops; burned pages of a Bible given to her by a neoconfederate at a racist rally while denouncing the Confederacy; and attends nearly every single meeting of the Charlottesville City Council and most of its committees, live-tweeting late into the night.

By the time we met in Charlottesville, we'd been corresponding for most of a year on Twitter, commenting on far-right shenanigans and rape threats we'd received. She was someone I deeply respected even before I saw her chain-smoking at the entrance of First Baptist, her petite form electric with tension, texting anyone she knew to come form a loose human chain around the church and surveil the surroundings for any threats—unbeknownst to most of the service attendees inside.

She explained that she was using the antifa phone tree to organize community protection. She has a dulcet, high voice and was wearing leggings; she was several inches shorter than my five-foot-three. Sometimes, as it turned out, antifascists come up just past your shoulder, and like to dress up their dogs in party hats.

People, mostly men, in inconspicuous clothing had begun to line up around the church, a few hundred feet apart, glancing around alertly. Molly told me she'd seen a man with a suspicious bulge in his jacket shaped like a holster and stopped him; it turned out to be an oversized cell phone holder in the end.

By the time I finished my fifth cigarette and stepped back inside, a sermon had finished, and another song began. The interfaith, mixed-race congregation began to clap along and the sound rose through the red-carpeted nave of the church, up past the mezzanine, to the ceiling and the spire and the hot August night.

Over the next few days, I spoke to street medics, anarchists, and antifascists who had fought on the streets of Charlottesville for the entirety of the long, hot, and dreadful summer of 2017—which local activists have dubbed the "Summer of Hate." They had combated a series of trial runs for the eventual, bloody Unite the Right rally—

from KKK delegations to hate-group torch marches. They had raised their voices against an acquiescent city government and a hostile police force and an apathetic public. They had been besieged, and had fought back anyway, in ways that still caused them palpable trauma and pain.

A local woman who is a member of an anarchist collective wept to me in a Mexican restaurant as she recounted begging for help during the white-supremacist torchlight march on the UVA campus that would horrify the nation, as her friends were assaulted by violent racists. Her partner recounted defending a comrade in a wheelchair from fire and fists. And still they fight on, for the very city that failed to heed their voices, and which has become a metonym for violent racism to the rest of the country. The overwhelming consensus from the activists I spoke to was that they refused to yield their small city to the forces of hate—that they would act as a dam against the flood, no matter what the cost to them, no matter what the odds of the fight. They had come through hell charred with their fists still balled to spar; they were scarred, but unbroken.

—

One thing to make clear at the outset, when describing antifascist activity, is that the vast majority of it is nonviolent. In fact, antifascism is a defensive posture—it rises as fascism rises, and falls as fascism falls, in a well-documented pattern that has lasted for decades. In the Trump era, antifascist organizing began to rise during the 2016 election season, as the white-nationalist movement grew unmistakably emboldened by the openly racist rhetoric spewing forth from the Trump campaign. As hate groups rose in prominence, antifascists began to coalesce around the idea of countering their organizing, protecting the vulnerable from violent hatred. The principal goals of most antifascist groups and individuals are to prevent violence from having to occur in the first place. Which isn't to deny that the movement condones some degree of violence in pursuit of quashing fascist organizing. Sometimes a thrown punch in a street brawl is a way to keep the next fight from happening with knives—or guns, always a potent factor in the American public sphere.

But long before that punch is thrown, antifascists act behind the scenes. Again, this doesn't make catchy B-roll for the news, and antifascists are famously press-shy in the first place—largely because they want to avoid harassment by their far-right foes. But much of antifascist activity takes place in the form of research, infiltration, and perhaps most of all "doxing"—revealing the names, locations, and occupations of members of hate groups.

This can entail everything from reviewing footage of hate rallies and matching faces to Facebook profiles, to elaborate plots involving undermining fascist groups from within by posing as their members online or in person. Antifascists aim to be wherever fascists are, working to sow discord, engender paranoia and discouragement, and ensure that there is, above all else, a social cost to fascism, racism, and virulent homophobia and transphobia.

In the Trump era, that social cost has been vastly eroded. As the writer David Roth noted in a *New Republic* article, one of the unofficial duties of a president is to "shape the culture in ways that reflect their own values or anti-values, politics, and vibe."[1]

Under Trump's presidency, the culture has a potent driving force that promotes—and thus erodes the social cost of—misogyny and a range of racism from the casual to the brutally open. From the early days of his campaign, Trump both advanced racist invective and displayed an unsettling degree of comfort with racist violence.

When supporters of his, during the campaign, violently beat and urinated on a Latino homeless man, the future president commended them as "passionate." A president who has openly flirted with white nationalism since the inception of his campaign, and has an openly white-nationalist chief immigration adviser in the form of odious Nosferatu figure Stephen Miller, imperils the fragile social contract that, for a few decades at least, made open white nationalism a socially unacceptable position to take. The gamble that antifascists make with their doxing is that, despite the corrosive effect of White House white nationalism, there are still neighbors, employers, and casual friends in communities across America who may be uneasy with members of organized hate groups in their midst.

Antifascists and the police have a particularly antagonistic relationship. At the tip of this iceberg of resentment is the street-theater aspect of antifascist organizing—the brawls and melees when fascist speakers or rallies invade a city. As white nationalist and far-right extremist events descend into violence between antifascists and fascists, police forces throughout the country have disproportionately focused their attentions on leftists. Excessive police violence, lopsided arrest counts, and the punitive posting of mug shots associated with leftist activists have added to the hostility that already exists between leftist organizers and the police. In turn, antifascists have refused to cooperate with police on numerous occasions, including in the cases of investigations into fascist and far-right violence.

This pattern has been documented in particular detail in Portland, Oregon, a city that has weathered an extraordinary, sustained, and bloody series of far-right incursions. Evidence emerged, reported in local publications like the *Willamette Week*, of extensive coordination between the Portland Police Bureau and far-right activists. One police lieutenant, Jeff Niiya, engaged in chatty, discursive, and even jokey texts with Joey Gibson, head of the far-right extremist group Patriot Prayer.

Patriot Prayer has staged numerous rallies since 2017 in Portland that attract openly white-supremacist groups, such as the neo-Confederate Hiwaymen and the racist group Identity Evropa. During the era of the coronavirus, Patriot Prayer became enthusiastic participants in "ReOpen Oregon" rallies that attracted a menagerie of militias, white nationalists, antigovernment extremists, and conspiracy theorists.

On one occasion, police discovered a group of Patriot Prayer supporters perched on a roof overlooking a protest route with a number of rifles, but made no arrests. Police have been far harsher with left-wing protesters: On August 4, 2018, at a Patriot Prayer rally, police threw stun grenades into a crowd of counterprotesters, causing a minor brain hemorrhage in a leftist protester when a grenade hit him directly in the head. The *Daily Beast*'s Arun Gupta, who was present at the far-right rally and counterprotest, summarized the views of leftist activists: "The city was turned into a war zone by a police force seeking to protect hundreds of outside extremists—Proud Boys, neo-Nazis and neo-Confederates among them—who came dressed for combat."[2]

It's worth noting that police forces in America are near-uniformly aligned with the political right—and that the political right, in turn, have adopted the "protection" and "respect" of police forces as part of their cause. In response to Black Lives Matter protests against police brutality, right-wingers adopted the "Thin Blue Line" flag, a color inversion of the American flag that emphasizes the colors black and blue; *New York Times* columnist Jamelle Bouie has called it a "fascist flag," for its unmistakable alignment with state violence, and the accompanying rhetorical push for unquestioning obedience to the state.

Law enforcement unions overwhelmingly supported Donald Trump during the 2016 presidential election, and the International Union of Police Associations, representing more than 100,000 police officers in the United States, the U.S. Virgin Islands, and Puerto Rico, endorsed Trump for reelection in 2020. The avowedly white-nationalist "law and order" presidency of Trump matched the IUPA's goals, and the association's statement cited with approbation the resumption of the federal death penalty and facilitation of police access to military equipment. Trump has also publicly endorsed police brutality against suspects in general and protesters in particular, expressing a public desire for the "good old days" of unchecked violence against leftist protest.

"Every top Democrat currently running for this office has vilified the police and made criminals out to be victims," the IUPA said in a statement endorsing Trump. "While his candor ruffles the feathers of the left . . . he stands with America's law enforcement officer and we will continue to stand with him."

Police rhetoric extends beyond support of right-wing candidates to an outright detestation of leftist political causes. This naturally sets the stage for profound conflict with antifascists, who are overwhelmingly politically aligned with the far left. One particularly unhinged exemplar of police rhetoric on antifascism came in the wake of a 2017 far-right rally in Boston, in which a number of far-right "free speech" activists assembled on Boston Common to make a stand. Coming a week after Charlottesville's infamous Unite the Right rally—and after a national furor over Trump's seeming endorsement of the far-right marchers—the event drew just a handful of right-wing attendees, while thirty thousand to forty thousand citizens marched in counter-protest. The event was hailed by press and attendees as largely peaceful, and a forceful rebuke to a newly emboldened far right.

Yet the views of the police starkly differed from those of the public. In the Fall 2017 edition of *Pax Centurion*, the publication of the Boston Police Patrolmen's Association, Officer James Carnell, a veteran of the Boston Police Department, let loose in an essay titled "ANTIFA/NAZIS: Want Six or a Half Dozen?" Calling the protest an "anti-police riot," Carnell condemned "ANTIFA savages" and "lemming-like college kids [who] chanted and sang like North Korean civilians at a rally in Pyongyang." Although no casualties were reported at the event, Carnell nevertheless fulminated in a striking advocacy of violence against protesters (emphasis in the original text):

> ANTIFA, which allegedly means "ANTI-fascist," is in fact *the epitome, the definition of fascism itself:* strongarm violence and intimidation by lawless groups seeking to impose their will on the silent majority. . . . The only way to defeat these savages is to fight fire with fire. *Good* can and must be allowed to defeat *evil,* but kind words and kisses are no match for strongarm violence and lawlessness. You **WILL BE** unmasked and arrested as a disorderly person if you do not disperse **NOW.** . . . Mad dogs and mobs can sense indecision and weakness. Only the surety of violence meeting violence and that they will be arrested and prosecuted deters rioters.[3]

Antifascists are thus faced with a dual foe: both the violence of far-right groups whose goals are explicitly oriented toward violence and genocide, and the hostile forces of the state. The structure of the conflict is often referred to as a "three-way fight." The three points of the triangle are the state; anti-statist far-right groups who seek the violent overthrow of civil society; and antifascists themselves, who perceive themselves as the sole bulwark of community defense against both a police force aligned with government-sanctioned white-nationalist violence, and the far-right groups that seek to engage in vigilante violence.

In his eloquent (and much-loathed on the far right) book *Antifa: The Antifascist Handbook*, the scholar Mark Bray lays out a capsule history of the antifascist movement, placing its beginnings with militant anarchists who rose up against Benito Mussolini's fascist Black Shirt squads in 1921. The movement, led by the dashing Argo Secondari, called itself the Arditi del Popolo—the People's Daring Ones—and at its height had some twenty thousand members, though it was ultimately overwhelmed by a confluence of Mussolini's repression and movement infighting. In the mid-1930s, as fascism ascended in Europe, foreign volunteers converged to defeat the incipient forces of Francisco Franco in the Spanish Civil War, from 1936 to 1939. One of the chief mottos of antifascism stems from the Spanish Civil War—¡*No pasarán*! or "They shall not pass," famously employed during the Siege of Madrid by Spanish communist Dolores Ibárruri in 1936. Antifascism had many other loci in Europe in the 1930s, as the rise of authoritarian governments menaced the continent, and communists, socialists, anarchists, and targeted minorities fought back in bloody street brawls. It also surfaced in the United States, as Jews brawled with fascist Silver Shirts and members of the German American Bund.

World War II often stands as an emotional point of appeal among those who oppose the far right today. Many liberals use the talking point that America, or their grandparents or parents, fought Nazis in that war, which looms so large in the American imagination as the most just and triumphant conflict of the twentieth century. However, Bray and others largely skip over this chapter when recounting the history and ideology of antifascist work. This is, above all, for the simple reason that antifascist work as it is understood by most contemporary antifascists is, by definition, performed by nonstate actors. You can't have an antifascist, government-sponsored army with tanks and a budget in the billions. Stalin wasn't an antifascist; he was a dictator fighting off a threat to his absolute rule, and using a massive army to do so. Many antifascists are anarchists; they work to create community defenses and impose a social penalty on far-right organizing without the intervention of the state. Across the world, since the end of World War II, antifascist groups have arisen from communities affected by far-right organizing, and engaged in activities from sabotage to street conflict in hopes of nipping it in the bud. A commonly used slogan is "We keep us safe": antifascists use the notions of community and solidarity as driving forces for their activities. Nonstate actors who consider themselves to be in community with one another, and more broadly with those at risk of harm from far-right organizing, form the core of antifascism in America today. Street fighting is only a small part of a much broader set of activities, from flyering neighborhoods where known neo-Nazis live to make residents aware of the neo-Nazis in their midst; to compiling dossiers and feeding the information to journalists; to blogging; to providing security for events and individuals who might be the targets of hate groups.

There are about eleven thousand slippery-slope arguments that have played out in the American press, particularly after a masked and still-unidentified antifascist very publicly punched white-nationalist ideologue Richard Spencer right in the kisser in 2017. Debates have raged among pearl-clutchers about the risk to democracy posed by protesting against far-right speakers like Milo Yiannopoulos and Heather MacDonald and Michelle Malkin—although retaliatory incidents, such as when a protester was shot by a fascist at a Yiannopoulos protest in Berkeley, California, requiring extensive surgery, have received far less airplay.

There is a sense in the liberal imagination that antifascists are roughly on the "same side" as liberalism's stuffiest pundits, who debate ideas largely in the abstract; thus, antifascists must be far more heavily policed and chastised than their neo-Nazi counterparts. "Free speech" arguments against antifascist organizing are particularly popular among mainstream media personalities and journalists.

These arguments belie the obvious facts of antifascist organizing on the ground. Antifascists have specific targets; act in self-defense and in defense of their communities; and, far from evolving into some enormous power that seeks to constrain speech to greater and greater degrees, antifascist organizing has waned or even disappeared when various waves of far-right organizing recede. As Bray notes in his book, this pattern has been observable since the 1950s, when Jewish Brits and their allies opposed to the remnants of Oswald Mosley's fascist movement in that country brawled with them for years until the Mosleyites ceased to publicly organize. Were the slippery-slope argument as plausible as finger waggers seem to believe, success would merely whet antifascists' appetite to suppress right-wing speech, or any speech deemed unacceptable to their nascent authoritarian impulses. But this has never been the case; for more than seventy years, antifascists have sought to dog and drown the threat posed by fascist and far-right organizing, and have been content to disband when the immediate threat subsides.

Antagonism between antifascists and the mainstream press is high because of a broad institutionalist bias from the media itself. This is not necessarily a partisan impulse, but rather the understandable preference of journalists and news organizations to rely on official—

and seemingly authoritative—sources. Given the antagonism between police, federal authorities, and antifascists, official sources are wont to classify antifascists as a violent, chaotic force of disorder. While journalists frequently pride themselves on speaking truth to power, many local news outlets rely on robust relationships with police forces to report events as they occur. Antifascists, who, for the most part, prefer to remain anonymous, rarely offer up granular alternative narratives in a press-friendly manner, and lack the authority of officialdom in any case. They are wary of the police and the press because they've traditionally not been treated particularly well by either institution. Images of antifascists in the popular consciousness envision a mostly white, mostly male crew of commandos, or college students playing tough. In reality, while the demographics are necessarily difficult to parse in a group that keeps itself intentionally under the radar, most of the antifascists I've interacted with were women, people of color, or both. One antifascist source with knowledge of the matter told me that most major antifa crews in the United States are led by women.

Neo-Nazi groups also take advantage of the media in ways that date back to the 1960s heyday of George Lincoln Rockwell—and which are equally effective in the present. To return to Portland, national media coverage of the violent political street melees that have broken out in that city has often focused exclusively on the fact of violence between political groups—without sufficient examination of its causes. Patriot Prayer rallies in Portland have attracted so many skinheads and white nationalists that the city has functionally been subject to periodic invasions by violent right-wing ideologues. I say *invasions* because, as in Charlottesville, far-right groups have repeatedly employed the strategy of purposefully rallying in cities that are broadly liberal and have a strong left-activist presence. Joey Gibson himself is a resident of Vancouver, Washington, a suburb of Portland, but does not hold his rallies in that city or even in his home state.

Hoping to attract headlines from the press, these rallies explicitly aim to prompt strong reactions in the communities they invade, busing in far-right activists from the Pacific Northwest at large. Like George Lincoln Rockwell traveling to Boston and New York, far-right extremists choose their locations carefully. The idea is to create sympathy—the sense that "conservative activists," as figures like Gibson often euphemistically call themselves, are under siege by violent leftists. The racist, genocidal goals of many of the groups involved in these rallies, and the presence of right-wing street brawlers who repeatedly, and on film, assault left-wing protesters is hardly remarked upon.

What's more, the fact of right-wing activists being an invasion—and that antifascists are the residents of a city and perceive themselves as defending it from hostile outsiders—has been obscured entirely, in favor of an oversimplified "melee" narrative. This kind of omission is inevitable in an American populace that expects agents of the state, from the police to the military, to have a monopoly on the use of violence. Stories of police murder routinely vanish without a trace, but the specter of a black-clad, militant force of civilians bears the exotic mystique of homegrown guerrillas. There's an element of novelty to it that eclipses the phenomenon of armed and violent right-wing groups—a phenomenon that has existed in the United States for much of the twentieth century and into the twenty-first.

While antifascism itself is roughly a century old, it has evolved, in the twenty-first century, to embrace novel techniques and technological advances. In some ways, it has never been easier to participate in everyday antifascist work, provided you have a good internet connection, a measure of patience, and the ability to engage in pains-taking amateur detective work. Significant antifascist operations have focused on massive data leaks from fascist websites, such as the now-defunct neo-Nazi web forum Iron March, which operated from 2011 to 2017.

Iron March was openly anti-Semitic and racist, calling itself a "Global Fascist Fraternity," utilizing the fourteen words and proudly displaying press clips that called the site "Nazi Facebook" and an "international network that promotes race war." The site folded in 2017 for reasons that have not yet been clearly reported. On November 6, 2019, an anonymous antifascist going by the handle "antifa-data" released an info dump that revealed the email addresses, usernames, forum posts, messages, and IP addresses of Iron March's user base. Immediately, other internet users affiliated with antifascism, as well as journalists, began to comb through the data. The leftist Jewish publication the *Jewish Worker* created a searchable version of the database, which enabled anyone to find Iron March users in their city, search any term, and provide public comments on the data. And antifascist groups across the world began digging in.

From Alabama to Pennsylvania, from teenage neo-Nazis to members of the American military, participants in the fascist forum found themselves unmasked in public—to their neighbors, friends, and employers. The goal was simple: to check the cancerous growth of far-right organizing by imposing a social cost on the individuals who engage in it. From cybersleuthing to street melees, that is the sole goal of antifascists across the country; antifascism's goal is community protection, not genocide. And while any decentralized movement has its renegade factions and regrettable incidents, to establish a moral equivalency between those who combat Nazis and those who engage in Nazism is a profound societal mistake.

To those who find themselves uncomfortable with the operation of antifascists outside the comfortable bounds of institutions and, at times, the law, I remind you that the French partisans of World War II were acting illegally, while the Einsatzgruppen had the full support of German law. We tend to like our noble lawbreakers to be comfortably in the past, where time and death have sanitized them into heroes, and to suffer those who struggle against injustice in the present only grudgingly, if at all. Those who oppose a white-nationalist president, his allies in law enforcement, and a militarized state might consider moving beyond letter-writing campaigns to their congresspeople and engaging in the life-or-death struggle that motivates antifascists around the country and the world: the struggle of communities defending themselves against the nihilistic forces of violence, to build a better world by keeping the agents of genocide at bay.

AFTERWORD

Around the time I was finishing the writing of this book, making it the sole focus of my attentions, I started cooking again. For a long, difficult time, I had been in the grips of a depression, all through the spring, summer, and early autumn of 2019. Immersing myself in the worst of human nature while researching this book made me want to shrink inside the mollusk shell of my body, surrounded by air and hollow bone. I wanted to be sealed off. Every word felt painfully extracted from me: Rows of bad teeth grinned at me from the page. I hated myself, the world, and my words. Everything felt suffused with ugliness and I wanted to sleep all day. I made my world so small, a few blocks in diameter. I couldn't eat; my throat seemed soft and vulnerable, so swollen with anxiety that I feared it. I had to trick myself into eating. I had to be intoxicated, or eat soft, very swallowable things, tasteless or sweet. When I did eat, I ate too much.

Writing about hate changes you. Living in a world where organized hate is aware of you changes you, too. Suddenly, I had friends—comrades in arms, whom I talked to every day, whom I loved—who were being put on anonymous hit lists. I had to think about self-defense plans, and paid for a service that erased my family's addresses from the internet. Before I even began this book, a federal agency had condemned me for exploring a potential link between one of its officers and white nationalism, and I'd been the subject of neo-Nazi propaganda. As I dove in further, I could feel the borders between my life and the hate I studied becoming porous. I went to sleep thinking about neo-Nazis—sometimes making a grim Arya Stark–ish enemies list, sometimes imagining ways to defeat them, sometimes trying to draw connections in my mind, or ideological delineations. I woke up thinking about how to synthesize it all for you, the reader. During the day I drifted from café to café, reading hate speech, hunched over my computer as I made my rounds of neo-Nazi websites and chats. I sang less and drank more. All the world's colors were pale as unsteeped tea.

Every day I was reading and writing about hatred: hatred of my people. Nearly everyone I loved was a Jew—my parents, my sisters, their children, the children I might have someday. I read about the people who hated kikes, and I talked to them. Although I opposed it, I internalized the depth of their hate and its vitriol: It changed the way I saw myself when I looked in the mirror. Suddenly I was the Jewess they derided: heavy, stooped, wretched, big of hair and nose. The things I loved about myself felt grotesque. It warped my mouth into bitterness. I wanted no part of my own body and all its works. I wanted no part of myself.

The way I love is to cook for those I love, and the best weapon against hate, they say, is love. Not the false love of airy social proclamations, or the acquisitive love of new desire, but a fierce, abiding love. If I couldn't summon that for myself I could summon it for others, fierce love served in hot dishes. And after all those months of uncharacteristic quietude, of powerful self-loathing, I wanted to cook like a Jew.

From the medieval era and beyond, anti-Semitic texts have warned that you can distinguish the Jew by her smell of garlic. According to the sociologist Celia S. Heller, Gentiles in prewar Poland derisively referred to Jews as "onion-eaters, herring eaters, and as garlic-smelling." When I was done with the book, I brought home onions and garlic, minced, tumbling them into a sizzling pan of olive oil or butter or schmaltz, filling my kitchen with their aromatic steam. I made Jewish food, too—cholent, kishke, a doughy umami mix of buckwheat groats and noodles, chicken soup. It was food to live on, that finally hung warm and heavy in my belly. A dash of coarse salt, a sprinkle of pepper, a few piney scraps of fresh rosemary, steamed in hot fat. It made a corresponding sizzle in my blood, an awakening.

Living in the bowels of hate, it is easy to forget life. You're constantly gesturing toward the dark, into the private darkness in yourself. I felt lifted off the earth by fear, kept high where the air is thin and bitterly cold. It's heady there in the stratosphere, just you and the data you're gathering on the people who hate you the most. All that is good feels cut off from you. Hundreds of feet below you, that's where life exists, and green things live, and bodies sigh warmly against one another. Not where you live.

In *The Ethics of Our Fathers*, a book of the Talmud, Rabbi Tarfon says: "You are not obligated to complete the work, but neither are you free to abandon it." By the end, this is how I came to feel about my work. Dismantling the rise of fascism is best not left to lone vigilantes, nor to the punitive mechanisms of the state, but to people working together to stamp out hate wherever it arises. In the meantime, I cook like a Jew: paprika, dill, onions, garlic, warm broth, and company. The herring is optional, but love is not optional. It is what we must marshal to break the back of the beast. To do so we must break bread together: a prickle of salt, a pat of melting butter, a bite, a kiss, a homily in the mouth about what's worth fighting for.

ACKNOWLEDGMENTS

Thank you to my parents, who allowed me to drape myself on their couch with the grace of a geoduck clam for months at a time, and taught me that the best love is ferocious. To C. and the ladies, for the liverwurst sandwiches. To Ellie for being my first, best, and most constant reader. Thanks to Dan Mandel, my agent, who can schmooze with the best of them and offer great comfort. To Paul Whitlatch for acquiring the book and Krishan Trotman for shepherding it to reality and believing in it. To the Writers Hype Grotto for picking me up from various states of despair and reading various bits of this book at various stages. To the Anti-Nazi Femme Collective for teaching me how to be tough and smart and giving me so much insight. To loving friends like Moshe, Sara, Megan, and the Rope Bandits. To Alex for being part of my soul and helping me stay alive. To my sisters and the babies for never letting me forget what I am fighting for.

ENDNOTES

CHAPTER 1: ON HATING

1   Jan-Willem van Prooijen and Karen M. Douglas, "Conspiracy Theories As Part of History: The Role of Societal Crisis Situations," National Institutes of Health (June 29, 2017). https://www.ncbi.nlm.nih.gov/pmc/articles/PMC 5646574/.

CHAPTER 2: THE JEWS

1   Adam Serwer, "The Coronavirus Was an Emergency Until Trump Found Out Who Was Dying," *The Atlantic* (May 8, 2020). https://www.theatlantic.com/ideas/archive/2020/05/americas -racial-contract-showing/611389/.

2   Leonard Dinnerstein, *Antisemitism in America* (New York: Oxford University Press, 1994), 14.

3   "Pogroms," *YIVO Encyclopedia of Jews in Eastern Europe*

(New Haven, CT: Yale University Press, 2008). http://www
.yivoencyclopedia.org/article.aspx/Pogroms.

4   Bernard K. Johnpoll, "Why They Left: Russian-Jewish Mass
    Migration and Repressive Laws, 1881–1917," *American Jewish
    Archives* (1995). http://americanjewisharchives.org/publications
    /journal/PDF/1995_47_01_00_johnpoll.pdf.

5   "From Haven to Home: 350 Years of Jewish Life in America: A
    Century of Immigration, 1820–1924," *The Century*, New Series,
    vol. 88 (New York: The Century Co., 1914). https://www.loc.gov
    /exhibits/haventohome/haven-century.html.

6   Michael Barkun. *Religion and the Racist Right: The Origins of the
    Christian Identity Movement* (Chapel Hill: University of North
    Carolina Press, 1997), 34.

7   Burton J. Hendrick, "The Great Jewish Invasion," *McClure's
    Magazine* 28, 1907, 317.

8   Edward Ross, "The Hebrews of Eastern Europe in America," *The
    Century* 88, 1914, 790.

9   Ross, *The Century*, New Series, Volume 88, The Century Co,
    New York, 1914.

10 Leo P. Ribuffo, "Henry Ford and 'The International Jew,'" *Amer-
    ican Jewish History* 69, no. 4 (June 1980): 437–177. https://
    www.jstor.org/stable/23881872?seq=1.

11 Ken Silverstein, "Ford and the Führer," *The Nation* (Janu-
    ary 6, 2000). https://www.thenation.com/article/ford-and
    -fuhrer/.

12 Will Schultz, "William Dudley Pelley: 1885–1965," North Caro-
    lina History Project (2016). https://northcarolinahistory.org
    /encyclopedia/william-dudley-pelley-1885-1965/.

13 Jason Daley, "The Screenwriting Mystic Who Wanted to Be the
    American Führer," *Smithsonian* (October 3, 2018). https://

www.smithsonianmag.com/history/meet-screenwriting-mystic
-who-wanted-be-american-fuhrer-180970449/.

14   Dinnerstein, *Antisemitism in America*, 112.

15   Diane Bernard, "The Night Thousands of Nazis Packed Madison Square Garden for a Rally—and Violence Erupted,"
Washington Post (December 9, 2019). https://www.washington
post.com/history/2018/12/09/night-thousands-nazis-packed
-madison-square-garden-rally-violence-erupted/?utm_term
=.8803d3a11de5.

16   J. Y. Smith, "The Rev. Charles E. Coughlin Dies: Noted as 'The
Radio Priest,'" *Washington Post* (October 28, 1979). https://
www.washingtonpost.com/archive/local/1979/10/28/the-rev
-charles-e-coughlin-dies-noted-as-the-radio-priest/baded71c
-2d5e-4bd7-b0b4-89c1ae33fe7a/?utm_term=.ecb23f231522.

17   Arthur Meier Schlesinger, *The Politics of Upheaval: 1935–
1936,* The Age of Roosevelt, vol. 3 (Boston: Mariner Books,
2003).   https://books.google.com/books?id=vC5HJloBWugC
&pg=PA17&lpg=PA17&dq=%22christ+or+the+red+fog+of
+communism%22&source=bl&ots=oRbfKHanFg&sig=ACf
U3U3_SI6DHCMVf5RL6QfR-GPX4iOtYg&hl=en&sa=X&v
ed=2ahUKEwi415vR7_PiAhWFmlkKHQAvBkcQ6AEwAHo
ECAkQAQ#v=onepage&q=%22christ%20or%20the%20red
%20fog%20of%20communism%22&f=false.

18   Keith Somerville, *Radio Propaganda and the Broadcasting of
Hatred: Historical Development and Definitions* (London: Pal-
grave Macmillan, 2012). https://books.google.com/books?id
=t6-37XD0yicC&pg=PA37&lpg=PA37&dq=%22The+Golden
+Hour+of+the+Shrine+of+the+Little+Flower,%22&source
=bl&ots=l-VLpLPQ2r&sig=ACfU3U000jGB03YGl9BT70
-YFUBDY9z8pw&hl=en&sa=X&ved=2ahUKEwjL2p7j7fPi

AhVKHqwKHWYDB7EQ6AEwDnoECAkQAQ#v=onepage &q=naturalistic&f=false.

19   Transcript of Address by Father C. E. Coughlin (November 20, 1938). https://cuomeka.wrlc.org/files/original/50b004fa185e86 c9079c4ad288f49ac1.pdf.

20   Dinnerstein, *Antisemitism in America*, 136.

21   Christian Anti-Jewish Party, "Defend the White Race" (1955). https://archive.org/details/ChristianAntiJewishPartyJ.B.Stoner Atlanta1004976/page/n33.

22   Tim Funk, "Fuses Were Lit: Decades Before Pittsburgh, 2 Charlotte-area Synagogues Escaped Tragedy," *Charlotte Observer* (November 14, 2018). https://www.charlotteobserver.com/living /religion/article221205950.html.

23   Dinnerstein, *Antisemitism in America*, 146.

CHAPTER 3: BOOTS ON FOR THE BOOGALOO

1   Andrew Anglin, "We Won," Daily Stormer (November 9, 2016). https://dailystormer.name/we-won/.

2   John Woodrow Cox, "'Let's Party Like It's 1933': Inside the Alt-Right World of Richard Spencer," *Washington Post* (November 22, 2016). https://www.washingtonpost.com/local/lets-party-like-its -1933-inside-the-disturbing-alt-right-world-of-richard-spencer /2016/11/22/cf81dc74-aff7-11e6-840f-e3ebab6bcdd3_story.html.

3   Alan Gomez, "Democrats Grill Trump Administration Officials over Family Separation Policy on the Border," *USA Today* (February 7, 2019). https://www.usatoday.com/story/news/politics /2019/02/07/democrats-trump-administration-family-separation -policy-border-immigration/2794324002/.

4   Anna Schecter, "White Nationalist Leader Is Plotting to 'Take Over the GOP,'" NBC News (October 17, 2018). https://www.nbcnews.com/politics/immigration/white-nationalist-leader-plotting-take-over-gop-n920826.

5   Francis Aidan Gasquet, *The Black Death of 1348 and 1349* (London: George Bell and Sons, 1908), 52–54.

6   Portions of this section appeared on the *GQ* magazine website under the headline "Why White Nationalists Are Turning on Trump Republicans" on November 25, 2019. https://www.gq.com/story/white-nationalists-trump-republicans

7   Michael Shear and Maggie Haberman. "Trump's Temporary Halt to Immigration Is Part of Broader Plan, Stephen Miller Says." *The New York Times*. April 24, 2020. https://www.nytimes.com/2020/04/24/us/politics/coronavirus-trump-immigration-stephen-miller.html

CHAPTER 4: OPERATION ASHLYNN

1   Ruth Thompson-Miller and Leslie H. Picca, "There Were Rapes!: Sexual Assaults of African American Women and Children in Jim Crow," *Violence Against Women* 23, no. 8 (2016): 934–950. https://sci-hub.tw/https://journals.sagepub.com/doi/abs/10.1177/1077801216654016.

2   Kathleen Mary Davis, "Fighting Jim Crow in Post–World War II Omaha 1945–1956" (master's thesis, University of Nebraska, 2002).

3   One Drop Rule, *Encyclopedia of Arkansas* (2019). https://encyclopediaofarkansas.net/entries/one-drop-rule-5365/.

4   Molly Conger, @socialistdogmom, Twitter (November 24,

2019). https://twitter.com/socialistdogmom/status/119866365
1730870273?s=20.

5　Stephen Harrison, "How Katie Bouman Shook Wikipedia," *Slate*
(April 16, 2019). https://slate.com/technology/2019/04/katie
-bouman-wikipedia-page-deletion-black-hole.html.

CHAPTER 5: ADVENTURES WITH INCELS

1　Simon Parkin, "Zoë Quinn's Depression Quest," *New Yorker*
(September 9, 2014). https://www.newyorker.com/tech/annals
-of-technology/zoe-quinns-depression-quest.

2　Alice Marwick and Rebecca Lewis, "Media Manipulation and
Disinformation Online," *Data and Society* (May 15, 2017), 9.

CHAPTER 6: THAT GOOD OLD-TIME RELIGION

1　Marc Caputo, "Libertarian Party Drama: Goat Sacrifice, Eugenics
and a Chair's Resignation," *Politico* (October 1, 2015). https://www
.politico.com/states/florida/story/2015/10/libertarian-party-drama
-goat-sacrifice-eugenics-and-a-chairs-resignation-026236.

2　Federal Election Commission, "Candidates for President, 2020."
https://www.fec.gov/data/candidates/president/?q=invictus&ele
ction_year=2020&cycle=2020&election_full=true&party=REP.

3　US District Court District of Kansas, *United States of America v.
Curtis Wayne Allen et al.* Jury Trial Transcript vol. IV. (2018).

4　Ibid., Exhibit 18.

5　Ibid., Government's Reply to Defendants' Response to Notice of
Authorities Relevant to U.S.S.G. § 3A1.4 (Document 472).

6   "Manifesto" (December 3, 2018). https://www.documentcloud .org/documents/5694091-Manifesto.html.

7   Ryan J. Reilly, "Exclusive: 'Everyday Guy' Describes How He Brought Down an American Terrorist Cell," *HuffPost* (April 21, 2018). https://www.huffpost.com/entry/right-wing-terrorism -dan-day-fbi-informant_n_5ad80fa7e4b03c426dab314c.

8   *United States of America v. Curtis Wayne Allen et al.* Exhibit 25.

9   Roxana Hegeman, Associated Press, "Militia Members Get Decades in Prison in Kansas Bomb Plot," reprinted in *U.S. News & World Report* (January 25, 2019). https://www.usnews.com/news/us/articles/2019 -01-25/3-militia-members-face-sentencing-in-kansas-bomb-plot.

10   Becky Little, "How Hate Groups Are Hijacking Medieval Symbols While Ignoring the Facts Behind Them," History Channel (December 18, 2017). https://www.history.com/news/how-hate -groups-are-hijacking-medieval-symbols-while-ignoring-the -facts-behind-them.

11   "Knights of the Ku Klux Klan," Southern Poverty Law Center Extremist Files. https://www.splcenter.org/fighting-hate/extremist -files/group/knights-ku-klux-klan.

12   *The Histories and Legends of Old Castles & Abbeys* (London: John Dicks, 1850). https://books.google.com/books?id=XZN SPtrFi-QC&pg=PA410&lpg=PA410&dq=earl+of+arran+fiery +cross&source=bl&ots=9bXHl9QdAF&sig=ACfU3U2GZ2JQ 2LifbUs3TzTKgKuCMkfCjw&hl=en&sa=X&ved=2ahUKEwjd 9baEoePjAhUJhOAKHVTBCC8Q6AEwBHoECAgQAQ#v=o nepage&q=earl%20of%20arran%20fiery%20cross&f=false.

13   Amy Kaufman, "Race, Racism, and the Middle Ages: The Birth of a Nation Disgrace: Medievalism and the KKK," *Public Medievalist* (November 21, 2017). https://www.publicmedievalist.com/birth -national-disgrace/.

ENDNOTES

14 Hailey Branson-Potts, "In Diverse California, a Young White Supremacist Seeks to Convert Fellow College Students," *Los Angeles Times* (December 7, 2016). https://www.latimes.com /local/lanow/la-me-ln-nathan-damigo-alt-right-20161115-story .html.

15 Mattias Gardell, *Gods of the Blood: The Pagan Revival and White Separatism* (Durham, NC: Duke University Press, 2003).

16 Damon T. Berry, *Blood and Faith: Christianity in American White Nationalism* (Syracuse, NY: Syracuse University Press, 2017).

17 Gardell, *Gods of the Blood*, 165.

18 "Tenets of the Folk Right," Folkrightvalues.com. https://www .folkright.com/folkrightvalues.html.

19 The Ásatrú Folk Assembly, *Ásatrú Book of Blotar and Ritual* (self-pub, 2011).

20 Peter Beste, "Wolves of Vinland." Photo essay. peterbeste.com /wov.

21 Agence France-Presse. "Suspect in Norway Mosque Shooting to Remain Jailed." August 12, 2019. https://www.courthouse news.com/suspect-in-norway-mosque-attack-to-remain-jailed/

22 Libby Watson. "London Has Fallen, According to This Racist Wall Street Journal Op-Ed." Splinter News. August 30, 2018. https://splinternews.com/london-has-fallen-according-to-this -racist-wall-street-1828725242

23 https://dailystormer.su/austria-five-vibrants-convicted-of-gang -enriching-a-13-year-old-girl/.

ENDNOTES

CHAPTER 7: TWEEN RACISTS, BAD BEANIES, AND THE GREAT CASINO CHASE

1   Kevin Roose, "The Making of a YouTube Radical," *New York Times* (June 8, 2019). https://www.nytimes.com/interactive /2019/06/08/technology/youtube-radical.html.

2   Robert Evans, "From Memes to Infowars: How 75 Fascist Activists Were 'Red-Pilled,'" Bellingcat (October 11, 2018). https://www.bellingcat.com/news/americas/2018/10/11/memes -infowars-75-fascist-activists-red-pilled/.

3   Laura Smith, "In the Early 1980s, White Supremacist Groups Were Early Adopters (and Masters) of the Internet," Timeline (October 11, 2017). https://timeline.com/white-supremacist -early-internet-5e91676eb847.

4   Christopher Miller, "Azov, Ukraine's Most Prominent Ultranation-alist Group, Sets Its Sights on U.S., Europe," Radio Free Europe/ Radio Liberty (November 14, 2018). https://www.rferl.org/a/azov -ukraine-s-most-prominent-ultranationalist-group-sets-its-sights -on-u-s-europe/29600564.html.

CHAPTER 8: GETTING TO THE BOOM: ON ACCELERATIONISM AND VIOLENCE

1   Elizabeth Zerofsky, "Letter from Europe: A Terrorist Attack on Yom Kippur in Halle, Germany," *New Yorker* (October 13, 2019). https://www.newyorker.com/news/letter-from-europe/a -terrorist-attack-on-yom-kippur-in-halle-germany.

2   Jeremy Jojola, "A Prominent Neo-Nazi Lives in an Apartment Not Far from Downtown Denver," 9 News (November 25, 2019). https:// www.9news.com/article/news/investigations/neo-nazi-lives-in-capitol -hill-downtown-denver/73-bb42d1d2-2762-4e60-bf64-3a2e5f739347.

3   Ibid.

4   Sam Levin, "Police Thwarted at Least Seven Mass Shootings and White Supremacist Attacks Since El Paso," *Guardian* (August 22, 2019). https://www.theguardian.com/world/2019/aug/20/el -paso-shooting-plot-white-supremacist-attacks.

5   Joe Sexton, "Las Vegas Man Arrested in Plots Against Jews Was Said to Be Affiliated With Atomwaffen Division," ProPublica (August 14, 2019). https://www.propublica.org/article/las-vegas -man-conor-climo-was-said-to-be-affiliated-with-atomwaffen -division.

6   Janet Reitman, "U.S. Law Enforcement Failed to See the Threat of White Nationalism. Now They Don't Know How to Stop It," *New York Times Magazine*, November 3, 2018. https://www.nytimes.com/2018/11/03/magazine/FBI-charl ottesville-white-nationalism-far-right.html.

CHAPTER 9: ANTIFA CIVIL WAR

1   "Bob Avakian," Revolution. https://revcom.us/avakian/bob _avakian_official_biography/Bob_Avakian_(BA)_Official _Biography-Part-1-en.html.

2   Erin Blakemore, "Five Things to Know About the Case That Made Burning the Flag Legal," *Smithsonian* (November 29, 2016). https://www.smithsonianmag.com/smart-news/five -things-know-about-case-made-burning-flag-legal-180961229/.

3   Dylan Scott, "What the Heck Is the 'Revolutionary Com- munist Party' Doing in Ferguson?" Talking Points Memo (August 21, 2014). https://talkingpointsmemo.com/dc/left -wing-radicals-ferguson-missouri-protests.

ENDNOTES

4   Sean Adl-Tabatabai, "ANTIFA Plan Nationwide Riots on Nov. 4th to Forcibly Remove Trump," News Punch (August 18, 2017). https://newspunch.com/antifa-riots-november-trump/.

5   Josh Boswell, "Mother Churns Out Stories for Master of Fake News," *Sunday Times* (January 29, 2017). https://www.thetimes.co.uk/article/mother-churns-out-stories-for-master-of-fake-news-fcmzc05sx.

6   Craig Silverman, Jane Lytvynenko, and Scott Pham, "These Are Fifty of the Biggest Fake News Hits on Facebook in 2017," *BuzzFeed* (December 28, 2017). https://www.buzzfeednews.com/article/craigsilverman/these-are-50-of-the-biggest-fake-news-hits-on-facebook-in.

7   Lucian Wintrich, "ANTIFA Leader: 'November 4th . . . Millions of Antifa Supersoldiers Will Behead All White Parents,'" Gateway Pundit (October 30, 2017). https://www.thegatewaypundit.com/2017/10/antifa-leader-november-4th-millions-antifa-supersoldiers-will-behead-white-parents/.

CHAPTER 10: WE KEEP US SAFE

1   David Roth, "The Vainglorious Eternals Go Golfing," *New Republic* (November 13, 2019). https://newrepublic.com/article/155733/trump-clinton-bloomberg-giuliani-golf-photo-vainglorious-eternals.

2   Arun Gupta, "Protester Maimed by Portland Police: 'I Thought I Was Going to Die,'" *Daily Beast* (August 9, 2018). https://www.thedailybeast.com/portland-protester-wounded-by-police-i-thought-i-was-going-to-die.

ENDNOTES

3   James Carnell, "The ANTIFA/NAZIs: 'Want Six or a Half Dozen?'—The Nazis They Were Looking for . . . Were Right Next to Them," *Pax Centurion* (Fall 2017): 34–35. https://www.bppa.org/wp-content/uploads/pax-centurion/2017/fall/.

INDEX

INDEX

INDEX

INDEX

INDEX

INDEX

INDEX

INDEX

INDEX

INDEX

INDEX

INDEX

INDEX

INDEX

INDEX